A Great Deception

A Great Deception

The Ruling Lamas' Policies

Western Shugden Society

This edition published in 2010 by the Western Shugden Society

The Western Shugden Society is the international coalition of practitioners of the enlightened Deity Dorje Shugden

Western Shugden Society
Studio 177
56 Tavistock Place
London
WC1H 9RG
Tel: +44 (0) 7717 209418
efax: +44 207 0001 322

Company Reg No: 6631434 (UK)

British Library Cataloguing in Publication Data
A catalogue record for this book is available from the British Library

ISBN 978-0-9563918-0-3 – paperback

Set in Garamond, and printed on Soperset 80 gsm
Printed and bound in the UK by CPI William Clowes Beccles NR34 7TL

Contents

List of plates:

1. The first statue of Dorje Shugden, made by the Fifth Dalai Lama with his own hands. The statue is now at Pelgyeling Monastery, in Nepal.
2. Trode Khangsar, the Temple dedicated to Dorje Shugden by the Fifth Dalai Lama.
3. Line drawing of the Fifth Dalai Lama, Ngawang Losang Gyatso, 1617-1682.
4. The Thirteenth Dalai Lama, Thubten Gyatso, 1876-1933.
5. Yapshi Langdun, a Tibetan minister who Reting regarded as a rival and outmanoeuvered in the search for the new Dalai Lama.
6. Reting Rinpoche with Bruno Beger in 1938, during one of several German SS expeditions to Tibet.
7. An SS expedition to Tibet in 1938. Reting sent them home with a letter to 'King Hitler', praising the Nazi leader and requesting that they strengthen the relationship between the two regimes. [377]
8. Lhamo Dondrub, as a child in the Muslim village of Takster before being brought to Lhasa.
9. Enthroned as the Fourteenth Dalai Lama and given the name Tenzin Gyatso.
10. Nowadays the Dalai Lama lives in exile, but who is the real Dalai Lama behind the mask?
11. The Dalai Lama meeting Chairman Mao in 1955.
12. The Dalai Lama voting at the First National People's Congress, 1954.
13. The Dalai Lama praised Mao as being like a God.
14. A division of the Tibetan army on parade in 1938.
15. Bayonet wielding soldiers on guard at the Norbu Linka, the Dalai Lama's summer palace.
16. This top secret CIA field diary was kept by Douglas MacKiernan and Frank Bessac. It proves that the CIA were in Tibet as early as 1949, before the People's Liberation Army entered Tibet in 1950. CIA covert operations in Tibet continued until the early 1970s. In recent decades the National Endowment for Democracy has continued CIA activities with respect to Tibet. [378]
17. The Dalai Lama with Tibetan Resistance fighters in 1959. He authorised the Tibetan units of the Indian Special Frontier Force to fight the war in East Pakistan in 1971.
18. Monks surrendering the guns and explosives they were using against the Chinese.
19. Gyalo Dondrub, the Dalai Lama's brother, involved - in his own words - in 'very dirty business'.
20. The Dalai Lama inspecting troops at Chakrata. He authorised the Tibetan units of the Indian Special Frontier Force to fight the war in East Pakistan in 1971.
21. John Kenneth Knaus a CIA operative who was involved with the CIA funded Tibetan guerrillas.
22. Norbu Dorje, a US-trained former Tibetan guerilla.
23. Torture implements from the Dalai Lama's era on display in Lhasa. This photo shows tools for gouging out eyes, and crushing fingers.

24. A Tibetan with his severed arm.

25-26. Stocks. These were in common use in Shol prison at the base of the Dalai Lama's 1000-room Potala Palace.

27. A Tibetan whose arm was cut off as punishment.

28. A Tibetan whose Achilles tendons were severed as punishment.

29. A Tibetan in leg-irons, left to wander the streets begging for food.

30. The Dalai Lama with Shoko Asahara, leader of the AUM Cult, who masterminded the sarin gas attack on Tokyo's subway that killed 13 people.

31. The Dalai Lama with Jorg Haider, leader of Austrian extreme rightwing (FPÖ) party.

32. The Dalai Lama with Bruno Beger, a convicted Nazi war criminal, who conducted experiments on Jews in German concentration camps; 86 of his subjects were murdered.

33. The Dalai Lama with his friend and mentor Heinrich Harrer. Harrer was a Nazi and an SS sergeant. He joined the SA (Sturm-Abteilung) in 1934 when it was illegal in Austria.

34. The Dalai Lama in January 2008: 'These monks must be expelled from all monasteries. If they are not happy, you can tell them that the Dalai Lama himself asked that this be done, and it is very urgent.' Subsequent to this, the persecution, already started in 1996, became more intense. [380]

35. Entry is denied to the monasteries and their facilities.

36. Hundreds of monks are expelled and made homeless. Indian Police provide temporary protection for them.

37. Even children are forced to make public oaths denouncing Dorje Shugden.

38. Wanted posters appear around Dharamsala inciting violence to Dorje Shugden practitioners.

39. Hospitals ban Dorje Shugden worshippers from receiving treatment.

40. The public 'referendum' that forces monks from their monasteries.

41. A wall is built at Ganden Monastery to segregate the Shugden monks from the rest of the monastery.

42. Application for identity documents require the person to have denounced Dorje Shugden.

43. The Identity card received by those who publicly denounce Dorje Shugden, without this there is no access to food and medicine.

44. Samdhong Rinpoche, the Prime Minister of the Tibetan Government in Exile and principally responsible for trying to fulfil the Dalai Lama's wish to 'clean' society of Shugden practitioners.[381]

45-47. These young tulkus from Shar Gaden Monastery were beaten up because they worship Dorje Shugden.

48-59. Demonstrations & Protest Marchs in Australia, France, Germany, India, United Kingdom and the United States against the Dalai Lama's religious persecution.

60-65. Having just received spiritual advice from the Dalai Lama at a talk he gave in Radio City, New York, the attendees left the auditorium and immediately began attacking the peaceful protest being held by members of the Western Shugden Society. The Police called in horse-backed reinforcements and heavily armed riot police; finally they closed down several blocks of Manhattan.

Preface

The purpose of this book is to achieve the following four aims:

- to liberate millions of innocent practitioners of the Buddhist Deity Dorje Shugden and their families from suffering;
- to restore peace and harmony between Shugden and non-Shugden practitioners;
- to re-establish the common spiritual activities of Shugden and non-Shugden practitioners; and
- to free Buddhism from political pollution.

Achieving these aims depends solely upon whether the present Dalai Lama will accept the four points set out at the conclusion of Chapter 4 of this book.

The Dalai Lama wishes to ban Shugden worship in general; and in particular to remove Tibetan Shugden worshippers from their communities, and Western Shugden worshippers from the international Buddhist community. Since 1996 the Tibetan exile government has continually applied effort to fulfil these wishes. In February 2008 alone, 900 monks who are Shugden practitioners were expelled from their monasteries in India.

In 1996 the Tibetan exile government publicly decreed to the Tibetan communities of each country, including Tibet, that Shugden practitioners were their national enemies and were against the Dalai Lama's wishes. The decree stated that unless Shugden practitioners promised to stop Shugden worship they would not receive any official position or job, nor any help or support, even medical assistance, either from the Tibetan exile government or from individual members of the Tibetan community. Further, any connection at all with Shugden practitioners should be cut. Children of Shugden practitioners were no longer permitted to attend Tibetan schools, and Shugden practitioners themselves could not join community meetings, social events and so forth.

The Tibetan exile government put the Dalai Lama's wishes into practice directly in India, and in the same way the Dalai Lama's official representative in each country throughout the world has directly and practically followed the orders of the exile government. These representatives have organised vigilante groups in their respective regions and directly prevailed upon such groups to defame, threaten, and sometimes physically harm Shugden practitioners. In this way many Shugden temples have been closed and shrines destroyed, individual Shugden practitioner's houses have been burned down, practitioners have been brutally beaten, and children have been banned from their schools. Tibetan Shugden practitioners are repeatedly accused unjustly of being 'the Tibetan national enemy' and ostracised from their communities.

This inhumane treatment directly violates basic human rights and principles of democratic law, but nevertheless pervades almost every Tibetan community today, whether in the East or West. For example, in Tibet itself where the Chinese now give basic equal rights to everyone, all Shugden practitioners still suffer from a lack of religious freedom caused by other Tibetans who continue to work within Tibet to fulfil the Dalai Lama's wishes there. And in Switzerland, a democratic country, which hosts a large Tibetan exile community, Shugden practitioners suffer from a lack of religious freedom caused by the unjust and discriminatory actions of groups organised by the Office of the Dalai Lama's Representative, which acts directly against democratic law in continually working to fulfil the Dalai Lama's wishes. It is the same in all other countries. The Dalai Lama himself, the Tibetan exile government, the present and former abbots of the main monasteries of the Gelug Tradition, and the Dalai Lama´s official representatives in each country throughout the world, have all broken international law and are abusing basic human rights. They are criminals wearing spiritual masks.

The source of all these problems is just one single person – the Dalai Lama himself. It is very clear that the Dalai Lama's people are acting against Shugden practitioners simply out of blind faith, and only to fulfil his wishes.

Since the Dalai Lama first created this international problem in 1996, the world's media, including the BBC in the UK, have continually received information about it. In many countries in 1996 and 2008 they directly witnessed thousands of Shugden practitioners engaging in international public demonstrations against the Dalai Lama, protesting 'Dalai Lama give religious freedom!' and 'Dalai Lama stop lying!'. There is no doubt that, for example, the BBC understands this international problem, including the inhumanity of the situation; the violation of basic human rights; the fact that it is entirely caused by the Dalai Lama, who acts like a 21st century dictator; and the fact that the suffering is experienced by millions of innocent people throughout the world. However, the BBC does not broadcast any true information about this international problem, but instead always supports the 21st century dictator, the Dalai Lama. Why is this?

From the very beginning until now, the Dalai Lama and his exile government have striven to hide this international problem that the Dalai Lama himself has created. Whenever a journalist asks the Dalai Lama 'Why have you banned Shugden worship and caused so many problems?' he replies saying that it is not true that there is a ban, it is merely rumour; there is no problem. Following this lie, when journalists ask the same question of the Dalai Lama's representatives in each country, they again receive the same bland reply 'This is not true, it is just a rumour; there is no problem'. If you were to telephone the Dalai Lama right now and ask him 'Why have you banned Shugden worship and caused so many problems?' he would still reply saying 'This is not true, it is rumour; there is no problem'.

There is no greater liar or a person more powerfully deceptive than this in the world today. So far the international community has had no opportunity to receive clear and true information about Tibetan ruling lamas in general, nor about this present Dalai Lama in particular, who keeps the name of Avalokiteshvara, the Buddha of Compassion, whilst harming peoples' spiritual life and causing suffering to millions of innocent people. It is for these reasons that the Western Shugden Society has prepared this book to provide this information, and we hope that the world's media will investigate more fully and publicise the issues raised in this book.

The book mainly focuses on the source of this ban – the Dalai Lama himself – and on the ancient flaw in the system of the Tibetan government – the 'Lama Policy' – that continues in the Tibetan exile community today, a fundamental flaw which allows this one man to use his position as religious leader to exercise political power, and his position as political leader to enforce his own religious prejudices.

Part One begins by examining the nature of Lama Policy, which, far from bringing enlightened Buddhist values into politics, corrupts the practice of Buddhism and makes it a tool in the ruthless power struggles of Tibet. The second chapter focuses on the present Dalai Lama. Based on personal testimonies it shows how his selection as Dalai Lama was due to political corruption in Tibet at that time. The Dalai Lama has through his persuasive speech become revered worldwide as a supposedly wise and compassionate leader, but the next two chapters of the book examine his actions and expose the truth, that he is a religious dictator and hypocrite. The remaining two chapters of Part One are a chronicle of events relating to his ban on the practice of Dorje Shugden, and a brief selection of newspaper and magazine reports on the issue of Tibetan independence and the ban on Dorje Shugden.

Part Two is a more detailed examination of the major themes raised in *Part One*. It begins with an examination of the 'union of religion and politics' system of Tibetan government, first established by the Fifth Dalai Lama and from which the Fourteenth Dalai Lama derives his present power, and reveals how this system is a great deception, which from generation to generation has brought nothing but suffering to millions of people. The next chapter is a review of the history and institution of the Dalai Lamas, showing how the Fifth Dalai Lama first came to hold dual political and religious power in Tibet, not through spiritual qualities but through the might of supporting armies and the cynical ruthlessness of his ministers. It also looks at the Fifth Dalai Lama's role in the murder of Ngatrul Dragpa, who arose after death as the Dharma Protector

Dorje Shugden; and shows how the Fifth Dalai Lama's shameful example as a Buddhist monk was emulated by the Thirteenth Dalai Lama. Chapter 9 looks at how the present Dalai Lama has continued this shameful example, examining his political views and failures, and showing how his ban on Dorje Shugden is connected with his failed political policies. The following chapter focuses in particular on this ban itself. Chapter 11 exposes the present Dalai Lama's role in the many scandals that have damaged the Tibetan exile community, revealing a criminal face behind a spiritual mask, and the final chapter is a summary assessment of the Dalai Lama's harmful activities.

We hope that all Buddhist traditions will grow and develop strongly and purely in the future, free from all such political interference as exposed in this book.

Western Shugden Society
September 2009

PART ONE

The Tibetan Situation Today

CHAPTER 1

Lama Policy

The explanations given in this book are to encourage people not to follow or be influenced by 'Lama Policy', which like a drug causes people to be confused about the real nature of Buddhist practice. In this context, 'Lama' refers to the Fifth, Thirteenth and Fourteenth Dalai Lamas of Tibet. The policy of these lamas has been to use religion for political aims, thus causing suffering to millions of people from generation to generation. Because of the Fifth Dalai Lama's policy of mixing religion and politics, the Nyingma, Sakya and Kagyu traditions of Tibetan Buddhism rapidly declined and, as a result, for hundreds of years millions of people who followed these traditions experienced great difficulties. Today, some people from these traditions say that it was followers of the Gelug tradition who caused their tradition to decline, but this is untrue. The Gelugpas themselves had no political power. It was the Fifth Dalai Lama who alone used his political power to destroy the development of these traditions, both spiritually and materially.

The Fifth Dalai Lama always showed two faces. One was that of a Nyingmapa and the other was that of a Gelugpa. In fact, he did not follow either tradition, but remained between them without ever finding a pure spiritual path. In this he was like the present Dalai Lama, the Fourteenth, who also shows two faces and likewise has never found a pure spiritual path.

The Fifth Dalai Lama achieved political power in the 17th century through the military support of Gushri Khan, the ruler of the Qoshot Mongols, who helped him fight a war against Karma Tenkyong Wangpo, then the principal ruler of Tibet. At the request of the Fifth Dalai Lama, Gushri Khan sent his Mongol armies into Tibet, and as a result won the war. Karma Tenkyong Wangpo was captured and later executed, and the Fifth Dalai Lama achieved political power and became the ruler of Tibet. This event alone shows the nature of Lama Policy. The Fifth Dalai Lama was an ordained Buddhist monk having the commitment not to kill or otherwise harm others. He therefore acted directly against the spiritual commitments laid down by Buddha. This is a very shameful example, for a Buddhist monk holding the position of a high lama, a supposedly holy being.

In their teachings the Fifth and Thirteenth Dalai Lamas talked about compassion, but they behaved like dictators creating so many problems for their society. This is true also of the present Dalai Lama. Despite this hypocrisy, many people because of their extreme religious view and blind faith still believe that these lamas are holy beings. In Tibetan society, anyone who has views and intentions that are different from those of the Dalai Lama is immediately accused of not being Tibetan; they are criticised, threatened and ostracised. This happened in the past and is happening to Dorje Shugden practitioners today. From this alone we can see that this Lama Policy continues to have a devastating effect on society. This problem cannot be solved unless the lama himself changes his own attitude.

The Fifth Dalai Lama was the founder of Lama Policy, which he called 'the union of religion and politics'. The nature of Lama Policy is deceptive; its function is only to mislead people and to use religion for political aims. It is like a rainbow, which from a distance looks beautiful but upon closer examination is seen to be completely empty and hollow. The lamas who have principally upheld the policy established by the Fifth Dalai Lama are the Thirteenth and Fourteenth Dalai Lamas, and of these two the policy of the present Dalai Lama is the worst.

During the Fifth Dalai Lama's time there was a lama called Ngatrul Dragpa, who was recognised as an emanation of the Buddha of Wisdom. Even though the Fifth Dalai Lama had political power, Ngatrul Dragpa had spiritual power, and people throughout Tibet had great faith in Ngatrul Dragpa, as also did Gushri Khan. These two lamas had different views and intentions; Ngatrul Dragpa rejected the Lama Policy of the union of religion and politics. He wanted Buddhism to be maintained purely without being used for worldly aims, but the Fifth Dalai Lama was opposed to this. Afraid that Ngatrul Dragpa would usurp his position through the help of Gushri Khan's ministers, the Fifth Dalai Lama and his ministers secretly murdered Ngatrul Dragpa. It is commonly accepted that Ngatrul Dragpa then appeared as a Deity called Dorje Shugden, a protector of pure Buddhism who prevents the Buddhist religion being used for political aims. This belief is based on commitments made by Ngatrul Dragpa himself before he died, and on many predictions.[1] A more detailed account of the Fifth Dalai Lama's involvement in the murder of Ngatrul Dragpa is presented later in Chapter 8.

After Ngatrul Dragpa's death the Fifth Dalai Lama began to experience many difficulties and inauspicious signs. Because of this he believed that Ngatrul Dragpa had become Dorje Shugden and was wishing to retaliate, and he was terrified that Dorje Shugden would now kill him. The Fifth Dalai Lama first sought refuge in other lamas and requested them to burn Dorje Shugden with a magic ritual fire practice. When this failed, he strongly made many request prayers to his own protector, the Nechung spirit, to destroy Dorje Shugden, but his experience of inauspicious signs and hallucinations grew even stronger. Eventually he realised that he had made a great mistake in opposing Ngatrul Dragpa. Regretting his previous actions, he began to respect the instructions of his root Guru, the First Panchen Lama, Losang Chokyi Gyaltsen, who had indicated that Ngatrul Dragpa was of the same mental continuum as the previous holy beings Sonam Dragpa, Duldzin Dragpa and Je Tsongkhapa Losang Dragpa. With strong regret the Fifth Dalai Lama confessed his wrong deeds and, recognising Dorje Shugden as an enlightened Deity, finally decided to rely upon him. For his daily practice the Fifth Dalai Lama wrote the following request prayer to Dorje Shugden, called *Lhundrub Doma* in Tibetan:

'HUM
'Though unmoving from the sphere of primordial
spontaneity,

With wrathful turbulent power, swifter than lightning,
Endowed with heroic courage to judge good and bad,
I invite you with faith, please come to this place!

'Robes of a monk, crown adorned with rhinoceros
leather hat,
Right hand holds ornate club, left holds a human heart,
Riding various mounts such as nagas and garudas,
Who subdues the mamos of the charnel grounds,
praise to you!

'Samaya substances, offerings and tormas, outer, inner and
secret,
Favourite visual offerings and various objects are arranged.
Although, previously, my wishes were a bit dense,
Do not stop your powerful apparitions, I reveal and confess!

'Now respectfully praising with body, speech and mind,
For us, the masters, disciples, benefactors and entourages,
Provide the good and avert the bad!
Bring increase like the waxing moon in spiritual and temporal
realms!

'Moreover, swiftly accomplishing all wishes,
According to our prayers, bestow the supreme effortlessly!
And like the jewel that bestows all wishes,
Always protect us with the Three Jewels!'[2]

Later he ordered a Shugden Temple to be built in Lhasa called 'Trode Khangsar', which still exists today, and he even crafted the first statue of Dorje Shugden himself.[3]

From this account we can understand that the present Dalai Lama's actions are completely opposite to those of the Fifth Dalai Lama. Due to ignorance, the Fifth Dalai Lama first rejected the enlightened Deity Dorje Shugden, but later his mind changed from ignorance to wisdom and he came to believe in and rely upon Dorje Shugden for the rest of his life. In contrast, the present Dalai Lama at first relied upon the enlightened Deity Dorje Shugden, during this period writing a prayer of request, the first and last verses of which read:

> 'You are the powerful protector of Saviour Manjushri,
> Who have the powerful wealth of the wisdom and
> compassion of innumerable conquerors,
> And who arose as the king of all powerful wrathful ones;
> Please come from Tushita, Pure Dakini Land, and so
> forth.
>
> 'In summary, I request you, O Protector,
> Who are the synthesis of all Protectors, Yidams and
> Gurus,
> Please be the embodiment of all my Protectors, Yidams
> and Gurus,
> And please send rain from the great gathering of clouds
> of the four types of actions, to fulfil the two
> attainments.'[4]

Later, having received advice from the oracle of the Nechung spirit, the present Dalai Lama's mind changed from wisdom to ignorance. Using his political power he has now imposed a ban on the practice of Dorje Shugden, causing suffering to millions of people. Despite this difference in their actions, the present Dalai Lama still says publicly that he is rejecting Dorje Shugden because he is following the Fifth Dalai Lama. This is clearly a lie.

Shugden practitioners want to practise the Gelug tradition purely without mixing it with the Nyingma or any other tradition, and because of this the present Dalai Lama says that Shugden practitioners are sectarian. In truth, Nyingma practitioners also want to practise their tradition purely without mixing it with the Gelug tradition, and this is also true of Sakya and Kagyu practitioners. Thus, according to the Dalai Lama's view, the practitioners of these other traditions would also be considered sectarian, but he accuses only Shugden practitioners of this. This shows how dishonest and biased he is.

What the present Dalai Lama really wants is to become the leader of all traditions of Tibetan Buddhism by making all the practitioners of these traditions throughout the world follow only one tradition that he has newly created. Doing this would naturally destroy the pure lineages and blessings of the Nyingma, Sakya, Kagyu and Gelug traditions. This would be a very great loss to the world, when people more than ever need access to the Buddha's supreme methods for finding true peace and happiness, and it is for this reason that the Western Shugden Society is encouraging people to stop being deceived by the drug of Lama Policy.

CHAPTER 2

Reting Lama – How he chose the false Dalai Lama

The following information has been compiled from various sources, including *Ocean of Truth Explained* and personal testimonies.[5]

Reting Lama was the reincarnate Lama of Reting Monastery in Tibet, and also one of the most important lamas of Sera Jey Monastery near Lhasa. After the death of the Thirteenth Dalai Lama in 1933, Reting Lama became Regent of Tibet. A few years later a relative of the Thirteenth Dalai Lama, a high government minister called Langdun, told Reting Lama and other ministers that the son of one of his (Langdun's) relatives was the reincarnation of the Thirteenth Dalai Lama, and gave evidence to prove this.

The relationship between Reting Lama and Langdun was strained and difficult, and Reting rejected Langdun's claim that the son of his relative was the reincarnation of the Thirteenth Dalai Lama. However, the majority of ministers supported Langdun, and this made Reting anxious about his position. If the son of Langdun's relative was recognised as the reincarnation of the Thirteenth Dalai Lama, he would then lose his own power and position.

To solve this problem and protect his position, Reting devised a plan with his close friend, Ketsang Lama, another lama from Sera Jey Monastery. They made three decisions, the first of which was that the reincarnation of the Thirteenth Dalai Lama would be chosen from a faraway place such as the Amdo Kumbum region near the Chinese border. Secondly, Reting should go to the holy lake of the Deity Shridevi, in accordance with tradition, pretend to see visions of the Tibetan letters A, KA and MA in the water there, and record this in writing. These letters A, KA and MA would indicate that the mother (MA) of the reincarnation of the Thirteenth Dalai Lama would appear in Amdo (A) Kumbum (KA). And thirdly, after completing the second preparation, Ketsang should go to Amdo Kumbum and choose a suitable boy as the Thirteenth Dalai Lama's reincarnation.

When Ketsang and his two assistants arrived in Amdo Kumbum they began searching for a suitable boy. One day Ketsang met an old monk of Kumbum Monastery and explained that he was looking for a suitable boy to be recognised as the reincarnation of the Thirteenth Dalai Lama. He asked if the monk could recommend anyone. The old monk replied that in the nearby village of Taktser there was a boy who might be suitable, and offered to take Ketsang to see him. The old monk was actually a relative of the boy's family, so he was trying to guide Ketsang in the direction of his own family! Taktser was a Muslim village.

Two days later, Ketsang visited the family with the old monk, and was introduced to the boy. Ketsang showed the boy many different objects that had belonged to the Thirteenth Dalai Lama, but the boy showed no interest at seeing these things. Even when Ketsang handed him something saying, 'This is yours' the boy would immediately throw it away. However, Ketsang found that the boy was attractive looking, and thought that this would be good enough. As detailed in *The Ocean of Truth Explained*, Ketsang lied about the results of his examination of the boy.

A few days later Ketsang visited the family again and told the boy's parents, 'We are representatives of the Tibetan government, and if you are happy we want to recognise your son as the reincarnation of the Thirteenth Dalai Lama.' The parents happily accepted. The boy later wore the saffron robes of a Buddhist monk, and the local people jokingly nicknamed him 'The Saffron-Robed Muslim'. In this way, he received the position of the Tibetan Dalai Lama, and because of this Tibetan people began to worship him and keep his photograph on their shrines.

Having made these preparatory arrangements, Reting then informed the Tibetan government ministers and announced to the public that he and Ketsang Lama had found the authentic reincarnation of the Thirteenth Dalai Lama. In saying this he publicly lied.

The ministers of the Tibetan government were unhappy to accept someone from a non-Buddhist background as the reincarnation of the Thirteenth Dalai Lama. However, some monasteries supported Reting, and in particular the Abbot of Sera Jey Monastery forcefully threatened that there would be civil war if the ministers did not accept the reincarnation chosen by Reting. Also, as Reting himself had great political power, the ministers eventually had no choice but to follow whatever he said.

The boy was called Lhamo Dondrub, and to receive permission for him to be released from the Muslim community, Reting asked the Tibetan government to pay 400,000 silver coins to the local Muslim leader of the area around Taktser, a man called Ma Pu-fang. Eventually the Muslim boy Lhamo Dondrub was brought to Lhasa, arriving together with his search party, his family and a large group of Muslim merchants. Reting organised a great welcoming ceremony for the boy's arrival.

Later, when the time came for Lhamo Dondrub to receive ordination vows, he should have received them from the Regent Reting himself. However, Reting did not have the confidence to grant ordination vows because of having seriously damaged his own moral discipline. It was generally known that he was having a sexual relationship with the wife of his brother, and that he was engaging in many other actions that were inappropriate for a monk. Because of this he requested his own Teacher, the elderly Taktra Rinpoche, to hold the position of Regent for three years, and during that time to teach the Buddhist way of life and grant ordination vows to Lhamo Dondrub. Taktra agreed to this request.

After Taktra became Regent he tried to care for and teach the boy, but soon found that Lhamo Dondrub was very different from other boys. Whenever Taktra taught him how to practise the Buddhist way of life, the boy rejected these teachings and showed no interest in any spiritual practice. The boy was bad tempered, and often shouted at Taktra. Taktra was very disappointed and one day told some of his close disciples, 'This boy Lhamo Dondrub does not have any good imprints of a Buddhist way of life. I am worried about our country and what the future will hold for the Tibetan people.' Taktra then appointed two other teachers for the boy – Ling Rinpoche and Trijang Rinpoche.

Later, Taktra received further information that clearly showed that Reting was still having sexual relations with a woman and was engaging in many other actions that were inappropriate for a monk, and he became even more disappointed with Reting. Generally, in the very beginning, many government ministers including Langdun had understood that Reting had lied when he claimed to have received a vision of the three letters A, KA and MA in the holy lake of the Deity Shridevi. At the time one of Reting's assistants had told a friend that Reting had lied, and the friend in turn had passed this information to government ministers. When Taktra's term as Regent was almost finished, the Tibetan government Kashag ('Cabinet of Ministers') received many reports from different people about how Reting and Ketsang had chosen a false reincarnation of the Thirteenth Dalai Lama, and for this and other reasons the government sent soldiers to Reting Monastery to arrest Reting and bring him to Lhasa.

While in prison, Reting was brought one day under guard to the Kashag's meeting room. The Chief Minister asked Reting to tell the truth about his vision of the letters A, KA and MA in the water of the holy lake. Fearing for his life, Reting admitted that he had lied, and made a full confession. He died soon afterwards in prison; some say that he was executed on the orders of the Tibetan Government.

Having learnt the truth, the government then publicly announced that any person who had received a special position from Reting, including Lhamo Dondrub, would be removed from office. However, this was a time of great upheaval in Tibet. There was great fear that the Chinese army would soon invade Tibet and enter Lhasa. Also, many people were unhappy at hearing that Lhamo Dondrub would be removed from his position; and Lhamo Dondrub had apparently begun to improve his qualifications through receiving special care and teachings from Trijang Rinpoche and Ling Rinpoche. For these reasons, a number of lamas strongly requested the government through Taktra Rinpoche to delay the removal of Lhamo Dondrub from the position as Dalai Lama, and this request was accepted. Shortly afterwards, in 1950, the elderly Taktra Rinpoche was himself forced to resign. The Chinese army invaded Tibet in the following year, entering Lhasa a year later. The Tibetan government gradually ceased to function, and finally in 1959 Lhamo Dondrub – or Tenzin Gyatso as he was then called – escaped to India.

In India the false Dalai Lama created the Tibetan exile government. This exile government has hidden the truth about previous events in Tibet, and for fifty years has spread throughout the world only false information that has exaggerated the good qualities of this false Dalai Lama. They have made this false Dalai Lama famous throughout the world, but what have they gained from this? They receive a lot of money every year, but where does all this money go? Their policy of mixing religion with politics has achieved nothing for Tibet, but has greatly damaged the reputation of Buddhism. Although Lhamo Dondrub is a Muslim, throughout his life he has maintained the pretence of being a Buddhist holy being, giving Buddhist teachings that he stole from his root Guru Trijang Rinpoche. In this way he has cheated people throughout the world.

There are innumerable examples of how this false Dalai Lama has cheated people through lying. One example concerns a Spanish boy called Osel Hita Torres who was recognised by the Dalai Lama as the reincarnation of a Tibetan Lama. In May 2009 an article about Osel, 'Boy chosen by Dalai Lama as reincarnation of spiritual leader turns back on Buddhist order' appeared in the British *Guardian* newspaper. The article said:

> 'As a toddler, he was put on a throne and worshipped by monks who treated him like a god. But the boy chosen by the Dalai Lama as a reincarnation of a spiritual leader has caused consternation – and some embarrassment – for Tibetan Buddhists by turning his back on the order that had such high hopes for him.
>
> '… He is now studying film in Madrid and has denounced the Buddhist order that elevated him to guru status. "They took me away from my family and stuck me in a medieval

situation in which I suffered a great deal," said Torres, 24, describing how he was whisked from obscurity in Granada to a monastery in southern India. "It was like living a lie," he told the Spanish newspaper *El Mundo*.[6]

Another article called 'Osel´s awakening, a kid against his destiny' in *Babylon*, an English/Spanish magazine, says:

> 'However, he had no recollection of his supposed earlier life. "My earliest memory is of being four years old in Dharamsala, walking alone through a wood, but nothing about past lives."
>
> '... "I returned to Spain because I had arrived at a point where I no longer fitted into that life. I couldn't find myself, because for me it was a lie being there living something that was imposed from outside." For a person who has lived eighteen years in a bubble, stepping back into reality was a brutal shock.'[7]

Osel finally managed to liberate himself from this false life created by the Dalai Lama and some of his close followers. This is one of many examples of how the Dalai Lama deceives and manipulates people at different levels.

All of Lhamo Dondrub's opportunities came from the supreme kindness of his two Teachers – Ling Rinpoche and Trijang Rinpoche – yet how did he return their kindness? In *The Ocean of Truth Explained* it says:

> 'Later, in Dharamsala, India, Ling Rinpoche died with deep disappointment because the Dalai Lama refused his request to stop encouraging Gelugpas to practise the Nyingma Tradition. And Trijang Rinpoche died with deep disappointment, because the Dalai Lama refused his request to stop banning the practice of Dorje Shugden.'

It is commonly known that in this age the great Lama Je Phabongkhapa and his heart disciples Ling Rinpoche and Trijang Rinpoche are the lineage holders of the Gelug Tradition – a spiritual tradition that was founded by the Wisdom Buddha Je Tsongkhapa and which has flourished extensively throughout the world. The 'Saffron-robed Muslim', this false Dalai Lama, acts directly against the views, intention and deeds of these three precious lamas. The main wish of this false Dalai Lama is to destroy the pure lineage of the Gelug Tradition.

To avoid losing their own position within the monasteries, the present and ex-abbots of the main monasteries of the Gelug Tradition apply effort to fulfil the wishes of the false Dalai Lama. They have directly caused great division within the Sangha (the Buddhist ordained community), have removed thousands of monks from their monasteries, and have destroyed the internal trust, harmony and peace of every Gelug monastery. In this way they have caused many thousands of monks and their families to suffer.

It is shocking that they support the false Dalai Lama in his work to destroy the pure lineage of the Gelug Tradition. How shameful these present and former abbots are: they are truly criminals hiding behind spiritual masks.

The principal of these criminals is Samdhong Tulku, the Prime Minister of the Tibetan exile government and former Speaker of the Tibetan National Assembly. Previously he was Trijang Rinpoche's close disciple, but now he has become a criminal who acts directly against Trijang Rinpoche's view, intention and deeds. On behalf of the false Dalai Lama Samdhong actively encourages Tibetan people to act against Shugden practitioners. After the false Dalai Lama, Samdhong is the source of this international problem.

CHAPTER 3

A Dictator

Like a dictator, the present false Dalai Lama has complete control over both religious and secular life within the exile Tibetan community. One of his dictatorial actions has been to expel Tibetan Shugden practitioners from the Buddhist community, claiming that they are not Buddhist because they worship Dorje Shugden, who he believes is an evil spirit; and at the same time he is preparing to remove Western Shugden practitioners from the Buddhist community for the same reason. With blatant religious discrimination and extreme view, he has already expelled thousands of Shugden practitioners from Tibetan society. Not satisfied with this, he has ordered the collection of signed declarations from Tibetans in the East and West stating that they personally will abandon or never engage in Shugden practice, and that they will not support materially or spiritually, or maintain any connection with, anyone who does engage in Shugden practice.

His aim in collecting these signed declarations is to protect his own reputation, by claiming that he is not breaking the law but simply acting in accordance with the wishes of his people. His acts of religious discrimination are violations of basic human rights, and they defy any rule of democratic law. This is his own fault, not the fault of other people; he is being deceitful in blaming others for his breaking the law. Many people have signed this declaration only because they were afraid of being punished if they did not. These punishments have been clearly reported in many newspapers. Other people have signed because they are the Dalai Lama's supporters and are trying to protect his reputation.

On 29 February 2008 the Western Shugden Society asked the Dalai Lama to produce evidence to prove that Shugden is an evil spirit, saying: 'If you are not telling lies and you have valid evidence to support your actions you should show such evidence publicly, and you should do this yourself not through your people who until now you have hidden behind, having them perform your dirty work'.[8] The Dalai Lama did not reply. His silence proves that he is lying and has no valid evidence.

To fulfil this false Dalai Lama's wish to remove all Shugden practitioners from the worldwide Buddhist community, Robert Thurman has been quoted publicly as saying that Shugden practitioners are 'the Taliban of Tibetan Buddhism'[9] and also that Shugden practitioners are working for the Chinese. To clarify this issue, the Western Shugden Society wrote the following open letter to him:

> '10th September 2008
> An Open Letter
> To Robert Thurman,
> 'We the Western Shugden Society are writing this letter regarding your previous public statement that Shugden people are sectarian, naming them "the Buddhist Taliban"; and your recent public statement that the Western Shugden Society protestors are "working for the Chinese".
>
> 'As you know, Shugden people want to practise the Gelug tradition purely, without mixing with the Nyingma tradition. Because of this the Dalai Lama has said to Shugden people that they are sectarian. In truth, the Nyingmapa also want to practice their Nyingma tradition purely without mixing with the Gelug tradition; and it is the same for the Sakyapa and Kagyupa. So according to the Dalai Lama's view, the Nyingmapa, Sakyapa and Kagyupa are also sectarian, but he only says that Shugden people are sectarian. In reality he is lying.
>
> 'If you, Robert Thurman, are not yourself lying, then you must show your evidence to prove your public statements: that Shugden people are sectarian, "the Buddhist Taliban" as you named them; and that the Western Shugden Society

is working for the Chinese. You should show your evidence publicly through the internet before 25th October 2008. If your evidence does not appear by this date then we will conclude that you have lied publicly and are misleading people.

'Sincerely,
Western Shugden Society'[10]

The Western Shugden Society did not receive any reply from Robert Thurman. Again, his silence indicates that his statements are lies.

Since 1996 the Dalai Lama has stated publicly again and again that Shugden practice is harming his life and the cause of Tibetan independence. Because of their blind faith in the Dalai Lama many Tibetans believe what he says without investigating the actual truth. Consequently they have become extremely angry with Shugden practitioners and have tried to expel them from Tibetan society by many different means. These measures have included public humiliation, acts of provocation and intimidation, and threats; dismissing Shugden practitioners from jobs and positions, and denying them services; spreading lies and manipulating public opinion against them; not allowing other people to have material or spiritual relationship with them; withdrawing essential supplies to monks who engage in Shugden practice, not allowing them to attend classes or services at their monasteries, and forcing them to sign promises that they will abandon Dorje Shugden practice.

Through the Dalai Lama's acts of religious discrimination, Tibetans throughout the world are now divided into those who accept what he says concerning Dorje Shugden and who are consequently angry with Dorje Shugden practitioners, and those who reject what he says about Dorje Shugden and who are consequently experiencing great suffering within their communities. This situation pervades throughout the world, both in the East and in the West.

The entire Tibetan community has lost its internal trust, peace and harmony, and is experiencing a very dangerous situation. The single source of all these problems is the Dalai Lama himself. Through his destructive policies, the Gelug Tradition is divided into those who follow his view and believe that Shugden is an evil spirit, and those who believe that Shugden is a Wisdom Buddha. In this way the Gelugpas have lost their trust, peace and harmony, as well as their common spiritual activities, and are experiencing many dangers. Because of other actions of the Dalai Lama the Kagyupas are also divided into two groups, and have likewise lost their trust, peace and harmony, and their common spiritual activities (see Chapter 11: *The Karmapa Affair*).

For many years the Dalai Lama repeatedly said that he was not seeking Tibetan independence and that he has not done anything to promote it, yet in 2008 he suddenly organised demonstrations in Tibet against China for this purpose. Although the demonstrations were intended to embarrass the Chinese government in the year when the Olympic Games were held in China, the widely-distributed video footage of Buddhist monks involved in looting and violence brought Buddhism into disrepute. He himself enjoys life in his luxurious palace in India, while the poor Tibetan people experience great suffering and danger. His senseless actions have caused Tibetans living in Tibet many difficulties, again through destroying their internal trust, peace and harmony.

As soon as he arrived in India as a refugee in 1959 he made plans to transform the four traditions of Tibetan Buddhism – Nyingma, Sakya, Kagyu and Gelug – into one single tradition. This was his method to destroy the pure lineages of the Nyingma, Sakya, Kagyu and Gelug, and make himself alone the head of them all by establishing a new combined tradition. In this way he sought to achieve complete power to control everything within Tibetan society at a spiritual, political and material level.

At that time, the Tso Kha Chusum ('Thirteen Groups of Tibetans') opposed his plans and because of this for many years the Tibetan community lost its harmony and peace. In 1977 the leader of the Thirteen Groups, Gungtang Tsultrim, was shot dead (see Chapter 11: *The Assassination of Gungtang Tsultrim*). It is commonly accepted that the assassin was paid by people working for the Dalai Lama, in particular the Dalai Lama's notorious brother Gyalo Dondrub (see

Chapter 11: *The Dalai Lama's Brother, Gyalo Dondrub*). Later, other important members of the Thirteen Groups also died suddenly and in suspicious circumstances, again causing many people to believe that organisations behind the Dalai Lama caused their deaths. It is said that there is a secret organisation based in New Delhi led by his notorious brother, whose function is to threaten, destroy the reputation of, or even kill those who oppose the Dalai Lama's plans.

Although the Dalai Lama received an advanced education in Buddhism from his kind Teacher and root Guru Trijang Rinpoche, who was the lineage holder of Je Tsongkhapa's teachings, after he arrived in India his behaviour towards his root Guru sadly changed. He continually acted against the intentions of Trijang Rinpoche, and worked hard to destroy Trijang Rinpoche's spiritual tradition, the pure tradition of Je Tsongkhapa's doctrine.

Since 1996, Shugden practitioners throughout Tibet, India and Nepal have suffered because many Tibetans followed the Dalai Lama's view and adopted the belief that Shugden practitioners are their enemy. In both India and Tibet, many Shugden temples, shrines, statues, paintings and texts have been unlawfully destroyed, and many monks have been expelled from their monasteries. Following the Dalai Lama's orders, the authorities within the monasteries and Tibetan settlements are continually making effort to expel those who have devotion for Trijang Rinpoche and who practise Dorje Shugden. In this way, the Dalai Lama has caused great sorrow and suffering to millions of people.

What is clear is that all these dreadful situations have developed through the power of the Dalai Lama's evil actions. By dictatorial decree he has caused great suffering to people throughout the world, threatened the continued existence of pure lineages of Buddhist practice, opened up deep divisions in the Buddhist community and rendered the cause of Tibetan independence hopeless by destroying the internal trust, peace and harmony of the Tibetan people.

CHAPTER 4

A Hypocrite

Although the Dalai Lama talks constantly about love and compassion, his own actions have brought and continue to bring misery and unhappiness. Since 1996, this false Dalai Lama has unceasingly inflicted heavy and unjust punishment on Dorje Shugden practitioners – all of whom are completely innocent of any crime or misdemeanour. Using his people like an army, the Dalai Lama has destroyed many Shugden temples and shrines, caused millions of people to experience inhumane situations and unbearable feelings of pain, and expelled all Shugden practitioners from the Tibetan community. He has caused innocent people to become severed from their families, friends, monasteries and communities. Thousands of Shugden practitioners have been forced into refugee status for the second time in their life, as they try to escape the inhumane treatment by seeking exile in other countries.

On 8 February 2008, this Dalai Lama caused the expulsion of 900 monks from their monasteries in India. Earlier, on January 9th, he had been invited to inaugurate a Prayer Hall for a large monastic community in South India. At this supposedly spiritual event he publicly announced a 'Referendum on the practice of Dolgyal' (Dolgyal is a false name for Dorje Shugden, which the Dalai Lama uses with a negative attitude), insisting on a collection of votes on this issue by the deadline of February 8th. Each monk was required to cast his individual vote. But since when did any spiritual practice become the object of a political vote like this?

The voting itself was held in public, in full view of monastery administrators, by casting coloured sticks indicating either 'yes' or 'no', with no possibility of abstention. As a direct result of this so-called referendum 900 innocent monks were then summarily expelled from their monasteries.

Most of these 900 monks were very poor and had no other place to live; many were fearful of the future and actually wept as they were forced to leave. The false Dalai Lama is clearly breaking the law by inflicting such blatant religious persecution. Making this difficult situation worse for the expelled monks is the message now being issued by his representatives to the Tibetan community, that anyone who helps Dorje Shugden practitioners will receive similar punishment. Furthermore, anyone who dares not to follow the orders of the Dalai Lama is publicly denounced by his government ministers and declared a 'Chinese supporter'. Not satisfied with this, his ministers encourage groups within the Tibetan community to humiliate, discredit and ostracise the people denounced, and to distribute 'wanted'-style posters giving their names, addresses and biographical details, and those of their families.

Becoming aware of the international public horror at these recent violations, which clearly stem from the single-minded policy of the Dalai Lama alone, the Tibetan Prime Minister and other officials within the exile Tibetan government then started a campaign to distance the Dalai Lama from this referendum, and from the resulting inhumane victimisation of a whole section of the Tibetan community. Such official deception, hypocrisy and duplicity is truly astounding.

One only needs to hear the speeches of the Dalai Lama and to witness current events within the Tibetan community to understand the truth. It should be clear to the international public, and to world leaders, governments and other organisations that it is the false Dalai Lama himself and no one else who solely initiated and who solely maintains the prevalent discrimination, persecution and intolerance within Tibetan society today.

The Dalai Lama has given two reasons for banning the practice of Dorje Shugden. He claims that Shugden practice shortens his lifespan, and harms Tibetan independence, but this is all complete nonsense. He has never produced one valid piece of evidence to prove his claims. He asserts that 'Shugden is an evil spirit', but where is his evidence to prove this? Until now the only evidence he has given has been recollections of his own dreams. But how can he think that such 'evidence' is credible? It is utter nonsense and would be thrown out of any court of law.

If the Dalai Lama is not lying and really has valid evidence to support his actions then he should make this evidence public; and he should do this himself, not through those whom he hides behind and makes perform his 'dirty work'.

The Dalai Lama has somehow been very fortunate in his deception and repressive behaviour. Even now, because he has inherited a high reputation and title from his predecessors, many people still believe what he says without checking its validity. It is only this inheritance that has given him the opportunity to use the title 'Dalai Lama of Tibet' and become known throughout the world. He has never earned this title through his own personal qualities or actions. This is clear from the way in which he has misused his position in this modern world. Instead of putting Buddha's teachings of universal love, compassion and equanimity into practice he continues to inflict discrimination, persecution and intolerance upon Tibetans and upon western Buddhists. He is cynically abusing the faith that people have in him.

If he really is a Buddhist 'holy being', then why is he directly acting against Buddha's teachings? Buddha said, 'You should never harm living beings because they are your kind mothers.' But for many years now the Dalai Lama has harmed millions of innocent people causing them completely unnecessary suffering, fear and dangers. And what benefits have been achieved from these actions? None whatsoever!

This false Dalai Lama is the only 21st century 'Buddhist' dictator. He is the only Tibetan 'lama' who uses Buddha's teachings for political aims. He is the only Tibetan 'lama' who is causing great suffering and sorrow to millions of innocent people. He is the only Tibetan 'lama' who has no compassion.

To liberate millions of innocent people from suffering we request everyone throughout the world, including world leaders, to ask the

Dalai Lama to accept the following four points:

1. to allow anyone who wishes to practise Dorje Shugden the freedom to do so;
2. to stop completely the discrimination against Shugden practitioners;
3. to allow all Shugden monks and nuns who have been expelled to return to their monasteries and nunneries; and to receive the same material and spiritual rights as non-Shugden practitioners;
4. to write to Tibetan communities throughout the world that they should apply practically the above three points.

CHAPTER 5

The Ban on the Practice of Dorje Shugden: a Chronicle of Events

Early 1950s

The Dalai Lama composes *Melody of the Unceasing Vajra: A Propitiation of Mighty Gyalchen Dorje Shugden, Protector of Conqueror Manjushri Tsongkhapa's Teachings.*

1978

The Dalai Lama speaks publicly for the first time against the practice of Dorje Shugden.

1980s

18 July 1980

During an address at Sera Monastery (near Bylakuppe, Karnataka State, South India), the Dalai Lama says 'To summarise my views, I am not saying Gyalchen [Dorje Shugden] is not an authentic Deity, but in any event, for those who mainly rely on Palden Lhamo or Gyalpo Kunga [Nechung], whether it be a great master or a monastery, it does not bode well to worship Gyalchen.'

The Dalai Lama orders the closure of a small Shugden Temple near the main hall of Sera Monastery. Lamas and senior monks from Sera-Jey and Sera-Mey monasteries have attended this temple. By command of the Tibetan exile government, a small new temple of the Nechung spirit is erected in the courtyard of the monastery, and similarly in all Tibetan settlements.

1983

The Dalai Lama orders the removal of the Dorje Shugden statue from the main prayer hall of Ganden Monastery (in Mundgod, Karnataka State, South India), the main monastery of the Gelug tradition of Tibetan Buddhism. When the Dalai Lama is told that the statue is too large to get through the door, he replies that the statue should be broken into pieces.

1986

The renowned Mongolian Lama Guru Deva Rinpoche, then living in Clementown near Dehra Dun, is forced to leave India because his printing press published a letter questioning the Dalai Lama's actions regarding Dorje Shugden.

Guru Deva donates his house in Drepung Gomang Monastery to the monastery itself. The abbot of the monastery manages to persuade a Tibetan mob not to destroy the house.

Under increasing pressure from Tibetans in Nepal, Guru Deva is forced to return to Mongolia, where he remained isolated from the Tibetan community until his death in 2009 at the age of 101.

In the past, he had made very generous offerings and donations to the Dalai Lama, the two tutors and the great monasteries of Sera, Drepung and Ganden at a time when the Tibetan exile community was experiencing serious shortages of everything.

1996

March 1996

The only independent newspaper in Dharamsala, known as *Democracy* is forced to stop publishing. (Dharamsala is the town in northern India where the Dalai Lama lives and where the Tibetan exile government is based.)

10 March 1996

During annual teachings at the Thekchen Choeling Temple in Dharamsala, the Dalai Lama for the first time imposes an outright ban on the practice of Dorje Shugden:

> 'Whether outside of Tibet or within Tibet, this Deity is [in] discord with [government Deities] … this is serious in the context of the common cause of Tibet. Therefore unless I remind you once again, there are ones who pretend they have not heard it. It will be good if you comply [with what we are saying] without our having to resort to this last step. It will be the last resort if [we] have to knock on doors. It will be good if [they] can heed without having to resort to this last step. Whether it be a monastery, or the residence of eminent spiritual masters, or private individuals themselves, it will be a different matter if they do not have the interest of the Tibetan cause [in their heart]. If you consider the cause of Tibet, if you agree to the leadership of the Dalai Lama, if you support my part in the [exile] government, your stand should not be otherwise [on this point].'

21 March 1996

During his talk at the preparatory session of Tamdrin Yangsang and Sangdrub empowerments, the Dalai Lama says:

> 'Basically the autobiography of the 5th Dalai Lama is explicit on the conflict between the Dalai Lama and Tulku Dragpa Gyaltsen. The 'Secret Vision' is also clear on this. Based on them, the 13th Dalai Lama issued a ban. Many things that remained anonymous during his lifetime, on the part of government ministers as well as the common public, started thrashing about after his death. Gyalchen [Dorje Shugden] is one of them. I have come to be counted amongst the line of the 5th Dalai Lama. I feel a definite karmic connection with my predecessor. It is my mandate to complete what was in practice during [the time of] the 5th Dalai Lama and my predecessor. This is my responsibility.'

The Dalai Lama then tells any Dorje Shugden practitioner present to leave the temple, barring them from attending the empowerments:

> 'We are to participate in the empowerment of Tamdrin [a Tibetan Buddhist Deity]. We require recipients who do not

worship Gyalchen ... it happens that Dolgyal [Dorje Shugden] relates to Chinese spirits, we actually mentioned him by name in our exorcism based on Tamdrin at the time. Although these exorcisms cannot be relied upon, I had strange dreams [since then]. [Therefore] I do not feel it will be comfortable for worshippers [of Shugden] to be here. That being the fact I have said it is impermissible to have worshippers of Dolgyal in this audience. If acrimony between deities results in disharmony between humans it will be spiritual ruination ... This will affect the life span of the spiritual master also.

'Hence yesterday we decreed that it will not be right for worshippers of Gyalchen to be among our audience ... If there are any people unknown to me who have crept into this audience who are nevertheless worshippers of Shugden, it is better for you not to stay among us. If you refuse, not only will it not benefit yourself but in the worst case may even become the cause of shortening the life of the Dalai Lama. If you wish for the speedy death of the Dalai Lama, then I have no objection. If there is anyone who wishes to continue worshipping Gyalchen, it is better that they stand up and leave. If there are no such people, it is alright.

'... if you private monks and spiritual masters continue making excuses and continue worshipping thus, you shall have a day of regret. Likewise, in the monastic colleges the majority are beyond criticism; I also see that there are some who remain firm. If you can think by yourselves it is good; as mentioned ... it will not be good if we have to knock on your doors.

'This is my responsibility, although some people may not like it ... I will carry through to completion the work I have begun. I will not back off because of a few disgruntled individuals. I am determined to implement the conclusions of my careful research and will not let it be.'

30 March 1996

The Private Office of the Dalai Lama issues a decree requiring everyone to stop practising Dorje Shugden, with instructions to make people aware of this through government offices, monasteries, associations, etc.

The Assembly of Tibetan People's Deputies (or the 'Tibetan National Assembly', the Tibetan exile parliament) passes a resolution banning the practice of Dorje Shugden by Tibetan government employees.

Letters from the Private Office of the Dalai Lama are sent to the abbots of various monasteries in South India:

> '... government oracles [such as Nechung] point towards there being a danger to the health of His Holiness the Dalai Lama, as well as to the cause of Tibet, due to the worship of Shugden. Banning this is also the conclusion reached by His Holiness after years of observation. There is also a rift between Shugden and the two principal deities of the government as well as with Dharmaraja. Moreover, this is a cause for instability within the Gelugpa tradition.
>
> 'Though aware of repeated addresses by His Holiness, there is continued [worship of Shugden] by Tibetan monasteries, and Tibetan incarnate Lamas and Geshes within India and Nepal. In certain cases, far from heeding this address, individuals have actually urged His Holiness to desist from raising this issue since, according to them, this is causing more harm than good in Tibetan communities.
>
> '... in his inaugural address to the Congress of the Cholsum [Three Provinces of Tibet] Association, he [the Dalai Lama] referred to his recurrent sore throat, mentioning that it may be an indication that he should stop raising this issue. This indicates that he does not wish to speak about this anymore since no one is paying any attention.
>
> 'On March 4th, at the concluding audience for these Congress members, the Dalai Lama remarked: "It is good that paying attention to my health you have passed a resolution regarding this matter. Danger to health does not exclusively mean armed attack. This type is extremely rare in Tibetan society. If there is continued indifference to my injunctions,

then there would not be any point in my continuing to live silently as a disappointed man. This would be a more apt interpretation."

'Therefore, under the auspices of all former Abbots, Disciplinarians, incarnate Lamas and Geshes, an announcement should be made of these talks by His Holiness regarding the worship of deities in such a way that no one can have the excuse of not having heard it. In addition, ensure total implementation of this decree by each and everyone.

'With the additional assistance by the house masters, also ensure the explicit announcement of this decree to all ordinary monks [in the monastery].

'In implementing this policy, if there is anyone who continues to practise Dolgyal, make a list of their names, house name, birth place, class in the case of students, and the date of arrival in case of new arrivals from Tibet. Keep the original and send us a copy of the list. Please share this responsibility and submit a clear report on the implementation of this circular.'

5 April 1996

The Dalai Lama addresses the Tibetan Youth Congress and the Tibetan Women's Association to encourage them to take up the cause of the ban and enforce it actively. During this talk, the Dalai Lama is reported as saying that there may be one or two persons willing to give up their life for him, thus emphasising the determination with which he intends to enforce the ban. Although this remark was later removed from the official record of the talk, it is believed that the full talk was videoed by a Japanese film crew that was present.

At 8 a.m. at Ganden Choeling Nunnery in Dharamsala, a group of nuns go into the abbot's chamber and drag a Dorje Shugden statue into the street with a rope attached to its neck. The main perpetrators – Lobsang Dechen, disciplinarian of the nunnery, Tenzin Tselha and Dolma Yangzom – spit at and sat on the statue before breaking it up and throwing the pieces into the town's garbage dump. This statue had been consecrated by Kyabje Trijang Rinpoche (the junior tutor of the Dalai Lama), Kyabje Ling Rinpoche (the senior tutor of the Dalai Lama), Kyabje Zong Rinpoche and Kyabje Rato Rinpoche.

9 April 1996

The Tibetan Freedom Movement bans the worship of Dorje Shugden by its members.

14 April 1996

The Guchusum Movement Organisation passes a resolution banning the practice of Dorje Shugden by its members.

All government employees are ordered to sign a declaration to the effect that they do not and will never practise Dorje Shugden.

18 April 1996

The Tibetan Department of Health posts a notice to its doctors and staff members:

> 'We should resolve not to worship Shugden in the future. If there is anyone who worships, they should repent the past and stop worshipping. They must submit a declaration that they will not worship in the future.'

19 April 1996

The Toepa Association (Regional Group) passes a resolution declaring Dorje Shugden to be a 'Chinese ghost' and banning its practice.

Employees of the Tibetan Children's Village (in Dharamsala, Himachal Pradesh, North India) are urged to take loyalty oaths.

A decree is sent by the Dalai Lama's Private Office to all major Tibetan monasteries making it mandatory for administrators and abbots to enforce the ban.

Representatives of the Dalai Lama's Private Office begin to arrive in the monasteries and Tibetan settlements to apply pressure and to supervise a signature campaign against Dorje Shugden practice.

22 April 1996

The decree banning the worship of Dorje Shugden is officially read out at Drepung Monastery (near Mundgod, South India), and the abbot confirms that everyone must abide by the ban. Drepung Loseling Monastery distributes a prepared form, saying that anyone who does not sign it will be expelled from the monastery immediately. Many monks, including Dragpa Rinpoche, move away to a nearby Indian town rather than give their signature.

That night, on behalf of some frightened Tibetans at Golathala Tibetan settlement near Bylakuppe, a large statue of Dorje Shugden together with smaller images and pictures of Kyabje Trijang Rinpoche are driven through the night to the Dorje Shugden Temple in Ganden Shartse Monastery, for safe-keeping.

In Bylakuppe, a search party looking for other Shugden images is told by an attendant of the young Lama Dakyab Rinpoche that he has thrown one statue into the lake near Tibetan Settlement No 2. It is reported that many other Shugden statues were thrown into the lake at this time.

23 April 1996

In the main assembly hall at Drepung Gomang Monastery, the abbot announces a strict ban on worshipping Shugden. That evening, the windows of the house of Kyabje Dagom Rinpoche, a prominent devotee of Dorje Shugden, are smashed, and an atmosphere of intimidation pervades the monastery. Kyabje Dagom Rinpoche's disciples complain to the abbot, but are ignored.

The abbot orders a declaration to give up the worship of Shugden to be signed. Later, two monks from Ngari Khangtsen (part of Drepung Gomang Monastery) arrive weeping at the Dorje Shugden Temple at Ganden Shartse Monastery, explaining that although they do not want to give up their religious belief, they have no choice but to sign this declaration or face immediate expulsion from their monastery. One of these monks leaves his monastery the next day.

25 April 1996

On the orders of their abbot, Achog Tulku, who was in Dharamsala at this time, Ganden Shartse Monastery convenes a meeting to discuss the status of its Dorje Shugden shrine. The meeting resolves not to curtail the religious freedom to practise Shugden.

26 April 1996

A Hayagriva puja group of Sera-Jey Monastery receives a special commission from the Private Office of the Dalai Lama to perform twenty-one days of exorcism by the Deity Hayagriva Tamdim Yangsang, against Dorje Shugden and its practitioners. Bari Rinpoche is asked to preside over the exorcism, and in return the Private Office offers to award him the position of 'Geshe Lharampa' (the highest geshe degree) in the following year, with exemption from the Geshe examinations normally required.

Late April, 1996

Zungchu Rinpoche collects signatures agreeing to the ban from Ganden Shartse schoolchildren. When an 11-year-old monk asks what the signed form is for, Zungchu replies that it is a form to find western sponsors for the schoolchildren.

27-30 April 1996

This is a period of great tension in the monasteries of South India. There is fighting between monks from Ganden and Drepung monasteries. At Ganden Jangtse Monastery, a monk is beaten by supporters of the ban and has to be taken to hospital; and windows of the houses of prominent Shugden practitioners are smashed.

1 May 1996

Under armed police protection, Tibetan exile government officials proclaim a decree of the ban at Ganden Monastery.

9 May 1996

Representatives from Tibetan monasteries all over India that traditionally practise Dorje Shugden meet in Delhi and resolve not to give up their faith. They submit their first appeal to the Private Secretary of the Dalai Lama.

10 May 1996

In the hope of a dialogue, Shugden practitioners send a petition to the Dalai Lama, followed by further petitions on May 20th, May 30th and June 5th. The petitions are all rejected.

Since then a number of other petitions and letters have been sent to the Dalai Lama, and requests for audiences have been made on several occasions. They have also all been rejected.

10-11 May 1996

The Tibetan Youth Congress convenes, and resolves to implement the ban in every Tibetan settlement. House-to-house searches start, and statues, paintings and other holy objects are burned or desecrated.

14 May 1996

The Kashag (Cabinet of ministers of the Tibetan exile government) releases a statement denying any religious suppression.

15 May 1996

Kundeling Rinpoche, Director of Atisha Charitable Trust in Bangalore, India, organises peaceful demonstrations against the ban.

The Tibetan exile government in Dharamsala makes the baseless allegation that Kundeling Rinpoche is a Chinese spy, and a warrant for his arrest is issued. He has to leave the country temporarily because of threats made to his life.

23 May 1996

The Dorje Shugden Devotees Charitable and Religious Society (now usually called 'the Dorje Shugden Society') is formally registered in Delhi. Documents including Tibetan government decrees relating to the ban on the practice of Dorje Shugden are mailed by the Society to about 75 human rights groups around the world, as well as to Tibet support and cultural groups.

24 May 1996

The Dorje Shugden Society receives a letter dated May 22nd under the name of Kalon Sonam Topgyal, Chairman of the Kashag, announcing that now there will be a complete ban on Shugden practice. The ban emphasises that:

> '... concepts like democracy and freedom of religion are empty when it concerns the well-being of H.H. the Dalai Lama and the common cause of Tibet.'

28 May 1996

The Kashag Secretariat restricts permission for Geshe Chime Tsering – the general secretary of the Dorje Shugden Society – to travel abroad to lead a cultural tour to raise funds on behalf of his monastery, Ganden Shartse.

5 June 1996

During the 12th session of the Tibetan National Assembly held in Dharamsala between May 31st and June 6th the Chairman of the Kashag, Kalon Sonam Topgyal, addresses the assembly as follows:

> 'Now, on the matter of propitiation of Dharma protectors, I think we first have to come up with explanations on whether this [ban] infringes upon human rights or not. Therefore, it is clear that no one is dictating "dos and don'ts" to all our religious traditions, including the four Buddhist Traditions and Bön. Anyone in our Tibetan society can engage in the religious practices of Islam, Christianity, Buddhism or Bön. However, once having entered a particular religious faith, [one has to] conform to the standard practices pertaining to that religious faith; it is not proper, however, for Buddhist monks to enter and practise [Buddhism] in mosques in the name of freedom of religion. This being the case, this [ban] is imposed without infringing upon religious freedom. In particular, since we are a dual-system nation, we have to proceed in accordance with this religio-political structure [of our nation]; it is not proper to engage in whims in the name of religious freedom.

> In short, the great monastic institutions and those under the [Tibetan exile] administration are not allowed to rely [on Dorje Shugden].'

6 June 1996
An eight-point resolution is passed by the Tibetan National Assembly, imposing a ban on the worship of Dorje Shugden.

19 June 1996
The Tibetan Women's Association sends a letter to Ganden Tripa, the head of the Gelug Tradition:

> 'We heartily appreciate and praise that many monks and monasteries have obeyed H.H. the Dalai Lama's speech against Shugden. We do our best against Geshe Kelsang, some geshes and Westerners. They did protest. You must reply to letters and books written by them. This is the only best way to solve the Tibet issue.'

June 1996
A retired Tibetan minister, Mr. Kundeling, is stabbed and badly wounded at his house. At a meeting in Dharamsala a few days before this, he had mentioned his concern about the course of this new policy of the exile government.

July 1996
A Tibetan Democratic draft constitution for a future free Tibet is amended to read that no judge or juror can be an adherent of Dorje Shugden.

During the preparation for a Kalachakra initiation in Lahul Spiti, the Dalai Lama's female oracle Tsering Chenga alleges that some thirty members of the Dorje Shugden Society will attack the Dalai Lama during the initiation. Elaborate security measures are taken and searches are made, but it is shown to be a false prophecy and a false alarm. No one from the Dorje Shugden Society is present.

7 July 1996

Geshe Losang Chotar from Sera-Jey Monastery burns a thangkha [religious painting] of the wrathful aspect of Dorje Shugden that came from Tawang Monastery in Arunachal Pradesh.

8 July 1996

A Public Notice is posted in Dharamsala:

> 'On July 8th, at 9 a.m. there will be the preparatory rite for the empowerment of Avalokiteshvara [Buddha of Compassion]. And on July 9th there will be the actual empowerment. However, those who worship Dolgyal [Shugden] are not allowed to attend this empowerment. By order of the Private Office of H.H. the Dalai Lama.'

11 July 1996

In the Tibetan community in Shillong, Meghalaya, ten Tibetans (eight men and two women) are expelled from the Tibetan Youth Congress and Tibetan Women's Association for refusing to give up their religious faith in Dorje Shugden.

13 July 1996

Samdhong Tulku, Speaker of the Tibetan National Assembly, talks to local Tibetan dignitaries in New Delhi. He advises them not to use pressure or violent language when persuading Tibetans in the Delhi area to give up the practice of Dorje Shugden, but to ask them to choose between Dorje Shugden and the Dalai Lama.

13-14 July 1996

In Mundgod, South India, over 700 monks, devotees of Dorje Shugden, conduct a peaceful protest against the suppression of Dorje Shugden. Eleven monks from Serkong House of Ganden Jangtse Monastery participate in the march. As a result, these monks are expelled from their college.

On August 6th, in the name of the Tibetan settlements in Mundgod, the Tibetan government sends a letter to Ganden Jangtse

Monastery expressing appreciation for the expulsion of the eleven monks.

14 July 1996

In a closed meeting held in Caux, Switzerland, the Dalai Lama speaks to the legislative members of the Tibetan exile community in Switzerland. An extract from his talk reads:

> 'Everyone who is affiliated with the Tibetan society of Ganden Phodrang government, should relinquish ties with Dolgyal. This is necessary since it poses danger to the religious and temporal situation in Tibet. As for foreigners, it makes no difference if they walk with their feet up and their head down. We have taught Dharma to them, not they to us. ...
>
> 'Until now you have done a good job on this issue. Hereafter also, continue this policy in a clever way. We should do it in such a way to ensure that in future generations not even the name Dolgyal is remembered.'

16 July 1996

The Dalai Lama speaks on *The World Tonight*, BBC Radio:

> 'I myself, in early age, I also did practise this. I was also a worshipper of the Deity [Dorje Shugden]. Then about 20 years ago I found through my own investigation, not suitable. So therefore, you see I also started some restriction. Then, beginning of this year, once more I repeated this. This time our exile parliament and many big monasteries made some effort. That is why a few individuals here and there complain.'

17 July 1996

A resolution is passed by the Tibetan National Assembly (proposed by Yonten Phuntsog and seconded by Tsering Phuntsog):

> '8: In essence, government departments, organizations, associations, monasteries and their branches under the direction of the Tibetan exile government should abide by the ban

against the worship of Dolgyal ... however, if a person is a worshipper of Dolgyal, he should be urged not to come to any teachings such as Tantric empowerments given by H.H. the Dalai Lama.'

Mid-July, 1996

A 70-year-old widow, Mrs Chogpa, from the Rajpur Tibetan settlement near Dehra Dun in Uttar Pradesh, is harassed beyond tolerance by local Tibetans including her immediate neighbours. Helpless against abuse by so many people, she is forced to sell her home, kitchen, and small vegetable garden for a fraction of their value, and takes shelter in Tibetan Camp No 1 in Mundgod, Karnataka State.

25 July 1996

A letter is sent to various monasteries recruiting monks for the Buddhist School of Dialectics in Dharamsala. One of the four qualifications required is: '4: The candidate should not be a worshipper of Dolgyal.'

29 July 1996

900 monks from Sera-Mey Monastery conduct a peaceful demonstration against the ban on Dorje Shugden.

Samdhong Tulku, Speaker of the Tibetan National Assembly, gives a speech to monks gathered in the assembly hall of Sera Lachi, saying during the speech: '... Dorje Shugden and Nechung [state protector] are both Bodhisattvas who have reached high grounds.' This is an example of contradictory statements made by members of the Dalai Lama's government at this time.

August, 1996

An organisation calling itself 'The Secret Society of Eliminators of the External and Internal Enemies of Tibet' makes public its death threat against the two young reincarnations of high Lamas who rely on Dorje Shugden: Kyabje Trijang Rinpoche (aged 13) and Kyabje Zong Rinpoche (11). An extract reads:

> 'Anyone who goes against the policy of the government must be singled out, opposed and given the death penalty ... As for the reincarnations of Trijang and Zong Rinpoche, if they do not stop practising Dolgyal and continue to contradict the words of H. H. the Dalai Lama, not only will we not be able to respect them but their life and activities will suffer destruction. This is our first warning.'

8 August 1996
Tibetan school children are taught for the first time a new song called *Tibetan Cause*, which includes the lines:

> 'All Tibetans, listen to the advice of the Dalai Lama and rely on pure protectors. This is the Tibetan cause.'

4-6 October 1996
The Board of Gelug Teachers in Europe (19 members) meet and resolve to request an audience with the Dalai Lama to discuss this issue. The audience is denied, with a letter from the Private Office of the Dalai Lama stating, 'You have nothing else to say apart from taking care of the 18 volumes of Je Tsongkhapa's works.' Since then the members of the board feel too intimidated to meet again.

The Dorje Shugden Society meets with abbots from Sera, Drepung and Ganden monasteries in New Delhi. The abbots request an audience with the Dalai Lama to discuss the issue. The audience is denied, like all such previous requests by the Dorje Shugden Society.

7-8 November 1996
The house of retired schoolteacher Mr. Losang Thubten is attacked and set on fire, with his daughter and another relative deliberately locked inside. Fortunately they all survive.

In an audio tape published earlier by the Dorje Shugden Society Mr. Thubten had given a number of historical accounts showing blatant injustice in the actions of the Tibetan exile government.

11 November 1996

In Dharamsala a notice is posted banning Dorje Shugden practitioners from attending a Guhyasamaja empowerment to be given by the Dalai Lama.

19-21 November 1996

The Dalai Lama visits Tibetan monasteries at Mundgod, South India, doing so without the traditional request, which is unprecedented for a Dalai Lama.

In the hope of more conciliatory speech by the Dalai Lama, Dorje Shugden practitioners call off a proposed peace march. This cancellation is publicised in the local newspaper, and the organisers also personally call the Deputy Commissioner and Superintendent of Police of Karwar to assure the authorities of this goodwill gesture.

The Dorje Shugden Society in Delhi sends a delegation to request an audience with the Dalai Lama in the hope of reconciliation during this visit. But the Dalai Lama's Private Secretary, Mr. Lobsang Jinpa, tells the delegates that there is no point in the delegates seeing the Dalai Lama if they do not want to give up their practice of Dorje Shugden.

On November 20th there is a monastic debate examination. Members of both Ganden Shartse and Jangtse monasteries (approximately 2,000 monks) participate. The programme begins at 2 p.m. and lasts until 7:30 p.m., and at about 6 p.m. the Dalai Lama speaks. Excerpts from this talk include the following:

> 'When I was visiting Sera Monastery [in Bylakuppe, November 15th-18th], a representative of Shartse and Jangtse monasteries called on me, formally inviting me to visit these two monasteries. I playfully asked them about the recent demonstrations against my officers.
>
> 'This time I will visit Shartse. In the future, however, if this monastery continues to practise Dorje Shugden and build images of this Deity, then I must decline to visit Shartse. In that case they should not invite me, nor will I come even if invited.

> 'Likewise, in Tibet in the future, if any monastery practises Dorje Shugden, they should not entertain any hopes of inviting me, and even if invited, I shall not feel comfortable accepting such invitations.
>
> 'Likewise if there are still people who feel they cannot give up this practice and who feel they will continue to practise Dorje Shugden, I do not see any benefit for them to remain under the auspices of the Ganden Phodrang Tibetan government.
>
> 'You might feel that by publishing letters, pamphlets etc. against this ban, that the Dalai Lama will revoke this ban. This will never be the case. If you take a hard stand, I will tighten this ban still further.'

After these pronouncements, the Dalai Lama stands up from his throne and, pointing to the left and right, asks 'Which is Shartse and which is Jangtse?' Then, pointing towards the Shartse section, he continued: 'I warn you, elder monks of Shartse. You must not say one thing and do another. The elder monks should change their mind, and guide the junior monks.'

1997

6 June 1997

An amendment to the Tibetan constitution is made:

> Original Version: 'The Chief Justice of the Supreme Court: The Chief Justice of the Supreme Court should be a Tibetan national, and in a court of law ... need not be referred to ... .'
>
> New Version: 'The Chief Justice of the Supreme Court: The Chief Justice and the two other justices of the Supreme Court, in addition to being a Tibetan national, should not be a devotee of Gyalchen Shugden and in a court of law ... need not be referred to ... .'

1998

January 1998

Tashi Wangdu, president of the Tibetan Regional Council, states on Swiss TV:

> 'There are governmental and non-governmental gods. To worship gods that are not recognised by our government is against the law.'

2 January 1998

During the Dalai Lama's inauguration of a new debating courtyard of Sera-Mey Monastery, the monks of Pomra Khangtsen (a section of the monastery), who constitute about three-quarters of the monastery and who all rely on Dorje Shugden, are prohibited from attending the ceremony. Under instructions from the Tibetan exile government in Dharamsala, these monks are prevented from leaving their rooms and kept under virtual house arrest by the local police. The Tibetan exile government allege that the monks are a threat to the Dalai Lama's security.

During the inauguration ceremony, there is on display a large thangkha painting of Tha-wo, the monastic protective Deity, who looks like Dorje Shugden. The Dalai Lama, mistakenly thinking that the Deity is Dorje Shugden, bitterly attacks the practice of Dorje Shugden in his talk to the monks. Later he calls the abbots together and begins to chastise them for displaying the thangkha, until it is pointed out to him that it is not of Dorje Shugden.

During this talk the Dalai Lama announces that the monks have to choose between the Dalai Lama and Dorje Shugden.

5-8 January 1998

The Swiss TV SFI news programme '10 vor 10' features four consecutive daily news reports on the Dorje Shugden issue, entitled *Dalai Lama: Discord in Exile.* These reports reveal the suffering and conflict within the Tibetan exile community caused by the ban on Dorje Shugden practice, as well as the hypocrisy of the Dalai Lama and the Tibetan exile government in seeking to suppress evidence of its persecution of Shugden practitioners.

22 March 1998

There is a public meeting in Delhi on the 'religious crisis precipitated by the Private Office of the Dalai Lama'. Participants number about 200, including Shri Rathi Lal Prasad Verma, Member of Parliament (BJP Party), Mrs. Dolly Swami, President of Delhi Mazdoor (Laborers), Prof. Dr. P. R. Trivedi, Chairman of Indian Ecological and Environment, Shri Dev Anand Mishra, prominent Human Rights Activist, Prof. Ashwani Kumar, Faculty of Law at Delhi University, and other dignitaries. Mr. Rathi Lal expresses genuine pain over the religious ban. He says this is a clear attack on religious freedom as guaranteed by the Constitution of India. He offers to discuss this issue with his colleagues in government, and to bring it on the floor of the parliament. Dolly Swami notes that as long as Tibetans live in India, their leadership has to live by Indian law. Every Indian leader or academic who speaks on the occasion expresses deep sympathy with all those Tibetans who worship Dorje Shugden, and offers their encouragement.

23 March 1998

In *Tages Anzeiger* (Switzerland's largest newspaper) the Dalai Lama says:

> 'I think that this Shugden-worship has been for 360 years like a painful boil. Now I have – like a modern surgeon – made a small operation that hurts for a moment but is necessary to solve this problem.'

19 May 1998

A letter is sent from the Department of Religion and Culture, Central Tibetan Administration of the Dalai Lama, signed by Tenzin Topgyal, Assistant General, and directed to all Tibetan 'Settlement and Welfare Officers' in India:

> 'Concerning monks and nuns who wish to travel to foreign countries, after obtaining recommendation letter from the local

> settlement and welfare officer on the strength of authorisation letter from their monasteries, after these are received at this office, (this office) has to obtain authorisation from the Cabinet Secretariat after verifying whether or not the candidate meets the following requirements ...
>
> '3. Attestation from their monastery and the abbot, that neither the host, whether private or organisation, as well as the invitee is a devotee of Dolgyal, that neither the host nor the invitee has any connection with Dolgyal.'

This requirement directly contravenes Article 13(2) of the United Nations Universal Declaration of Human Rights, Article 12(2) of the UN International Covenant on Civil and Political Rights, Article 21 of the Indian Constitution, and Article 18 of the Tibetan Constitution adopted by the Tibetan exile government.

1999

13 January 1999

The Dalai Lama pays a visit to Trijang Labrang (in Ganden Shartse Monastery), the residence of His Holiness the late Trijang Rinpoche (1900-1981), his root Guru. At a gathering of the Labrang's monks, the Dalai Lama says:

> '... during my visit to Switzerland, Lobsang [Chief Steward of Trijang Labrang] asked that the current Choktul Rinpoche [the Dalai Lama's recognised reincarnation of Trijang Rinpoche] be allowed to worship Dorje Shugden like his predecessor, without a decision through the dough ball divination. He also told me that the ban on Shugden practice is causing widespread suffering to everyone, and that it should be revoked. This is ridiculous talk. My reason for banning the Shugden Protector is in the interest of Tibetan's politics and religion, as well as for the Gelug tradition. In our face-to-face meeting, I also told Rinpoche to understand that we may be meeting each other for the last time.'

During this private audience with the Dalai Lama, Ven. Choezed-la, the eldest official at Trijang Labrang, humbly points out that the religious ban has created an unprecedented atmosphere of hostility against both Shartse Monastery and Trijang Labrang, which is not very different from the atmosphere of the Cultural Revolution in Tibet. He requests that, to end the suffering within the Tibetan public arising from this atmosphere, the Dalai Lama would kindly consider revoking the ban. To this the Dalai Lama angrily replies,

> 'There will be no change in my stand. I will never revoke the ban. You are right. It will be like the Cultural Revolution. If they [those who do not accept the ban] do not listen to my words, the situation will grow worse for them. You sit and watch. It will grow only worse for them.'

14 January 1999
During the first public address of a visit to Drepung Monastery, the Dalai Lama touches briefly on the Tibetan issue, and dwells on his ban on the practice of Dorje Shugden. An excerpt reads: 'The Dorje Shugden Society plays games with me wherever I go. They have published an announcement. They think that I will back off. That I will never do. If not in this life, a successor will be appointed to sustain this ban.'

15 January 1999
In Mundgod, representatives of the Dorje Shugden Society call on Mr. Pema Choejor, Tibetan Minister for the Department of Security in Dharamsala, and Mr. Khedrup, Secretary of the same department. The Society's representatives, in their face-to-face meeting, explain their situation in detail. Excerpts include:

> 'The exile government has already taken away both our political rights and religious rights. The Tibetan public has been induced to hate us even more than [they hate] the Chinese, with discrimination, defamation, abuse and baseless allegations. This has gone on for three years now. From our side, time and again,

> we have approached the Dalai Lama and the exile government through personal representation and delegations, as well as numerous petitions. To this date, however, there has been no sympathetic solution from the exile government's side. Today the Dalai Lama spoke out so angrily, violently and so abusively against us, and our faith in front of the entire settlement.
>
> 'According to you, the practice of Shugden in Tibetan society harms the well-being of the Dalai Lama and the cause of Tibet. We do not have any intention to undermine the well-being of the Dalai Lama; at the same time we cannot compromise our religious principles for the sake of political expediency.'

To these representations, the exile government officials respond:

> 'We understand your difficulty. We will convey your grievance clearly to the Kashag in Dharamsala. What you say is true, but since the ban comes from His Holiness, we are put into a very difficult situation. H.H. the Dalai Lama is taking a rock-like stand, and if you also take an equally rigid stand, we [the exile government] are caught helpless in between.'

First week of May, 1999
In an informal meeting of local Tibetan organisations in Darjeeling with a new representative Officer of the Dalai Lama, these groups unofficially announce to the local Tibetan people that henceforth no one is permitted to invite any member of the following three local monasteries to any Tibetan gatherings or Buddhist festivals in the area: Samten Choeling Monastery (established in 1952), Tharpa Choeling Monastery (1922) and Kharshang Monastery (1919). All three are Gelug monasteries that follow the practice of Dorje Shugden.

24 July 1999
An anonymous poster appears in Tibetan settlements in Nepal, reading:

'The Mahayana Gelug Monastery in Kathmandu sent around 152 monks to Pomra of Sera-Mey and Dhokang of Ganden Shartse monasteries.' The posters go on to ask Tibetan families in Nepal not to send children to these monasteries, because these monasteries practise Dorje Shugden.

2000

12 September 2000
Around 3,000 Tibetans descend on Dhokhang Khangtsen at Ganden Shartse Monastery, attacking the monastery and its monks with stones and bricks.

14 December 2000
The Delhi High Court directs the Delhi Police Department to investigate complaints of torture of Dorje Shugden practitioners by agents of the Dalai Lama.

2001-2008

During this period many Shugden practitioners escape from India and Nepal to various other countries as refugees. Other Shugden practitioners choose to stay in India, but in places where there are no supporters of the Dalai Lama. However, members of their families and relatives who still live within the Tibetan communities continue to suffer.

2006

14 February 2006
In Lhasa, Tibet, a statue of Dorje Shugden is forcefully removed from Ganden Monastery and destroyed along with a statue of Setrab (another Buddhist Deity) by a few monks in the Nyakri section of Ganden Monastery. Unrest occurs inside Tibet due to strong denouncements by the Dalai Lama at a Kalachakra empowerment (in India), and because of sending people to Tibet with the

mission to spread allegations that the Deity Dorje Shugden is harming Tibetan freedom and is a danger to the Dalai Lama's life. The houses of practitioners of Dorje Shugden and their relatives are attacked.

19 July 2006

In Lhasa, Tibet, the house of a family of well-known Dorje Shugden practitioners is attacked by four Tibetans wearing masks and claiming to be the Dalai Lama's messengers. The only person in the house at that time is their 20 year old son, who is tortured by having his fingers cut off. He is threatened that next time they will cut his hands off and then they will cut his head off if his family doesn't listen to the Dalai Lama.

January 2008

In a speech at a Tibetan monastery in South India, the Dalai Lama says with reference to Shugden monks:

> 'These monks must be expelled from all monasteries. If they are not happy, you can tell them that the Dalai Lama himself asked that this be done, and it is very urgent.'

A record of the Dalai Lama's continuing persecution of Dorje Shugden practitioners is maintained in the 'Chronicle of Events' on: www.westernshugdensociety.org.

CHAPTER 6

Newspaper and Magazine Articles

The world's media have been reporting on this growing crisis surrounding the Fourteenth Dalai Lama, a crisis that has led to a major tragedy of violence and bloodshed within the Tibetan Buddhist community in India, and which has now spread to Buddhist communities around the world. Two of the principal political issues underlying this crisis are: (1) the Dalai Lama's unilateral decision to abandon Tibetan independence as a political goal, and (2) his ban on the religious practice of Dorje Shugden.

Many newspapers and television networks have now reported on this situation, presenting in many cases the extreme views of the major contestants or the opinions of other journalists, usually unsubstantiated. Now that the public at large is aware that there is a problem, what is needed is a deeper investigation and analysis of the many complex issues involved, with the aim of ending this great tragedy of unnecessary human suffering.

16 June 1988 – 'Dalai Lama asks Home Rule, with Chinese Role, in Tibet', *The Washington Post:*

> 'The Buddhist spiritual leader proposed talks with China to make Tibet "a self-governing, democratic political entity . . . in association with the People's Republic of China [which] could remain responsible for Tibet's foreign policy."
>
> 'The Dalai Lama said he was "well aware that many Tibetans will be disappointed by the moderate stand" these new ideas represent.'

16 November 1988 – 'Dalai Lama offers Tibet Compromise', *The Boston Globe:*

'The Dalai Lama, revered by Tibetans, said yesterday he would settle for less than full independence for Tibet to prevent assimilation of the region by China. "I am not insisting we should be an independent country," the spiritual and temporal leader of Tibetans said in an interview.'

11 March 1996 – 'Refugees chafe at Dalai Lama's rule', *The Independent* (London):

'Tibetan refugees began an 18-day walk from their northern India headquarters to New Delhi yesterday, hoping to step up pressure on China for Tibet's independence. The march reflected growing impatience by a younger generation of Tibetans with the Dalai Lama, whose offer to compromise on independence has failed to win concessions from China.'

26 January 1997 – Paul Salopek, 'The CIA's Secret War in Tibet', *Chicago Tribune:*

'The Americans came, he said, in a big turboprop plane, a gleaming machine that he and other awed Tibetans called a "sky ship". They wore sunglasses and baggy flight suits. They packed shiny automatic weapons on their hips. And speaking through an interpreter, they asked Nawang if he wanted to kill Chinese.

' "I told them I would be very happy to kill many Chinese," recalled the 63-year-old rug merchant, one of thousands of exiled Tibetans living in this picturesque Himalayan capital.

' "I was very young and strong then. Very patriotic. I told them I would even be a suicide bomber."

'The strangers, Air Force pilots working with the CIA, must have liked what they heard because on that hot day back in 1963, at a secret air base in India, they took Nawang and 40 other Tibetan recruits on the first airplane ride of their lives. It was a journey that would stretch halfway around the world and into one of the murkiest chapters of the CIA's long history of covert activity in Asia: a secret war in Tibet.'

20 November 1997 – John Goetz and Jochen Graebert, 'Verklärt, verkitscht – Hollywood feiert den Dalai Lama' ('Modified and kitschified – Hollywood fetes the Dalai Lama'), *ARD* (German TV documentary):

'Things are not so harmonious and tolerant around the Dalai Lama – especially not when it comes to his own power.

'Shugden is one of many traditional Tibetan protector deities. For many years the Dalai Lama also worshipped this centuries old Deity. But now he has banned the worship of this Deity.

'It's alleged that Shugden worship endangers the personal safety and health of the Dalai Lama. There is a ban on any Shugden worshippers receiving employment in roles from Ministers to nurses. And on top of this the Dalai Lama demands that people spy on each other: [quoting government letter:] "Should anyone whosoever continue to worship the Shugden Deity, make a list of their name, address and place of birth. Keep the original and send us a copy of the list." Denunciation and spying have poisoned the atmosphere amongst the Tibetan exiles.

'The Dalai Lama is renowned throughout the world for his wisdom. But in reality he makes all his important political decisions in a highly dubious manner: he asks traditional Tibetan oracles for advice.

'Lhasang Tsering: "In terms of introducing democracy, I can only say that the exile government is half-hearted. In fact, almost embarrassingly so. The question of independence was decided by the Executive in isolation. Not even the parliament was consulted, let alone the people. So I say: the decision to give up the goal of independence was undemocratic." '

5 January 1998 – Beat Regli, '10 vor 10' *SF1* (Swiss TV documentary):

'A ban that shakes many Tibetan Buddhists at the core of their faith. In just one monastery in southern India about a thousand monks refuse to comply with the Dalai Lama's decision.

'Anonymous threats are spread against anyone who refuses to obey his directives: Whoever reveres Dorje Shugden, "... must be targeted and firmly opposed. We must bring them before the public. They have to be killed."

'The Thubten family was literally chased out of their residential area.

'Mrs Thubten: "About a hundred people attacked us. Had we gone out of our house, they definitely would have killed us."

'Fanatical followers of the Dalai Lama tried to burn down this family's house. They successfully forced these people who revere the Deity now banned by the Dalai Lama to flee. They lost everything. This family are pariahs of the Tibetan Community in India.

'Mrs Thubten: "They broke into our house and destroyed everything. They smashed the china; demolished the TV with stones; wrecked the fridge. All the windows, they destroyed everything. My husband worked thirty-five years for all this."

'Only few victims are willing to speak out against this persecution.'

March 1998, Laura Durango, 'Report – Bad Times', *Diario de Cordoba:*

'The media all over the world is taking notice of this conflict. The Swiss television SF1, the German television ARD and the Canadian magazine NOW have already reported on the supposed methods used by the Dalai Lama's Tibetan government in exile to ban the worship of Shugden: destruction of statues and images of this Deity, forced signature campaigns to make people promise to stop their worship, intimidation of those who refuse to do so, expulsion of monks from their monasteries and punishments compared to those of Hitler against the Jews.'

26 April 1998 – Julian West, 'Tibetans accuse Dalai Lama of spiritual betrayal', *The Daily Telegraph* (London):

'All is not well in Shangri-la. In the Dalai Lama's mountain headquarters the chanting of Tibetan monks has been disturbed by loud voices of dissent.

'Many members of the 130,000-strong Tibetan exile community are convinced that the Dalai Lama has betrayed their dream of a Tibet free of Chinese occupation.

'Some are even accusing "His Holiness" of sacrificing Tibetan independence for "his own spiritual ideology" by constantly changing his aims and failing to modernise their society.'

28 April 1998 – Karen Butler, 'Monks, nuns to protest Dalai Lama in NY', *United Press International* (UPI) (New York):

'Followers of the Dalai Lama will petition the Tibetan holy man during his visit to New York City this week asking him to reverse his ban on a traditional Buddhist practice, which they say is religious persecution.

'It is the first time that the Dalai Lama has been faced with a protest from his own followers while visiting the United States.

'The Dalai Lama, who arrives Friday, reportedly stopped Dorje Shugden as a protector deity in 1976 after an oracle told him that the deity was a malevolent spirit harmful to the leader's well being.

'A High Lama, Kundeling Rinpoche, says that on Saturday about 150 monks and nuns plan to present the Dalai Lama with a petition bearing 15,000 signatures objecting to the ban, which he compares to President Clinton forbidding Christians from worshipping the Virgin Mary.'

30 April 1998 – 'Major Change in Political Complexion as Tibetans Call for Militant Campaign', *East Asia Today Reports*, BBC World Service:

> 'The death of Thupten Nudup[sic], the fifty year old monk, who self immolated this week in Delhi, is, according to analysts, producing nothing short of a sea change among the followers of the exiled spiritual leader, the Dalai Lama.
>
> 'Tens of thousands of them came onto the streets of Dharamsala, the seat of their exiled government, to pay respects to the dead man.'

30 April 1998 – Nadine Brozan, 'Buddhists to Protest Dalai Lama during US Visit', *New York Times:*

> 'The Dalai Lama may be bearing messages of peace when he arrives in New York today at the start of a 15-day American tour, but he faces the threat of protests from a coalition of Buddhists who contend that he has kept them from worshipping a deity that they revere.'

30 April 1998 – Karen Michel, 'Protesting the Dalai Lama, All Things Considered', *National Public Radio,* (USA):

> 'The Dalai Lama, the exiled Tibetan spiritual leader, is starting another visit to the United States.
>
> 'This one could be less peaceful than previous visits. A group of dissident Tibetan Buddhists says the Dalai Lama's ban on the worship of a Buddhist Deity called Dorje Shugden amounts to religious oppression. The Dorje Shugden International Coalition is also criticizing the Dalai Lama for heeding the advice of an oracle to issue the ban.'

1 May 1998 – Costas Panagopoulos, 'Zero Worship: The Deity the Dalai Lama Doesn't Love', *New York Magazine:*

> 'The Shugden Coalition ... has collected some 15,000 signatures petitioning the Dalai Lama to lift the ban, which, the Coalition

'All the more jarring, then, that upon arriving in New York City last Thursday to start a 16-day American tour, the icon of enlightened harmony was met by demonstrators. And not just any protesters, but saffron- and maroon-robed Tibetan Buddhist monks and nuns hefting a sign that read DALAI LAMA, PLEASE GIVE RELIGIOUS FREEDOM and accusing him of suppressing devotions to a deity known as Dorje Shugden.'

11 May 1998 – Kenneth Woodward, 'A Scratch in the Teflon Lama', *Newsweek:*

'The reputation of His Holiness—despite constant trafficking with politicians, fund-raisers and media and movie stars—has remained as lofty as the Himalayas. He is the Teflon lama.

'Now there is a scratch. At the start of a religious visit to the United States, the Dalai Lama was picketed in New York City last week by a group of Buddhists charging him with—of all things—religious intolerance.'

13 July 1998 – Christopher Hitchens, 'His Material Highness', *Salon Magazine:*

'The Dalai Lama has come out in support of the thermonuclear tests recently conducted by the Indian state, and has done so in the very language of the chauvinist parties who now control that state's affairs. The "developed" countries, he says, must realise that India is a major contender and should not concern themselves with its internal affairs. This is a perfectly realpolitik statement, so crass and banal and opportunist that it would not deserve any comment if it came from another source. ...

'The greatest triumph that modern PR can offer is the transcendent success of having your words and actions judged by your reputation, rather than the other way about. The "spiritual leader" of Tibet has enjoyed this unassailable status for some time now, becoming a byword and synonym for saintly and ethereal values. Why this doesn't put people on their guard I'll never know.'

1 August 1998 – Sara Chamberlain, 'Deity Banned – Outrage as Dalai Lama denounces Dorje Shugden', *New Internationalist:*

'Buddhists picketed the Dalai Lama's recent visit to the United States and Europe. They protested against the ban on the worship of the 350-year-old deity, Dorje Shugden, whom they say is one of the most revered in the Buddhist religion. In 1996 the Dalai Lama announced that worship of Dorje Shugden was banned and explained that his oracle, Nechung, has advised him that the deity was a threat to his personal safety and the future of Tibet.

'According to P.K. Dey, a human-rights lawyer from Delhi: "Those worshipping Shugden are experiencing tremendous harassment … Dalai Lama supporters are going from house to house searching. For example, in Clementown, India, the house of a family of Shugden worshippers was stoned and then firebombed. Wanted posters describe people believed to be Shugden leaders as the top ten enemies of the state."

'Dorje Shugden worshippers say the ban and its implementation are in direct conflict with the proposed constitution of a free Tibet, laid down by the Dalai Lama in 1963. The constitution states that all religious denominations are equal before the law, and every Tibetan shall have the right to freedom of thought, conscience and religion. But when Dorje Shugden worshippers challenged the ban, the Tibetan Government-in-exile stated that: "Concepts like democracy and freedom of religion are empty when it comes to the well-being of the Dalai Lama and the common cause of Tibet."

'During recent peace vigils a petition with 15,000 signatures was handed to the Dalai Lama stating the need for all Tibetan traditions to flourish. Protesters asked him to sign a declaration of freedom to worship Dorje Shugden. The Dalai Lama refused.'

24 August 1998 – Archana Phull, 'Anti-Shugden agenda flares up conflict', *The India Express:*

> 'The "anti-Shugden agenda" of a convention to be hosted by the United Cholsum Organisation of the Tibetans in McLeod Ganj from August 27 has again flared up the Dalai-deity conflict with over 120 members of the Dorje Shugden Charitable and Religious Society, Delhi deciding to throng the venue, without any invitation, to seek direct "evidence of Cholsum accusations on Chinese funding to the hard core Shugden to divide the Tibetan community".'

2 September 1998 – Hema Shukla, 'Protest by religious dissidents reflects schism among Tibetan exiles', *Associated Press:*

> 'NEW DELHI, India: About 150 Tibetan protesters accused the Dalai Lama of religious repression Tuesday, reflecting a schism in the Tibetan exile society that was once seen as cohesive.
>
> 'The demonstrators were believers in Dorje Shugden, a Tibetan deity whose worship was banned by the Dalai Lama in 1996. They wore white masks during their protest march to symbolise what they called attempts to silence them.'
>
> 'Tibetan officials have indicated that the Dalai Lama believes the spirit of Dorje Shugden is working against him, hampering his goal of winning autonomy for Tibet from China.'
>
> ' "We want the world to know that Tibetan society has problems. There is religious repression," said Cheme Tsering, a spokesman for the marchers. ...'

15 September 1998 – Jim Mann, 'CIA gave Aid to Tibetan Exiles in '60s, Files show', *The LA Times:*

> 'For much of the 1960s, the CIA provided the Tibetan exile movement with $1.7 million a year for operations against China, including an annual subsidy of $180,000 for the Dalai Lama, according to newly released U.S. intelligence documents.

'The money for the Tibetans and the Dalai Lama was part of the CIA's worldwide effort during the height of the Cold War to undermine Communist governments, particularly in the Soviet Union and China. In fact, the U.S. government committee that approved the Tibetan operations also authorized the disastrous Bay of Pigs invasion of Cuba.'

November 1998 – Brendan O'Neill, 'Dalai Lama "a religious dictator"', *Living Marxism:*

'... There is no outlet in Tibet or northern India for Shugden worshippers to protest about what is happening. The only independent newspaper in Tibetan exile society, Democracy, was forced to close in March 1996 after it criticised government-in-exile policy. ...

'Perhaps it is not surprising that the Dalai Lama should be able to suppress debate in Tibetan society. More disturbing is that the Western media has also been largely silent about this. It seems that for many the Dalai Lama is beyond reproach; as Hollywood's and the liberal media's favourite good guy he can do no wrong.

' "It's not the politically correct thing to do, to criticise the Dalai Lama", says Dan Coote of the British branch of the Dorje Shugden Coalition. When Coote sent out press releases at the beginning of this year he was told by some journalists that "they would not touch this story", because it was "too critical" of the Buddhist leader. "There seems to be a double standard", says Coote, 'where some freedoms are seen as worthy of support, while others are ignored".'

10 January 1999 – 'Dorje Shugden worshippers barred from Dalai Lama meet', *The India Express:*

'Theological differences among Tibetan Buddhists reached a climax here on Saturday with the arrival of the Dalai Lama with worshippers of Dorje Shugden deity demanding that they be derecognised as Tibetans so that they can apply for Indian citizenship.

'Before the Dalai Lama's arrival in Hubli where he will conduct a series of religious classes, a notice was sent to all the communities stating that followers of Dorje Shugden, addressed as Dolgyal (a derogatory term), would not be allowed to attend the seminar. Passes were issued only to those people and monks who gave a written statement that they were not followers of this deity.'

10 March 1999 – Iain S. Bruce, 'The Dark Side of the Dalai Lama', *The Scotsman:*

'To much of the Western world he is the very embodiment of kindness and peace, a gentle robed figure of great wisdom and limitless virtue. Feted by politicians, pop stars and Hollywood stars, the seemingly undisputed spiritual and political leader of the movement to free Tibet has always seemed like a pretty safe bet in a diplomatic arena populated by rogues and charlatans.

'The cracks in the Dalai Lama's impeccable image, however, are beginning to show and accusations are being levelled with increasing frequency which link the 1989 Nobel laureate to religious repression, despotism and murder.

' "The Dalai Lama has two faces. In the West he enthusiastically creates an atmosphere of liberalism and open dialogue; in the East he treats people as a monarch does his subjects", says Lama Kundeling, the abbot of the Atisha monastery in Bangalore and a respected member of the exiled Tibetan community. "There is no freedom for us – he has a total monopoly over all spiritual and secular matters and spreads confusion and distress among the Tibetan people.'

5 January 2001 – 'Of the Dalai Lama and a witch-hunt', *Frontline* (India's National Magazine):

'What has been the impact of the ban?

'Kundeling Rinpoche: "Severe. I call it the Tibetan Inquisition initiated worldwide, but particularly in India. For example, the house of every Tibetan was searched, pictures and images of Dorje Shugden were trampled upon, desecrated, burnt or destroyed publicly. The houses of prominent people – followers of Dorje Shugden – were attacked during the nights, and death threats issued to all those who did not follow the dictates of the Dalai Lama. A number of monks were expelled from the monastery at the Mundgod settlement for having participated in a peaceful protest march organised by me on May 15, 1996 in the Mundgod settlement. When the Dorje Shugden Society was established in April 15, 1996 in Delhi, the Dalai Lama and his so-called ministry used threats, money, and the Indian bureaucracy to close it down forcibly." '

18 September 2003 – Laurie Goodstein, 'Dalai Lama says Terror may need a violent reply', *New York Times:*

'The Dalai Lama, a winner of the Nobel Peace Prize and one of the world's most prominent advocates of nonviolence, said in an interview yesterday that it might be necessary to fight terrorists with violence, and that it was "too early to say" whether the war in Iraq was a mistake.

' "I feel only history will tell," he said. "Terrorism is the worst kind of violence, so we have to check it, we have to take countermeasures."

'The Dalai Lama spoke in his first visit to New York City since the 2001 terrorist attacks. He is on the last stop of a United States tour that has highlighted his dual roles as Buddhist teacher and head of state.'

10 October 2003 – Colman McCarthy, 'The Dalai Lama is no Gandhi', *National Catholic Reporter:*

'If you've ever had suspicions that the Dalai Lama is a lightweight, suspect no more. He is.

'Recently finishing a U.S. lecture tour that attracted rock-concert crowds in major cities, the 68-year-old Tibetan Buddhist came up against a pesky New York Times reporter who asked questions about terrorism and the war in Iraq. In a story headlined "Dalai Lama Says Terror May Need a Violent Reply," the monk said: "Terrorism is the worst kind of violence, so we have to check it, we have to take countermeasures."

'Soothing words to the Bush war makers as they seek $87 billion for countermeasures to bolster earlier countermeasures that failed. No amount of Buddhist incense smoked over the lama's words can hide their meaning: Kill people to solve conflicts. Here is one more religious leader who is a pacifist between wars, akin to being a vegetarian between meals ...

'The Dalai Lama joins a long list of people who, in the parlance of celebrity, are famous for being famous. He is an entertainer, a headliner, a showman—complete with maroon robes and a bare shoulder. Nothing wrong with that. A shtick's a shtick. But he's nowhere close to being in the company of Gandhi, who said, "I do not believe in any war," or the Mennonites Church of the Brethren or Quakers who don't hedge their antiwar convictions, much less wait for history.'

23 May 2007 – Michael Backman, 'Behind the Dalai Lama's Holy Cloak', *The Age* (Melbourne):

'Rarely do journalists challenge the Dalai Lama.

'Partly it is because he is so charming and engaging. Most published accounts of him breeze on as airily as the subject, for whom a good giggle and a quaint parable are substitutes for hard answers. But this is the man who advocates greater autonomy for millions of people who are currently Chinese citizens, presumably with him as head of their government. So, why not hold him accountable as a political figure? ...

'What has the Dalai Lama actually achieved for Tibetans inside Tibet?

'If his goal has been independence for Tibet or, more recently, greater autonomy, then he has been a miserable failure.

'He has kept Tibet on the front pages around the world, but to what end? The main achievement seems to have been to become a celebrity. Possibly, had he stayed quiet, fewer Tibetans might have been tortured, killed and generally suppressed by China.'

5 February 2008 - French Politician Jean Luc Melanchon on the Olympic Protests, Telematin, *France 2* (French TV):

'Jean Luc Melanchon: "If people want to protest against the Olympics, it means they accept the Dalai Lama's claims about Tibet. But there we need to look carefully and not be naive. I find it unbelievable, really, to see French people, who would argue forcefully for the separation of church and state, finding it desirable to have a theocracy in Tibet ...

'We know how these things work. It's not a simple affair about an association or an NGO. There are strategic interests being played out. Kosovo didn't demand independence, but ended up with a US military base. So let's not pretend to be naive, and say that this isn't about geo-political or geo-strategic issues. People are being manipulated." '

6 March 2008 – Brendan O'Neill, 'Why Tibetophilia won't set Tibet free', edited version first published on *Comment is Free* on 6th March 2008 (available on www.spiked-online.com/index.php/site/article/4852/, March 10th 2008):

'At the same time, [free Tibet] campaigners' unquestioning support for the Dalai Lama suggests they see Tibetans as an immature people who need a godlike figure to lead them. The Dalai Lama was never elected by anybody; rather, in a process that makes Britain's House of Lords seem almost modern and democratic (I said almost), he was handpicked by a tiny sect of monks who believed that he represents one of innumerable incarnations of the Buddhist entity Avalokitesvara.

'Indeed, some writers on Tibet have pointed out that the idolisation of the Dalai Lama by Western activists and officials, and of course by some Tibetans, might actually undermine the development of democracy in Tibet. In her book *The Tibetan Independence Movement: Political, Religious and Gandhian Perspectives*

[Routledge, 2002], Jane Ardley writes: "[It] is apparent that it is the Dalai Lama's role as ultimate spiritual authority that is holding back the political process of democratisation. The assumption that he occupies the correct moral ground from a spiritual perspective means that any challenge to his political authority may be interpreted as anti-religious."

'In elevating the Dalai Lama to the position of unquestionable representative of the Tibetan people, pro-Tibet activists are helping to stifle "the opportunity for opposition and the expression of different views" – the very lifeblood of democracy. Indeed, some Tibetan Buddhist groups that have challenged or questioned the authority of the Dalai Lama have found themselves denounced and suppressed by the Dalai Lama's people.'

21 March 2008 – Somini Sengupta, 'Some Tibetan Exiles Reject Middle Way', *The New York Times:*

'Since March 10 the Dalai Lama has stuck to his "middle way" script and appeared remarkably affable, at least publicly, even as China accused him of masterminding the uprising and called him "a devil with a human face." ...

'Yet, a handful of radical Tibetan exile groups have said angrily that the "middle way" has achieved nothing in nearly 30 years. They have called for an Olympic Games boycott, burned Chinese flags and refused to call off a march from here to Lhasa, Tibet's capital, which he has called impractical in opposing a mighty state intent on using force.

'So the question arises of whether the Dalai Lama, who has spent the last 49 years here in India and built one of the most powerful exile movements in the world, is out of touch with his own people.'

31 March 2008 – Pankaj Mishra, 'Holy Man: What does the Dalai Lama actually stand for?', *The New Yorker Magazine:*

'Since the Dalai Lama speaks English badly, and frequently collapses into prolonged fits of giggling, he can also give the

> impression that he is, as Pico Iyer reports a journalist saying, "not the brightest bulb in the room."
>
> 'His simple-Buddhist-monk persona invites skepticism, even scorn. "I have heard cynics who say he's a very political old monk shuffling around in Gucci shoes," Rupert Murdoch has said. Christopher Hitchens accuses the Dalai Lama of claiming to be a "hereditary king appointed by heaven itself" and of enforcing "one-man rule" in Dharamsala, the town in the Indian Himalayas that serves as a capital for the more than a hundred and fifty thousand Tibetans in exile. ...
>
> 'His critics may have a point: the Dalai Lama's citizenship in the global cosmopolis seems to come at a cost to his dispossessed people.'

6 May 2008 – Venkatesan Vembu, 'Dalai Lama's Middle Way has failed', *DNA* (India):

> 'Jamyang Norbu: "There's now a very strong voice among Tibetan people, especially among young people. ... A lot of them, who are coming out of Tibet into exile, are not so reverent of the Tibetan government-in-exile. They are now saying that the Tibet government's policy – and the Dalai Lama's 'Middle Way' approach – is a failure. The Dalai Lama in some ways is desperate. He doesn't comprehend the nature of modern politics – and I don't think he has an understanding of totalitarian regimes." '

17 May 2008 – Stefan Kornelius, 'A politician in Monk's Robes', *Suddeutsche Zeitung* (Germany):

> 'Even in the first hours of his journey through Germany the spiritual leader of the Tibetans, the Dalai Lama, didn't want to utter a thoughtless word. In countless interviews, accompanied by cameras at every step, and in his speeches to followers and believers he patiently repeated the same old claims and assertions: No, this is not a political visit, he is just a simple monk, it's about religious and cultural autonomy for

the Tibetan People and protecting the environment. The unity of China is not being challenged and all his efforts are based in non-violence.

'Whoever examines this flow of words for their political substance will quickly realise that, according to the Constitution of the Tibetan Government in Exile, enacted in the Tibetan year 2218 (1991). The Dalai Lama is the lord over the executive and the legislative. Nothing goes in the world of the Tibetan Exiles without his say so.'

17 May 2008 – 'Stop Lying', *Suddeutsche Zeitung* (Germany):

'It sounds like a battle cry from the stadium, which is diagonally opposite, yet it is an accusation: "Dalai Lama, stop lying" Again and again the 300 robed protesters chant the sentence. Motorists wind down their windows, perhaps they cannot believe what they are hearing. Are there actually people outside China, even Tibetans who have something against the Dalai Lama? ...

'This is not about politics but about religious freedom. Nothing is being asked of the Dalai Lama other than what he is asking of the Chinese, but nobody is interested in what he's actually doing. "Here the Dalai Lama presents himself as a Spiritual Leader. We want people to look behind the mask".'

18 May 2008 – Mariam Lau, 'The Laughing King without a Country', *Die Welt am Sonntag* (Germany):

'Wherever the Dalai Lama shows up – and he shows up pretty much everywhere – a spiritual supermarket immediately pops up. For example, in front of the RuhrCongress in Bochum, the second stop on his long planned tour of Germany are stands selling Tibet Snowlion cushions, mousepads with his likeness, incense, wooly hats and "Free Tibet" ringtones. Across the way, in a gold and burgundy throng, are the monks from the Western Shugden Society accusing him of lying: "Dalai Lama, stop discrimination!"

'Indeed in an unusual act of political and religious constriction, a few years ago the religious leader of the Tibetans banned the worship of the Buddhist Deity Dorje Shugden that he felt was backwards and bloodthirsty. ...

'He isn't opposed to having his face on screen-savers. He happily writes forwards for embarrassing books and has made a dubious Temple of Hollywood. At the end of the day all he has is PR. If the Palestinians could have a figurehead like him instead of leaders intent on self-destruction they would have probably regained their country longer ago. But the Dalai Lama hasn't achieved much for his people up to now. Not one influential head of state in the world has given clear and concrete support to his campaign for cultural autonomy.'

18 May 2008 – from 'Rights pleas against Dalai Lama', *The Telegraph* (Calcutta):

Shimla, May 17th: 'A Delhi-based charitable trust has filed a human rights violation petition in Delhi High Court against the Dalai Lama and Samdong Rinpoche, the Prime Minister of the Tibetan government-in-exile.

' "The Dalai Lama is blackmailing Dorje Shugden worshippers into giving up their religious beliefs. ... " said the petition filed ... '

20 May 2008 – Brendan O'Neill 'Is the Dalai Lama a religious dictator?', *Spiked Magazine:*

'In her book *The Tibetan Independent Movement: Political, Religious and Gandhian Perspectives*, Jane Ardley argued that in terms of the development of internal political life in Tibet and Dharamsala, "[It] is apparent that it is the Dalai Lama's role as ultimate spiritual authority that is holding back the political process of democratisation. The assumption that he occupies the correct moral ground from a spiritual perspective means that any challenge to his political authority may be interpreted as anti-religious." ...

'The state of denial in the West about some of the Dalai Lama's alleged power-tripping, or at least the unquestioning attitude towards the Dalai Lama and everything that he does, highlights the role that he plays for many Western celebs, commentators and politicians today: he's a cartoon "good guy", giggling, pure and righteous, who apparently should be unconditionally applauded for standing up to the "Evil Chinese". All of the Dalai Lama's bad points – his origins in the stifling medievalism of 1930s Tibet; his archaic practices; his disregard for "concepts like democracy and freedom of religion"; his backing from the CIA in its Cold War with the Chinese – are simply ignored.'

22 May 2008 – Mario Cacciottolo, 'Peace and placards greet Dalai Lama', *BBC News:*

'Directly opposite, on the other side of the road, are a group of Buddhist monks whose argument is that the Dalai Lama has called for a ban on the worship of the Buddhist Deity Dorje Shugden, and particularly a prayer to him.

'The arguments are complicated, but basically His Holiness says that this particular Deity is un-Buddhist in its nature.

'These followers disagree, and according to Kelsang Pema, a nun taking part in the protest, what they want is a "meaningful discussion" with the Dalai Lama. "The only purpose of Dorje Shugden is to help people develop Buddhist minds of love, peace and compassion," she said.

' "We've sent him faxes, email and letters asking him to talk to us about it but they're all ignored. The Dalai Lama himself practised as we do until he was 50." '

23 May 2008 – from *The Metro* (London):

'The Dalai Lama's tour of Britain ran into multiple protests yesterday as demonstrators voiced their opposition to his political and religious beliefs. As the Tibetan spiritual leader spoke inside the Royal Albert Hall, hundreds lined the streets outside.

'They waved signs reading "Give us Religious Freedom" and "Hypocrisy".'

23 May 2008 – Ann Treneman, 'Dalai Lama drama as Westminster sees the Light', *The Times* (London):

'The Dalai Lama arrived at Westminster in a silver Merc accompanied by three other silver Mercs. His Holiness may be close to the heavenly light but he does not travel light. ...

'It has to be said that Mr Lama is pure box office. He is the crowd-pleaser to end all crowd-pleasers. He began by getting out the crimson man-bag that he always carries and which I thought contained something sacred or at least the meaning of life.

'Like a magician, Mr Lama brought out its contents: first he brandished a crimson visor (it matched his robes perfectly) and placed it at a rakish angle on his shaven head. Then he showed us his spectacles case with great delight. He brought out a tiny cellophane-wrapped item. "A sweetie!" he cried, giggling.

'Then he began to ramble. "Sometimes on the aeroplane, breakfast is quite small. I need not only quality but quantity because the Buddhist monk – no dinner. So I always carry some bread."

'It seemed a shame when we had to quit playing "Show Me Your Manbag" and talk about human rights. To start Mr Lama did a lot more bowing (he can bow while he sits)...

'Then he was off in a swirl of crimson. I tell you, if he wasn't a revered spiritual leader, he'd be a great ham actor. He's a Drama-Lama, that's for sure.'

27 May 2008 – John Hess, 'Protest over Dalai Lama', *BBC News:*

'These followers [belonging to the Western Shugden Society] came to Nottingham today to voice anger over his ban of an ancient Buddhist prayer.

'His [the Dalai's Lama's] visit to Nottingham has not only been politically controversial but this demonstration highlights the controversies within the Buddhist faith itself over his style of leadership.'

29 May 2008 – Brendan O'Neill, 'Down with the Dalai Lama', *The Guardian* (London):

'Has there ever been a political figure more ridiculous than the Dalai Lama? This is the "humble monk" who forswears worldly goods in favour of living a simple life dressed in maroon robes. Yet in 1992 he guest-edited French Vogue, the bible of the decadent high-fashion classes …

'The Dalai Lama says he wants Tibetan autonomy and political independence. Yet he allows himself to be used as a tool by Western powers keen to humiliate China. Between the late 1950s and 1974 he is alleged to have received around $15,000 a month or $180,000 a year from the CIA.

'In truth he is a product of the crushing feudalism of archaic, pre-modern Tibet, where an elite of Buddhist monks treated the masses as serfs and ruthlessly punished them if they stepped out of line.

'The Dalai Lama demands religious freedom. Yet he persecutes a Buddhist sect that worships a deity called Dorje Shugden.'

30 May 2008 – Matt Wilkinson, 'Update: Hundreds Protest at Dalai Lama Visit', *The Oxford Times* (Online), Oxford, England:

'The Dalai Lama is speaking at the Sheldonian Theatre and about 1000 members of the Western Shugden Society turned up outside. The protesters chanted "Dalai Lama Stop Lying" and other slogans as he arrived for the talk at 9.30am. The chanting reached fever pitch as the Dalai Lama arrived in a chauffeur-driven vehicle and was escorted into a building. The society claims the Tibetan leader has banned a traditional Bhuddist[sic] prayer, while his followers are abusing the human rights of Shugden Bhuddists[sic].'

5 June 2008 – Michael Backman, 'Selling Tibet to the World, *The Age* (Melbourne):

> 'Why is the Dalai Lama so hell-bent on moving against Shugden supporters? A reason might be that he genuinely believes Shugden worship is wrong. Another seems to derive from his desire to unite the four traditions of Tibetan Buddhism - the Nyingma, Sakya, Kagyu and Gelugpa. This has always been one of the Dalai Lama's problems. He is not the head of Buddhism; he is not even the head of Tibetan Buddhism. Traditionally, the Dalai Lamas are from the Gelugpa sect. But since leaving Tibet, the current Dalai Lama has sought to speak for all Tibetans and particularly all overseas Tibetans.
>
> 'To enhance his authority, he has sought to merge the four traditions into one and place himself at its head. But Dorje Shugden presents a roadblock.'

11 June 2008 – *SBS Worldnews Australia:*

> 'The Dalai Lama arrived in Australia today to a warm welcome from supporters but was branded a "liar" and a "hypocrite" by some 50 protesting Buddhist monks and nuns.
>
> ' "He is a hypocrite, and it's very sad to say that about a religious leader", said WSS spokesperson Kelsang Pema … "He is not practising what he preaches. He's here teaching about love and compassion but he endorses human atrocities, basically."
>
> 'She said the Dalai Lama's "inflammatory" campaign against a Buddhist Deity called Dorje Shugden had resulted in thousands of monks being expelled from monasteries, supporters denied food, medicine and travel visas, families being ostracised and Shugden temples being destroyed.'

12 June 2008 – John Stapleton, 'Adoration and Protests greet Dalai Lama', *The Australian:*

> 'While adoring crowds met the Dalai Lama in Sydney yesterday for the start of his six-day visit, there was also the predicted

rabble of protesters on hand accusing him of being a liar and hypocrite.

'But instead of the dissenters being Chinese nationals, the group deriding him were fellow Buddhists with barely an Asian face among them.

'About 100 Buddhists clad in the same scarlet robes as the Dalai Lama stood outside the Sydney Showground at Homebush chanting "Dalai Lama liar" and waving placards calling for religious freedom while the Tibetan spiritual leader inside preached love and compassion.

' "He is a hypocrite, and it's very sad to say that about a religious leader," Western Shugden Society spokeswoman Kelsang Pema said. "He is not practising what he preaches. He's here teaching about love and compassion but he endorses human atrocities, basically." Ms Pema said the Dalai Lama's "inflammatory" campaign against a Buddhist deity called Dorje Shugden had resulted in thousands of monks being expelled from monasteries, supporters denied food, medicine and travel visas, families being ostracised and Shugden temples being destroyed. "It's mainstream Tibetan Buddhism, but he is making us look like an offshoot because he has had a change of heart," she said. "He has banned a prayer which he himself engaged in for half of his life." '

15 June 2008 – 'The Tibetan Opposition', The Sunday Programme, *Nine Network* (Australian TV):

'Kelsang Lhachog: "One of the things about the Dalai Lama is that he has this extraordinary reputation that sort of puts a spell over the people of this world so that they don't question his actions and find it difficult to believe that he could make any mistakes or be faulty in any way. He speaks beautiful words but no one checks whether or not his actions actually match up to the words that he speaks. If you look into what is actually happening in his community that he is the leader of, you will see very clearly that he acts like a dictator. ...

' "I think that he's a political leader who is masquerading as a spiritual leader, and that is something that we all understand in the west is not an appropriate thing to mix. We all know: don't mix religion with politics because then it all gets very messy, and he's confused those two roles and is using his political power to enforce his own religious views on others." '

13 July 2008 – Tony Nauroth, 'Hundred Protest Dalai Lama', *The Express Times*, USA:

Bethlehem [Pennsylvania, USA]: 'Those looking for enlightenment Saturday from the Dalai Lama at Lehigh University's Stable Arena first had to manoeuvre past 400 monks and nuns protesting a 40-year-old arcane decree by the Tibetan-leader-in-exile that they said violates their religious freedom.'

18 July 2008 – David Van Biema, 'The Dalai Lama's Buddhist Foes', *Time Magazine*, USA:

'On Thursday afternoon, following a teaching by the Dalai Lama at New York City's Radio City Music Hall, a group of 500 or more audience members screamed at and spat at a mixed group of about 100 people, both Tibetan and Western, who had been peacefully protesting the high lama. Police felt it prudent to move in fast, with horses, and herded the smaller group into buses for their own protection. The pro-Dalai Lama crowd had also flung money at their foes, an insult indicating that they had been bought (presumably by the high lama's enemies in Beijing). Said one of the anti–Dalai Lama protesters, Kelsang Pema, who is British, has a Tibetan name and is the spokeswoman for the Western Shugden Society, "If this is what the Dalai Lama's people do to us in America, can you imagine what they would have done somewhere else?" '

8 August 2008 – 'The Dalai Lama's Demons', *France 24* (French TV documentary):

> 'Dalai Lama: "These monks must be expelled from all monasteries. If they are not happy, you can tell them that the Dalai Lama himself asked that this be done, and it is very urgent."
>
> 'The speech was a historic moment in the history of Tibetan Buddhism, and the beginning of a schism which could exclude the four million Tibetans followers of Shugden. A few weeks after the Dalai Lama's speech, Shugden monks could no longer enter monasteries. They regroup themselves outside village walls and meditate on why the Dalai Lama has excluded them.
>
> ' "Can the Dalai Lama really ban an entire religion?" asks one. "We are in the right, he's the one who is being incoherent. On one hand, he's always preaching freedom of religion and compassion, but on the other he's forbidding us to worship the god we choose", says another.
>
> 'Photos of Shugden leaders are posted on city walls, branding them as traitors. Signs at the entrance of stores and hospitals forbid Shugden followers from entry. It's apartheid, in a Buddhist land.'

28 August 2008 – Meindert Gorter, 'Why did the Dalai Lama ban Dorje Shugden?', *The New Statesman:*

> 'Gradually the pressure on Dorje Shugden practitioners got worse. Fanatical Dalai Lama followers began to demolish statues of the deity, the existing social solidarity amongst Tibetans was gone. Even in Tibet itself, where restoration of temples is in full swing and people enjoy new religious freedom, this ban created suspicion. Dorje Shugden worshippers were accused of being part of the 'Dorje Shugden sect' and became outcasts. The Dorje Shugden Society was founded, an ad-hoc group of people working together to oppose the ban – not to save the enlightened deity from harm but to help thousands of people from becoming outcasts.

'But numerous appeals and worldwide protests have not helped. The Dalai Lama has not responded and refuses all contact. If you think the Dalai Lama is only in the business of provoking positive sentiments, as most Westeners believe, you have to firmly close your eyes to imagine this less romantic reality.

'During speeches in India in January 2008, he has enforced the ban more strictly than ever before.'

30 September 2008 – 'The Dalai Lama: The Devil Within', *Al Jazeera* (TV documentary):

'With the help of rebel monk Kundeling Rinpoche, [the Dorje Shugden Society] are taking the most famous ex-Shugden practitioner, the Dalai Lama himself, to court.

'Kundeling Rinpoche: "So there is no democracy. The man, Dalai Lama, talks about democracy, talks about compassion, talks about dialogue, talks about understanding, talks about a solution, but for us there is no solution. There is no dialogue. There is no understanding. There is no compassion. Because in his perception we are not human beings. We are just evil. We are evil and we are agents of the Chinese. That is what it is. It is as simple as that."

'With just a few days to go before the Dalai high court hearing, Kundeling and Thubten meet with their lawyer.

'Shree Sanjay Jain (Human rights lawyer): "It is certainly a case of religious discrimination in the sense that if within your sect of religion you say that this particular Deity ought not to be worshipped, and those persons who are willing to worship him you are trying to excommunicate them from the mainstream of Buddhism, then it is a discrimination of worst kind."

9 October 2008 – 'Sur les traces du Dalaï Lama' ('Following the Dalai Lama's Tracks'), Envoye special, *France 2* (French TV documentary):

'Dalai Lama: "I don't want any more disorder in the monasteries. And to those who are not happy, tell them that the Dalai

Lama approves of the expulsions prescribed by the abbots in the temples."

'Reporter: For the first time, I discover an authoritarian face – himself the wise Tibetan is calling for the exclusion of the faithful. Why, and who is this Deity? To understand this, I am going to meet Dorje Shugden followers. ...

'Monk: "This Deity has never divided Tibetans. This is untrue. It is the Dalai Lama who has divided us, by banning Shugden practice. Before, everything was going well. The community was living in peace."

'Reporter: "Today, Shugden followers are expelled from their monasteries, and their photos are posted in the streets. A witch hunt has started in Southern India." '

7 March 2009 – David Eimer, 'Dalai Lama too soft on China say Tibetan Exiles', *The Daily Telegraph* (London):

'50 years on from his exile to India, the Dalai Lama is facing a growing tide of discontent over claims that his non-confrontational style of leadership is simply too soft.

'Militant Tibetan groups are increasingly challenging the spiritual leader's authority ahead of Tuesday's anniversary of the failed uprising against Chinese rule that led to him fleeing to Dharamsala in northern India.

'Mindful of the fact that half a century has passed and Tibet's independence has still not been achieved, they refer to his "failed" policies and talk of replacing the figurehead of the Free Tibet campaign with a more aggressive leader.

' "The Dalai Lama has been trying to resolve the situation through dialogue but, personally, I think the dialogue is getting us nowhere. The situation in Tibet is getting worse," said Dhondup Dorjee, the vice-president of the Tibetan Youth Congress ...

'Differences between the exiles forced the Dalai Lama last November to call a special meeting of the most prominent groups in Dharamsala, where he and the Tibetan government-in-exile have their HQ. "When the Dalai Lama called that meeting he was saying 'My approach has failed, tell me what to do next'," said Miss Tethong, who attended the gathering. "But the meeting was dominated by the Tibetan government-in-exile and they're not going to tell him 'Oh you've failed', so it ended up being an endorsement of His Holiness." '

26 March 2009 – South African Finance Minister Trevor Manuel on the Dalai Lama, *IOL* (South Africa):

' "To say anything against the Dalai Lama is, in some quarters, equivalent to trying to shoot Bambi," he said.

' "Let's put our cards on the table. Who is the Dalai Lama? I've heard him described as a god. I've heard him described as Buddha.

' "Is he just the spiritual leader of the Buddhists in Tibet, or is he the one who on March 28 1959 established a government-in-exile in the same way as Taiwan was established to counter the reality of a single China?"

'Manuel said Tibet's history had to be looked at, because the Lamas had been "feudal overlords" in that country.'

' "The reason why the Dalai Lama wants to be here ... is to make a big global political statement about the secession of Tibet from China and he wants to make it on the free soil of South Africa."

' "I'm sure he's welcome to come at any other time, but we shouldn't allow him to raise global issues that will impact on the standing of South Africa." '

30 July 2009 – Timan Muller and Janis Vougiokas, 'The Two Faces of the Dalai Lama: The gentle Tibetan and his undemocratic regime', *Stern Magazine* (Germany):

'The Dalai Lama smiles away all doubts. Almost everywhere he receives the same god-like veneration. In the West he appears as the idol of the new age but in the Himalayas he governs like a medieval potentate. A gentle do-gooder who can show surprisingly intolerant and dictator-like behaviour ...

'He will have to face confrontation as there is growing criticism in his own exile community. "His Holiness is living in a bubble without contact with the outside world," says Lhasang Tsering, a long term activist, now running a bookstore in Little Lhasa. "Religion and politics should finally be separated." '

PART TWO

The Dalai Lama of Tibet – Unravelling the Myth

CHAPTER 7

Mixing Religion and Politics

Part Two is a deeper examination of the points raised in Part One. It explains the Tibetan theocratic system of government, and presents a history of the Dalai Lamas, in particular the present Dalai Lama's political views and failures. This gives us the context in which to understand his ban on the practice of Dorje Shugden as another example of a dismal record of deceit and hidden scandals.

DHARMA AND POLITICS

As clearly shown throughout much of human history, mixing religion and politics in general is a great mistake. In the context of this book, religion refers to Buddha's teachings, or Dharma. Buddha taught that all living beings experience without freedom or choice, in life after life, the recurrent cycle of birth, ageing, sickness and death, known as 'samsara'. The fundamental purpose of all Buddha's teachings is to show how to achieve liberation from samsara by overcoming attachment to it, and how to help others to achieve this same liberation.

Although skilful political activity may bring temporary benefits, the main purpose of political activity is to find happiness within samsara through trying to change external conditions. Political activity and political objectives therefore lie within samsara.

The result of Dharma is to destroy samsara, whereas the result of politics is to keep us within samsara. Through practising Dharma, Buddhists try to overcome attachment to samsara, whereas through political activity people try to fulfil desires that increase their attachment to samsara. The desires underlying our attachment to samsara include desire for wealth, power, fame and pleasure, all of which are mistakenly viewed as sources of real happiness.

For these reasons, Dharma and politics are completely opposite in their views, aims and results. The consequences of mixing Dharma with politics will always be at best bad, at worst catastrophic.

THE MEANING OF 'MIXING RELIGION AND POLITICS'

Mixing religion with politics means using religious faith for political aims. Because of the terrible atrocities that have been perpetrated throughout history in the name of religion, it is often said that religion is the cause of much suffering in the world. However, when practised purely, religion cannot cause suffering. It is not religion itself but rather the exploitation of religion for political objectives that has caused and continues to cause so much suffering in this world. For example, in the West it is clearly understood that mixing religion and politics has been the cause of many problems, and of the sufferings caused by the Crusades, the Inquisition and the numerous European wars that have been fought in the name of religion, even in modern times. The western experience is that mixing religion and politics does not work. Because this is clearly recognised, in almost all countries throughout the West today there is a clear separation between 'Church' and 'State'.

THE TIBETAN SYSTEM OF GOVERNMENT

In direct contrast, in Tibetan society not only is there no clear separation between 'Church' and 'State', but the union of these two is the very basis of government, even today. The Tibetan name for their system of government is 'bö.zhung chö.si nyi.den' (bod zhungs chos sri gnyis ldan), which means the 'Tibetan Government of both Religion and Politics'. As Phuntsog Wangyal, who established the London-based Tibet Foundation, says:

> 'The term "Chö-si nyi-den" appears for the first time in the Seventeenth Century when the Fifth Dalai Lama reorganized

> the Government of Tibet as … the "Ever Victorious Tibetan Government of Ga-dän p'o-dr'ang".
>
> 'Religion is different from politics. But there was never any attempt in Tibetan history to separate the two. Rather the ruling class, first the aristocracy and later both the aristocracy and the monasteries, encouraged their union.'[11]

Although the system of 'Chö-si nyi-den' had previously existed in practice, it was the Fifth Dalai Lama who consolidated the existing arrangements and standardised them into hard-and-fast rules. As the self-proclaimed and infallible embodiment of the Buddha Avalokiteshvara and as the supreme secular head of state, the Fifth Dalai Lama made the institution of the Dalai Lama the core symbol for the union of ultimate political and religious power. As Phuntsog Wangyal again observes:

> ' … the supremacy of the Dalai Lama does not mean that the Dalai Lama always exercised supreme power, but it does mean that he is the ultimate authority in which supreme power over religion and politics rests.
>
> 'The institution of the Dalai Lama has a dual role, that of politics and religion. He symbolises the force that links two principles into a single institution.'[12]

Thus, the mixing of religion and politics was institutionalised by the Fifth Dalai Lama, and it is from this point in Tibetan history that the catastrophic decline begins that led to the loss of Tibet.

This intermingling of religion and politics can be seen in a whole series of the Fifth Dalai Lama's actions, including his construction and naming of the Potala Palace; his relationship with his Spiritual Guide, the Panchen Lama; his reliance upon and institution of Nechung as the State Oracle of Tibet; his twice-attempted invasions of Bhutan; and his military campaigns against the Jonangpas, Kagyupas and Bönpos, and their forced conversion to the Gelug Tradition.

The Fifth Dalai Lama's most significant creation from mixing Dharma and politics was the institution of the Dalai Lama itself. Through the fusion of supreme religious and political authority in one single person, the Fifth Dalai Lama became the self-appointed 'God-King' of Tibet. All of the actions of the Dalai Lama were thus to some extent contaminated by this union of religion and politics. None of his religious actions could be totally free of political implications, and likewise none of his political actions could be totally free of implication for the religious sphere. All of the Dalai Lama's religious and political actions, no matter how insignificant, carried the full weight of both his supposed religious infallibility and his absolute political authority.

The Potala Palace had the dual function of serving both political and religious objectives. On the one hand, the construction of the Potala itself was first intended to provide the Dalai Lama with an impenetrable fortress against military attack in the event that his powerful Mongol allies withdrew their support and second to serve as a potent symbol of his absolute political authority. On the other hand, in so naming the Potala, the Dalai Lama was identifying his residence as the earthly abode of the Buddha of Compassion, and himself as its resident, Avalokiteshvara.

Although from a religious point of view, even the human emanations of Buddhas need to accept and rely upon their Spiritual Guides, from a political point of view the Fifth Dalai Lama could not bridge the gap between his absolute authority and the propriety of relinquishing authority to his Spiritual Guide. How could the fountainhead of absolute religious and political power, to whom all others are subordinate, ever subordinate himself to a Spiritual Guide? This intrinsic contradiction within the Fifth Dalai Lama's position destroyed his spiritual relationship with his Spiritual Guide and created a poisonous precedent for future Dalai Lamas, especially the present Dalai Lama who claims to have a special connection with the Fifth.

One example of how the Fifth Dalai Lama regarded maintenance of his political power as more important than his duty as a Buddhist practitioner was his efforts to destroy the power of two important officials whom he considered to be rivals to his political authority. (These events are described below in Chapter 8.) When they took refuge in Tashi Lhunpo Monastery, the monastic seat of his own

Spiritual Guide, the Fifth Dalai Lama raised an army to attack it. He dismissed his Spiritual Guide's attempts at conciliation; and some years later, in an unprecedented act of public disrespect, the Fifth Dalai Lama did not even attend his Spiritual Guide's funeral.

Many of the actions of the Fifth Dalai Lama, through which he became known as the 'Great Fifth', were in fact from a spiritual point of view extremely negative political actions. Some of them were catastrophic for Tibet both spiritually and politically, and provided the stepping-stones that in the end led to the loss of Tibet as an independent Buddhist nation.

Oracles, Dough Balls and Divinations

The pronouncements of trance oracles have long played a crucial role in Tibetan politics and continue to do so today in Dharamsala. Indeed, these oracles are so revered that the State Oracle Nechung has the rank of a deputy minister in the Tibetan exile government today. An excerpt from the Tibetan government's official website reads:

> 'In the Tibetan tradition, the word oracle is used for a spirit which enters those men and women who act as mediums between the natural and the spiritual realms. The mediums are, therefore, known as "kuten", which literally means, "the physical basis".
>
> 'In early times it is believed that there were hundreds of oracles throughout Tibet. Today, only a few survive, including those consulted by the Tibetan government. … Nechung Kuten is given the rank of a deputy minister in the exiled Tibetan Government hierarchy.'[13]

To understand the Tibetan exile government it is necessary to understand the pervasive influence that oracles in general, and the Nechung oracle in particular, have on its decision-making. Loosely speaking, an oracle or spirit medium is a human being who believes their body can be used by a spirit; but the majority of people who claim to be oracles are merely pretending. They claim that the spirit puts their human mind into an unconscious state and then uses their body to speak directly to humans.

Nechung is a Bön (the pre-Buddhist religion of Tibet) spirit who was appointed by the Fifth Dalai Lama as the personal protector of the Dalai Lamas. In *Freedom in Exile* the present Dalai Lama extols the virtues of his relationship with the Nechung spirit:

> 'I seek his opinion in the same way as I seek the opinion of my Cabinet and just as I seek the opinion of my own conscience. I consider the gods to be my "upper house". The Kashag constitutes my lower house. Like any other leader, I consult both before making a decision on affairs of state.'[14]

The Dalai Lama explains that he is very close to the Nechung spirit, 'friends almost', but that he is essentially in command, 'My relationship with Nechung is that of commander to lieutenant'. As he says, despite objections from more 'progressive' Tibetans he continues to rely on this 'ancient method of intelligence-gathering' because in his opinion the answers he has received from the spirit medium have over time proven to be correct.[15]

The Dalai Lama graphically describes how the oracle enters into trance:

> 'Now the kuten's [spirit medium's] face transforms, becoming rather wild before puffing up to give him an altogether strange appearance, with bulging eyes and swollen cheeks. His breathing begins to shorten and he starts to hiss violently. Then, momentarily, his respiration stops. At this point the helmet is tied in place with a knot so tight that it would undoubtedly strangle the kuten if something very real were not happening. The possession is now complete and the mortal frame of the medium expands visibly.'[16]

While the medium is possessed, questions are put to the oracle first by the Dalai Lama and then by members of his government. In this way, just 'like any other leader', the Dalai Lama consults his upper house – a spirit – before making decisions on affairs of state. The Dalai Lama says that Nechung's answers are 'rarely vague … But I suppose that it would be difficult for any scientific investigation either to prove or disprove conclusively the validity of his pronouncements.'[17]

If any other politician in the world were to consult a spirit medium about matters of state he or she would be universally derided and dismissed from office.

At critical points in Tibetan history, experience has proven the spirit medium's advice to be both wrong and harmful. For example, in 1904 the British invaded Tibet under Colonel Younghusband, but they had no intention of openly attacking the Tibetans who were poorly equipped militarily. As the British force marched on Lhasa the Nechung oracle was consulted as to the best course of action. As Jamyang Norbu writes:

> 'The oracle declared that the "enemies of the Dharma" would be soundly defeated by a "heavenly army" which he would personally lead. The Tibetans were, of course, overwhelmingly defeated, around seven hundred peasant levies being massacred in a couple of hours at the hot springs near Guru.
>
> '… The next year during the New Year celebrations in Lhasa, when the state oracle came charging out of the Jokhang Temple in full trance, as was the annual custom, the exasperated citizens of Lhasa are reported to have booed the god – the women flapping their aprons, and the men shouting "Hey-le! Hey-le!" or "Shame on you!" '[18]

The Thirteenth Dalai Lama was so displeased with Nechung at that time that he forbade further consultations for a number of years.

It is commonly known that the Nechung oracle made a fatal error when prescribing wrong medicine to the Thirteenth Dalai Lama which resulted in his untimely death. It is believed that it was this medicine that worsened the Dalai Lama's condition and led to his death.[19] The Tibetan historian K. Dhondup, citing the testimony of the doctor present at the crucial diagnosis, tells us that due to fever the Dalai Lama's condition had become extremely critical:

> 'At that moment, I, Kuchar Kunphela, the medium of the Nechung Oracle and the Dalai Lama were the only persons present. The Nechung Oracle asked me if I had Chamjom Pawo 14, a medicine for cold disease. As this medicine was very strong, I could not risk giving it to the Dalai Lama. Therefore, I told the Nechung Oracle I did not have this medicine at all. Then the Nechung Oracle told us to ask his own attendant. Kuchar Kunphela quickly went outside and most probably met the attendant and obtained the medicine as he returned with a medicine bag with a spoon ready in it and offered the bag to the Nechung Oracle. The Oracle took a spoonful of medicine and offered it to the Dalai Lama. I did not know whether that medicine in that bag was Chamjom Pawo 14. Then the Oracle lost his trance. From that night onwards, the fever rose higher than before and the Dalai Lama was delirious. The illness went from bad to worse and on the 30th of the 10th month, [the next day], the Dalai Lama passed away.'[20]

Knowledge that this fatal error was made by the spirit medium – Nechung oracle – is also supported by the testimony of a clerk who worked for the Dalai Lama, as cited by Bell:

> 'That same night, between 1 and 2 a.m., the medium gave the Precious Protector some medicine in the form of a powder. When the medium came out, Champa La, the Presence's regular doctor, said to the medium, "You have made a mistake in the medicine" (Men di norra nangzha).'[21]

There is also an account in Bell that this mistake was the result of the Nechung oracle being taken over by an evil spirit. The spirit was the reincarnation of a tulku (incarnate lama) who some years before had been repeatedly flogged for alleged involvement in a plot to kill the Thirteenth Dalai Lama and had then taken his own life:

> 'At the end of February 1934, Palhese [Bell's great friend and informant], coming for his daily talk, asked me with suppressed eagerness, "Has Rai Bahadur Norbhu told you about recent

happenings in Lhasa concerning the passing of the Precious Protector to the Field?"

'[Bell replies:] "He has told me about the medium of the Nechung Oracle giving the Precious Protector medicine which injured him."

'Says Palhese, "It is about the medicine that I wish to speak. It was given at the instruction of a tulku from Nyarong (a province in Eastern Tibet), who has been reborn as a devil. It did indeed do injury; in fact, it made the Precious Protector [the Thirteenth Dalai Lama] an 'Is Not' [i.e., a dead person]." '[22]

Palhese gave Bell further details about this 'tulku' and his violent death, his rebirth as a 'devil' and of the failed attempts to subdue him, concluding 'Later on, it was noticed that the prophecies issuing through the prophet of the Nechung oracle were wrong and harmful.'[23]

Goldstein presents an even more damning indictment of the Nechung oracle's role in the Thirteenth Dalai Lama's death:

'On this occasion, the Nechung oracle said that the Dalai Lama should take a medicine known as 'the seventeen heroes for subduing colds' (chamjom pawo chupdün) and himself prepared the medicine in a cup with water. Most respondents report that the Dalai Lama refused the dose and that the state oracle had literally to pour it into his mouth. The Dalai Lama's condition immediately deteriorated, and by noon he was unconscious. He never said another word.'[24]

The Nechung oracle also had a negative role during the Chinese invasion in 1950:

'During the flight of the Dalai Lama to Dromo (Yadong) in the Chumbi Valley at the time of the invasion of Tibet by the Chinese in 1950, the Nechung Oracle was consulted repeatedly as to what course of action the Tibetan ruler should take. Should he take refuge in India or should he stay in Tibet? Twice the Oracle said that he should stay in Tibet despite attempts by the government to get him to say the contrary. It is said that it

> was eventually discovered that he had been bribed to deliver his message by the pro-Chinese monks of Sera, …'.[25]

In more recent times the Nechung oracle has made repeated prophecies that Tibet would gain independence within a few years. He also said on a number of occasions that he would send a 'heavenly army' to drive out the Chinese.[26] Of course these god-soldiers have failed to materialise and Tibet is still as firmly as ever under Chinese control. It is also well known that the Tibetan uprisings in Lhasa in the 1980s took place due to Nechung's advice. The results were devastating, many Tibetans lost their lives and the Chinese cracked down even more harshly.[27] The political bungling surrounding the recognition of the reincarnation of the Panchen Lama is also attributed to Nechung. He advised that the identity of the boy chosen by the Tibetans should be announced before the boy was officially recognised by the Chinese.[28] This decision infuriated the Chinese and the young Panchen Lama has been under virtual house arrest ever since, with very little chance of being allowed to leave Tibet.[29]

As Jamyang Norbu comments:

> 'What is mind-boggling in retrospect is the absolute faith of the public and even the Dalai Lama in these predictions that never even came remotely close to being realised.'[30]

It is primarily due to advice from the Nechung oracle that the present Dalai Lama has banned the worship of Dorje Shugden. It is known by many that the spirit medium of Nechung grew increasingly jealous of the Dalai Lama's reliance on Dorje Shugden.[31] Trijang Rinpoche, the Dalai Lama's own Spiritual Guide and principal advisor for many years, relied on Dorje Shugden and encouraged all his students to do the same.

However, in recent years a number of other oracles have emerged in Dharamsala that are of even more questionable authority than Nechung but upon whom the Dalai Lama nevertheless relies to make crucial political and religious decisions:

> 'Right now there is a glut of oracles in Dharamshala. Over and above the two state oracles there is the deity Dorjee Yudonma,

> one of the twelve Tenma goddesses, whose medium is a mild looking old amala [elderly woman]. There is also the oracle Lamo Tsangba, a local protective deity of Lhasa. His medium is a somewhat corpulent gentleman who was a trombone player in the Chinese military orchestra in Lhasa.'[32]

An event that occurred in November 1996 illustrates the confusion that these oracles are bringing to Tibetan society. In the main temple in Dharamsala, the Dalai Lama was attending the last day of six weeks of practices in connection with the invocation of a Deity known as Tamdrin Yangsang, the day on which the rituals including the 'taking out of the tormas' are performed. Those present included 75 monks from Sera Monastery, monks from Nechung Monastery, and also six or seven oracles of spirits chosen by the Dalai Lama. These oracles proceeded to go into trance, and a female oracle of the long-life protectoress Tsering Chenma, who had previously made virulent statements against the practice of Dorje Shugden, began attacking the Deity Dorje Shugden, saying that 'even within this congregation there are still those who practise Dorje Shugden.' Then:

> 'Another female oracle, Yudonma, then pointed to Jangmar Rinpoche from Drepung Loseling monastery, a Lama in his late 60s who was originally from Gyalthang province of eastern Tibet, and started shouting, "This Lama is bad, he is following Dorje Shugden, take him out, take him out!" She then starts pulling his robes and grabbing his head. The Lama gets up and slaps her twice. There was uproar in the temple: all taking place in front of the Dalai Lama. Jangmar Rinpoche was pushed out of the Temple, and the scuffle continued outside, with Jangmar Rinpoche being heard to say, "It is you spirits who are causing all this mess. It is you who are causing disharmony. You spirits cannot be trusted." Later, he threatened to take the medium to court, but was persuaded not to by the Dalai Lama. When he reported this incident to the Dalai Lama directly the next day the Dalai Lama says, "You have no fault, I know very well that you are not a practitioner of Dorje Shugden. Sometimes these oracles are a little too much. It is good you gave a slap." '[33]

So even the Dalai Lama himself, who relies upon the spirit medium of Nechung as his 'deputy minister' of government, recognises that oracles are not reliable sources of qualified information.

The oracle of the Deity Tsering Chenma is regarded so highly by the Dalai Lama that she was even allowed to live in his palace in Dharamsala. When she first arrived from Tibet, she was a young and attractive woman, and the Dalai Lama listened carefully to her pronouncements.[34] Unfortunately, she is just as unreliable as the other alleged spirit mediums.

In July 1996 during the preparations for a Kalachakra Initiation to be given by the Dalai Lama in Lahul Spiti, this same oracle, Tsering Chenma, alleged that thirty members of the Dorje Shugden Society from Delhi would attack the Dalai Lama during the initiation. Elaborate security measures were taken but no weapons were found, no plot was uncovered and it was discovered that there was no one even present from the Dorje Shugden Society![35]

Oracles have played a role in Tibetan history for a long time. Their influence, however, has never been as dominant as it is now in Dharamsala. Many ordinary Tibetans and distinguished lamas are concerned about this growing influence. Gonsar Rinpoche has been quoted on German television as saying:

> 'These days the State and other oracles – there are about four other oracles in India – play a great role in the different decisions of our exile government. Many of us think that this is somewhat of a risk.'[36]

The question naturally arises: if the Dalai Lama is an enlightened being – as some believe he is – why does he have to rely on the advice of spirits channelled through trance-oracles? An enlightened being would necessarily be able to make his or her own decisions based on their omniscient wisdom, and would not have to turn to such questionable methods. If other politicians in the world were to rely upon trance-oracles they would be laughed out of office. As Lukhangwa, a former Tibetan prime minister, told the Dalai Lama in 1956: 'When men become desperate they consult the gods. And when the gods become desperate, they tell lies.'[37]

These however are not the only dubious means by which the Dalai Lama makes his decisions. He openly admits that he uses dough balls, dice and dreams to help him come to important decisions,[38] for example, he is quoted as saying:

> 'I conducted a dough-ball examination and dice divination, which were so convincing that since 1975 I have completely stopped this practice [of Dorje Shugden]. I have not even had a portentous dream to make me wonder if the deity is vexed.'[39]

Considering that his political activities are based on these methods of discrimination we should not be surprised that in all these years he has not accomplished anything substantial for the Tibetan people.

In an interview for the Spanish magazine *Mas Alla* Geshe Kelsang Gyatso, the Founder and Spiritual Director of the New Kadampa Tradition – International Kadampa Buddhist Union, was asked:

> 'It is said that the Dalai Lama has more oracles (mediums) than ministers, that he is surrounded by oracles and that he does not take a step without consulting them. What do you think about such reliance? Do you think that there is a hidden power at the palace in Dharamsala?'

Geshe Kelsang Gyatso replied:

> 'This reliance is inappropriate. These methods of divination are often the source of many problems, conflicts and quarrels, and give rise to superstition. The person who gets into the habit of relying upon these methods ends up losing self-confidence, and there comes a time when he becomes incapable of taking a single decision by himself based on logical reasoning and using his own wisdom, or relying on the wisdom of other experts who could advise him. Buddha did not teach these methods, they are not Buddhist practices.'[40]

It is interesting to note the Fourteenth Dalai Lama himself is on record as saying that oracles have 'nothing to do with Buddhism … they should be looked upon as a manifestation of popular superstition'[41], but on the other hand he still sincerely relies upon them to make important decisions on political and religious matters that affect the lives of millions of people. For him spirit mediums are more important than his root Spiritual Guide, and Buddha Shakyamuni, the founder of Buddhism. In 1971 the Dalai Lama was quoted as saying about oracles:

> 'This has nothing to do with Buddhism. The oracles are absolutely without importance. They are only small tree-spirits. They do not belong to the three treasures of Buddhism. Relations with them are of no help for our next incarnation. They should be looked upon as manifestations of popular superstition which is deleterious to the health of human beings.'[42]

This is just one of many examples of the Dalai Lama contradicting himself – saying one thing but doing another. What is clear is that in relying upon the Nechung oracle the Fourteenth Dalai Lama is following a spirit with a history of false prophecies. The Dalai Lama is free to listen to a spirit-oracle when deciding his personal affairs, but it is clearly inappropriate, if not outrageous, that the fate of the Tibetan people and of millions of Buddhist practitioners should be decided in this way.

CHAPTER 8

History and Institution of the Dalai Lamas

To understand the destructive nature of the union of religion and politics as practised in Tibet, and how it continues to have a deeply harmful effect on Tibetan society, it is necessary to look briefly at an overview of Tibetan history and the role of the Dalai Lamas in it, in particular at the roles of the Fifth, Thirteenth and Fourteenth Dalai Lamas.

JE TSONGKHAPA AND THE GANDEN TRADITION

The founder of the Buddhist religion, or Dharma, was Buddha Shakyamuni. 'Shakya' is the name of the royal family into which he was born, and 'Muni' means 'Able One'. He was born a royal prince in northern India in the 7th century BCE, and given the name Siddhartha. At the age of 29 Prince Siddhartha renounced his kingdom and, turning to the life of a forest monk, meditated for six years until he achieved full enlightenment, or Buddhahood.

For forty years after his enlightenment, Buddha travelled throughout India and, motivated by great compassion, taught the meaning of what he had achieved and how to achieve it. It is said that during this period he gave 84,000 different teachings according to the different mental and spiritual capacity and inclination of those attending his teachings.

Buddhadharma then gradually flourished throughout much of Asia, and was first introduced into Tibet during the reign of King Songtsen Gampo (ca. 616-650 CE), although it was not until the reign of King Trisong Detsen (ca. 754-798 CE) that it flourished through the activities of Shantarakshita, Padmasambhava and other Indian Buddhist teachers. King Trisong Detsen first invited the renowned Buddhist teacher Shantarakshita to Tibet, but Shantarakshita soon met with opposition from many of the King's ministers who were followers of the Bön religion, and he was forced to leave for a while. Before he left he advised the king to invite another famous Indian master, the great Tantric practitioner Padmasambhava. Padmasambhava was able to pacify the non-Buddhist spirits of Tibet, thus removing the obstacles to the spread of Buddha's Mahayana and Vajrayana teachings throughout the country. The tradition that developed from this first dissemination of Buddhism in Tibet and which traces its origins to translations of scriptures produced at this time is called the 'Nyingma' or 'Old Tradition'.

The work of King Trisong Detsen, Padmasambhava and Shantarakshita, however, was soon undone by the anti-Buddhist King Lang Darma, who reigned from 838 to 842. Lang Darma destroyed Buddhist temples, closed monasteries and forced monks and nuns to disrobe, executing those who refused. In this way he eradicated all forms of organised Buddhist practice from Tibet. Lang Darma's persecutions eventually led to his own death; while watching a theatrical performance he was killed by an arrow shot by a Buddhist monk pretending to be one of the actors.

Although Buddhism gradually returned to Tibet, it was not until over a hundred years later that it began to flourish again there. One of the key figures in this second dissemination was Atisha (ca. 982-1054), another famous Indian Buddhist scholar and meditation master. Atisha was largely responsible for the re-establishment of Buddhism in Tibet, and his special presentation of Buddhist teachings, called the 'stages of the path to enlightenment' (Lamrim in Tibetan), attracted such interest and devotion that the dominance of Buddhism in Tibetan society was never threatened again. His tradition later became known as the 'Kadampa Tradition'. The followers of Atisha, known as Kadampa Geshes, were not only great scholars but also spiritual practitioners of immense purity and sincerity.

At the same time, through the extraordinary works of other great Tibetan masters, including Marpa the Translator (1012-1097); his disciple the famous Yogi Milarepa (1052-1135); and Milarepa's disciple Gampopa (1079-1153, also a practitioner of Kadam Dharma, the Kagyu Tradition was established.

The Sakya Tradition was established by Gonchok Gyelpo (1034-1102) who founded Sakya Monastery in 1073. One of the greatest masters of this lineage, Sakya Pandita (1182-1251), was invited to Mongolia in 1244 by the Mongolian Prince Godan, grandson of Genghis Khan. Sakya Pandita was able to spread Buddhism throughout Mongolia, and Prince Godan in turn established the Sakya lineage as the dominant political force in Tibet at that time. The Sakya, Kagyu, Kadam and later Gelug traditions all follow the translations of Tantric scriptures made during this second dissemination of Buddhism into Tibet, and are thus referred to in Tibetan as 'Sarma' or 'New Traditions'.

The institution of the Dalai Lama belongs to the Gelug (or Ganden) Tradition, which was founded by Je Tsongkhapa (1357-1419). The Gelug Tradition arose as a reformation of the original or 'old' Kadampa Tradition founded by Atisha; the Gelug practitioners ('Gelugpas') sometimes being called 'New Kadampas'. Je Tsongkhapa's legacy to Tibet is a very pure and special way of practising Buddha's teachings. Its source is the *Kadam Emanation Scripture*, which was transmitted directly to Je Tsongkhapa by the Wisdom Buddha Manjushri. The tradition that developed from this is known as the Ganden Oral Lineage.

The early masters who upheld this tradition, including the first four Dalai Lamas, led exemplary lives of pure practice and selfless devotion to the welfare of others.

THE FIRST FOUR DALAI LAMAS

Gendun Drub (1391-1474), who posthumously received the title 'First Dalai Lama', met Je Tsongkhapa when he was twenty years old and became one of his foremost disciples. Gendun Drub was a very pure spiritual practitioner, and renowned for combining study and practice. He spent more than twenty years in meditation retreat.

Although one of the youngest of Je Tsongkhapa's disciples, Gendun Drub became one of the strongest upholders of the Ganden tradition. With great energy, organisational skill and leadership ability he established the famous Tashi Lhunpo Monastery – the future seat of the lineage of the Panchen Lamas. In this and in many other ways Gendun Drub worked to secure the future protection and development of the Ganden Tradition. He died at the age of 84, seated in meditation.

Gendun Gyatso (1475-1542), whose recognition as the Second Dalai Lama was also posthumous, spent his whole life dedicated to upholding and spreading Je Tsongkhapa's tradition. In 1512 he became the abbot of Tashi Lhunpo Monastery, in 1517 the abbot of Drepung Monastery, and in 1525 the abbot of Sera Monastery. While at Drepung Monastery he built a residence known as 'Ganden Phodrang', also known as the 'Lower Residence', which became the principal residence of the Dalai Lamas until the time of the Fifth Dalai Lama. Having spread the teachings of Je Tsongkhapa throughout Central Tibet, he passed away in Drepung after a brief illness.

After Gendun Gyatso passed away, the high Lamas of Drepung set out in search of his reincarnation. They found a young boy, who was named **Sonam Gyatso** (1543-1588). He became greatly respected not only as a scholar and meditator but also as a negotiator of peace between factions of the Gelug and Kagyu traditions who were fighting at that time. Like his predecessor, he was so highly respected by his fellow monks that he was in turn elected abbot of both Drepung and Sera monasteries.

His fame eventually reached Mongolia and particularly Altan Khan – the leader of the Mongols and grandson of Dayan Khan, a descendant of Kublai Khan. Upon Altan Khan's invitations, Sonam Gyatso visited Mongolia in 1578. On hearing Sonam Gyatso's teachings, Altan Khan converted to Buddhism. During his three-year visit Sonam Gyatso taught Je Tsongkhapa's teachings throughout Mongolia, ordained thousands of Mongolians and brought an end to animal sacrifice and other inhumane practices there. Altan Khan conferred on Sonam Gyatso the title 'Dalai Lama', 'dalai' being a

Mongolian word for 'ocean', indicating that Sonam Gyatso's good qualities were as extensive as the ocean. Thus Sonam Gyatso became known as the Dalai Lama, with his previous reincarnations receiving the title retrospectively.

The Fourth Dalai Lama **Yonten Gyatso** (1589-1616) is unique in being the only Mongolian Dalai Lama, the grandson of Altan Khan. Attendants of the late Third Dalai Lama as well as representatives of the three great Gelugpa monasteries – Drepung, Sera and Ganden – travelled to Mongolia to confirm the reincarnation. At the age of twelve, Yonten Gyatso moved to Drepung to undergo religious training and at the age of nineteen was installed on the throne of the Ganden Phodrang at Drepung Monastery. Yonten Gyatso later became the abbot of Drepung and then Sera monasteries, but only for a short while. He died in 1616, at the age of only 27.

Until this time, the concept of a Dalai Lama with supreme political or even religious authority over all of Tibet did not exist. The first three Dalai Lamas were held in high regard as pure spiritual teachers. The fame of the 'Third' had spread throughout Mongolia, and he had received a Mongolian term of respect as well as the patronage of a strong military power. But there was no 'God-King', no one embodying the union of religious and political power, in these early Dalai Lamas. There was no institution of the Dalai Lama: the Dalai Lamas were more usually known as 'the reincarnations of the Lower Residence', and regarded as a lineage of famous reincarnate Gelugpa Lamas from Drepung who had simply been given an additional title by Mongolian patrons.

Through their activities of teaching and spreading the tradition of Je Tsongkhapa, and their exemplary lives of pure moral discipline and spiritual practice, these first four Dalai Lamas fulfilled their main responsibility of upholding the teachings of the Ganden Tradition.

Initially, the Ganden Tradition was not mixed with the politics of Tibet, but later this tradition gave rise to some of the most political lamas in Tibetan history: namely the Fifth, Thirteenth and Fourteenth Dalai Lamas. As John Powers remarks in *Introduction to Tibetan Buddhism*:

'... the fortunes of the Gélukpa order rose quickly, mainly because it continued to produce an impressive number of eminent scholars and tantric adepts. Another factor in its success was its initial reluctance to become involved in Tibetan politics. Instead, for several centuries after the death of Tsong Khapa, the Gélukpa order was mainly renowned for its strict adherence to monastic discipline, its accomplished scholars, and its intensive meditative training.

'This attitude of aloofness towards politics was not to last, however.'[43]

THE FIFTH DALAI LAMA

The institution of the Dalai Lama as we currently know it – mixing Dharma with politics as a method of government – begins with the Dalai Lama popularly known as the 'Great Fifth'. As a consequence of a complicated series of political-historical developments, as well as open warfare, 'the Fifth Dalai Lama made the institution of the Dalai Lama the core symbol of the state of Tibet.'[44]

Due to the rapid development and growing popularity of the Gelugpas, the kings of the Tsang region of Tibet, who were followers of the Karma Kagyu Tradition, felt increasing animosity towards the Gelugpas and subjected them to periods of persecution.[45]

In the years immediately before and following the death of the Fourth Dalai Lama, hostilities between the Gelugpas and the supporters of the king of Tsang intensified. It was into this environment of political and religious conflict that the Fifth Dalai Lama, **Losang Gyatso** (1617-1682) was born.

There were three candidates for the throne of the Fifth Dalai Lama. One was Dragpa Gyaltsen, whose later fame and stature as a great spiritual master were perceived as a threat by the Fifth Dalai Lama. The Fifth Dalai Lama's autobiography (Du ku la'i go zang in Tibetan) says that the Panchen Lama Losang Chokyi Gyaltsen (Losang Chogyen) performed a divination and chose him – Losang Gyatso – as the reincarnate Dalai Lama, although no date is given for the event and it is not even mentioned in the Panchen Lama's autobiography.[46]

Many doubts have been expressed about the confirmatory examinations made to test the authenticity of the Fifth Dalai Lama, which were carried out by a disciple of the Dalai Lama's Regent, Sonam Rabten. The nature of the relationship between the Dalai Lama and his Regent, as well as certain statements made by the latter which are recorded in the Fifth Dalai Lama's own autobiography, have fuelled speculation concerning the authenticity of the Fifth Dalai Lama's recognition.[47]

In any event, the times into which the Fifth Dalai Lama was born were so unstable politically that his discovery and whereabouts were kept secret for some time. In 1635, when the Fifth Dalai Lama was eighteen years old, the leader of the Chogthu Mongols, supporters of the ruler of Tsang, sent ten thousand troops 'to wipe out the Gelug-pa sect'.[48] This eventually led to war between the Chogthu Mongol armies and the Qoshot Mongol armies of Gushri Khan, supporters of the Fifth Dalai Lama, each intent on supporting their respective Buddhist tradition. Gushri Khan emerged victorious and in 1638 at a ceremony held in the Jokhang Temple in Lhasa he was placed on a throne and given the title 'Religious-King and Holder of the Buddhist Faith'.[49] Soon afterwards a letter sent by the pro-Bön chief of Beri to the ruler of Tsang accidentally fell into Gelugpa hands. Part of this letter read:

> 'It is a great disappointment that our allies, the Chogthu tribe, have been wiped out. However, next year, I shall raise an army in Kham and accompany it to Ü [the central region of Tibet, around Lhasa]. At the same time, you must bring in your army from Tsang. Together we will completely eliminate the Ge-lug-pa sect, so no trace of it will ever be found.'[50]

When this message was intercepted and passed to Gushri Khan he immediately went to the Dalai Lama, intent upon leading his army into battle, first against the chief of Beri and then against the ruler of Tsang. In the religious war that ensued the chief of Beri was captured and executed and then:

> 'Gushri [Khan]… attacked the Tsangpa King himself at his home base in Shigatse. The Geluk sect sent its own force of supporters and monks to assist him and in 1642 they captured Shigatse. The King of Tibet (the Tsangpa King) was executed.
>
> 'Gushri Khan gave supreme authority over all of Tibet to the Fifth Dalai Lama.'[51]

Having vanquished his enemies in Tsang, there were still other tasks to be accomplished if Losang Gyatso was to gain full power and control over Tibet. In his paper, *The Sovereign Power of the Fifth Dalai Lama*, Zuiho Yamaguchi writes:

> 'The first step along the path whereby the fifth Dalai Lama, no more than an incarnate lama of 'Bras-spungs [Drepung] monastery, came to view himself as king of Tibet and assumed the reins of government was the construction of the Potala.'[52]

On the advice of a Nyingma oracle, the Dalai Lama undertook the building of a massive fortress that would tower above the city of Lhasa and would secure his position in the event that the Mongols were to withdraw their military support. John Powers further explains the significance of the Potala Palace:

> 'During his reign, the connection between the Dalai Lamas and Avalokiteśvara was stressed, and this was reflected in the construction of the Potala, … The name that was chosen for the palace was taken from a mountain in southern India that is associated with Śiva in his incarnation as Lokeśvara, or "Lord of the World", who is considered by Tibetans to be an emanation of Avalokiteśvara. This association helped to establish the Dalai Lamas as incarnations of a buddha, and they are regarded as such by Tibetan Buddhists, who have traditionally looked upon the Potala as the residence of Avalokiteśvara in human form.'[53]

By destroying the opposing forces in Tsang and building the Potala Palace, the Fifth Dalai Lama secured some measure of political power. But, to secure supreme religious authority for himself as well, there were other obstacles to be removed. In the feudalistic society of those days, a sovereign's power could only survive if it was unchallenged and without rivals. Like the custom of medieval monarchies worldwide, rivals were murdered and all opposition to the ruler was crushed brutally.

This is clearly illustrated in the case of Tulku or Ngatrul Dragpa Gyaltsen. Yamaguchi continues:

> 'The Fifth Dalai Lama was an incarnate lama (sprul sku [tulku]) of 'Bras-spungs [Drepung] monastery, but there was another incarnate lama at 'Bras-spungs monastery, namely, sprul sku gZims-khang-gong-ma [the Tulku of the Upper Residence, Tulku Dragpa Gyaltsen], regarded as a reincarnation of Pan-chen bSod-nams-grags-pa [Panchen Sonam Dragpa] (1478-1544). For the Dalai Lama to become the supreme religious authority in all Tibet, it was imperative that only a single incarnate lama in the person of the Dalai Lama preside over 'Bras-spungs [Drepung] monastery from his headquarters at dGa'-ldan [Ganden] Palace.'[54]

Dragpa Gyaltsen was born in 1619, in the 10th month of the Earth Sheep year according to the Tibetan calendar. He was born in Tolung, into the prominent Gaykhasa family. At first he was considered a possible reincarnation of the Fourth Dalai Lama, but at the age of six he was instead recognised by Panchen Losang Chogyen as the reincarnation of Ngawang Sonam Geleg Pelsang (1594-1615). Accordingly he was enthroned formally as the reincarnate Lama of the so-called 'Upper Residence' of Drepung Monastery (the 'Lower Residence' being that of the Dalai Lamas). Being the reincarnate Lama of the Upper Residence meant that his reincarnation lineage went back to Panchen Sonam Dragpa (Tutor of the Third Dalai Lama) and because of his accomplishments of knowledge and spiritual proficiency, Dragpa Gyaltsen was considered equal in spiritual status to the Fifth Dalai Lama.

A graphic illustration of their equal spiritual status can be seen in a 17th century thangkha painting of the Buddhist Deity Palden Lhamo

(Shri Devi), reproduced in *Wisdom and Compassion: The Sacred Art of Tibet*. The description of this painting reads:

> 'In the upper left corner are three Gelukpa lamas, each with an identifying inscription. … the central figure is Losang Chökyi Gyaltsen (later made the first Panchen Lama by the Fifth Dalai Lama), the lama to his right is the Fifth Dalai Lama, and the lama to his left is Tulku Drakpa Gyaltsen, another reincarnate lama of Drepung monastic university.'

In this painting it is clear that the Fifth Dalai Lama and Tulku Dragpa Gyaltsen have equal status as disciples of the Panchen Lama. The explanation of this painting also reveals how political considerations would soon take precedence even in a religious painting:

> '[The painting can be dated]… with certainty to before 1642. Because the Panchen Lama is in the center and Drakpa Gyaltsen is present, it is clearly before the death of the latter, and before the rise to eminence of the Fifth Dalai Lama in 1642, after which time he would have been given the central position.'[55]

Tulku Dragpa Gyaltsen was two years younger than the Dalai Lama. His spiritual prominence, however, seemed to exceed that of the Dalai Lama. Pilgrims coming from Mongolia and the eastern Tibetan borders of Kham would first pay their respects to Tulku Dragpa Gyaltsen and then proceed to the Dalai Lama, sometimes making more offerings to Tulku Dragpa Gyaltsen than to the Dalai Lama; and when speaking of the Upper and Lower Residences, people often viewed both in equal terms.[56]

This was unacceptable to Sonam Rabten (who acted as the Fifth Dalai Lama's principal executive) and to the officials of the Dalai Lama's recently-established government (the Tibetan government is still called the Ganden Phodrang, after the Dalai Lama's residence in Drepung Monastery). Because of his strong resentment and hatred, Sonam Rabten and his associates began a campaign of persecution against the unsuspecting Tulku and his family.

Norbu, the governor of Tsang, was a close relative of Sonam Rabten, and participated in these intrigues against the Gaykhasa family with the indirect supervision, or at least approval, of the latter. He secretly invited the Mongols to create anarchy in the Tolung area, and contrived to leave the younger members of the Gaykhasa family with no option but to fight. In the event, a number of the family were killed. Norbu had intended this, and in 1638 he took the opportunity to seize their lands and property.

Another incident occurred in 1639, just a year later. In an unprecedented scheme to isolate Dragpa Gyaltsen further, Sonam Rabten personally tampered with the documentary records concerning the Tulku's predecessors, and destroyed some of them. Sonam Rabten regarded this as necessary because Dragpa Gyaltsen's prominence existed partly because of the claims that he was the reincarnation of famous Buddhist masters.

The Panchen Lama Losang Chökyi Gyaltsen (1570-1662), the Spiritual Guide of both Tulku Dragpa Gyaltsen and the Fifth Dalai Lama, had written a prayer listing Tulku Dragpa Gyaltsen's previous incarnations as including Venerable Manjushri, Mahasiddha Bhiravapa [Biwawa or Virupa], Sakya Pandita Kunga Gyaltsen, Buton Rinchen Drub, Duldzin Dragpa Gyaltsen, Panchen Sonam Dragpa, Sonam Yeshe Wangpo and Sonam Geleg Pelsang. The same line of predecessors has since been confirmed by Kyabje Phabongkhapa Dechen Nyingpo (1878-1941), and Kyabje Trijang Rinpoche (1900-1981).

According to the Fifth Dalai Lama's own account in his autobiography, Sonam Rabten's tampering with the names of Tulku Dragpa Gyaltsen's predecessors took place in 1639 on the 15th day of the fifth Tibetan month. Sonam Rabten said that the name of one of the recognised predecessors, Buton Rinchen Drub, had been misunderstood by Panchen Sonam Dragpa when Panchen Sonam Dragpa was writing the colophon of one of his texts. This being so, Sonam Rabten said, Buton's name should be removed from the common supplication prayer to Tulku Dragpa Gyaltsen. Because of his tampering with the records in this way, even the name of Panchen Sonam Dragpa could not be included in the prayer.

This was clearly an act of defamation on the part of Sonam Rabten, because the Panchen Lama Losang Chökyi Gyaltsen's own prayer composed to the Tulku stated the Tulku to be an incarnation of both Buton Rinchen Drub and Panchen Sonam Dragpa. The fact that Sonam Rabten disposed of documents that he wanted to suppress is clearly stated even in the Fifth Dalai Lama's autobiography.

That Sonam Rabten openly lied to achieve his ends is clear evidence of his efforts to isolate and denigrate Tulku Dragpa Gyaltsen. Later, in 1642, the Tulku's status was officially 'downgraded', again by decision of Sonam Rabten. In these and other ways Tulku Dragpa Gyaltsen was persecuted for over ten years, and was driven more and more into isolation.

Regardless of these circumstances, Dragpa Gyaltsen continued his spiritual engagements. Besides taking the Fifth Dalai Lama as one of his spiritual mentors, the Tulku honoured and made copious material offerings to him. On a number of occasions, when the Dalai Lama was departing from or returning to Lhasa, Dragpa Gyaltsen would personally see him off, or give welcoming receptions accordingly.

Tulku Dragpa Gyaltsen suddenly became ill on the 25th day of the fourth Tibetan month of the 'Fire Monkey' year, 1656. Using the illness as a cover, Sonam Rabten and Norbu contrived several attempts on Dragpa Gyaltsen's life. Finally, on the 13th day of the fifth month, Dragpa Gyaltsen was brutally murdered in his residence. To allay suspicion of murder, silk scarves were stuffed deeply down his throat. In this way a great and pure spiritual being, loved and venerated by the mass of ordinary Tibetans, was made to suffer humiliation and death at the hands of the Fifth Dalai Lama's ministers.[57] Tulku Dragpa Gyaltsen was 38 years old when he died.

As Kundeling Rinpoche says:

> 'This was the most scandalous event of an unprecedented nature that ever took place in the history of Tibet in general and the Gelugpas in particular. Judging from these events, many conclusions can be drawn about the nature of the Dalai Lama's own position, the role of his aides, and the monopoly of the newly established Ganden Phodrang Government.'[58]

Some writers have tried to attribute sole blame for the murder to the Fifth Dalai Lama's ministers, especially Sonam Rabten, and claim that the Fifth Dalai Lama did not know of their actions, but as Yamaguchi writes: 'it is patently clear from his undisguised criticism of Panchen Sonam Dragpa in his *Chronicle of Tibet*, written in 1643, that the Dalai Lama detested the incarnate lama.'[59] After Dragpa Gyaltsen's death, the Fifth Dalai Lama ordered a stop to the lineage of reincarnations of this great lama.

Many Gelugpa lamas believe that Dragpa Gyaltsen, and not Losang Gyatso, was the actual reincarnation of the Fourth Dalai Lama and that when Dragpa Gyaltsen died he became a Protector of Je Tsongkhapa's Ganden tradition. Indeed, before his death, Dragpa Gyaltsen himself predicted that he would become the Dharma Protector, Dorje Shugden.[60]

When giving the blessing empowerment[61] of Dorje Shugden to over five thousand disciples in England on 25 July 2009, Geshe Kelsang Gyatso explained:

> 'First you should know who Dorje Shugden is. Dorje Shugden is an enlightened Deity who is the manifestation of the wisdom Buddha Je Tsongkhapa. It is commonly believed that after the death of the great Lama Tulku Dragpa Gyaltsen he appeared as Dorje Shugden. The first Panchen Lama, who was the living Buddha Amitahba, listed some of Dragpa Gyaltsen's former incarnations, which are, during Buddha's time Bodhisattva Manjushri, and later Mahasiddha Biwawa, the great Sakya Pandita and Buton Rinchen Drub. These holy beings were also Je Tsongkhapa's former incarnations.
>
> 'Later, the great Yogi Kelsang Khedrub and many other Lamas including Kyabje Trijang Rinpoche listed Dorje Shugden's former incarnations, which are the same holy beings I have just listed from Bodhisattva Manjushri through to Buton Rinchen Drub. This proves that Dorje Shugden and Je Tsongkhapa are the same mental continuum, which means one person but different aspect. For these valid reasons I say

> that Dorje Shugden is a manifestation of the Wisdom Buddha Je Tsongkhapa – no doubt.
>
> 'Je Tsongkhapa himself appears as Dorje Shugden to prevent his doctrine of the Ganden Oral Lineage from degenerating. He does this by pacifying obstacles, gathering necessary conditions and bestowing powerful blessings upon practitioners of this doctrine.
>
> 'If we continually rely upon Dorje Shugden with faith, he will care for us as a mother cares for her child. He will guide us to the correct path, the liberating path. He will pacify our obstacles and gather necessary conditions for us, and we will receive his powerful blessings through which our wisdom, compassion and spiritual power will increase. Through this we can easily make progress along the quick path to enlightenment that is shown to us by Je Tsongkhapa.'[62]

Later in his life, the Fifth Dalai Lama realised that he had misunderstood the real nature of Dorje Shugden and he began to engage in the practice of Dorje Shugden and composed prayers to him (see Chapter 1). In these, the first prayers ever written to Dorje Shugden, he invites Dorje Shugden to come from the Dharmakaya, clearly indicating that he had come to regard Dorje Shugden as an enlightened being.[63]

Having destroyed the life of Tulku Dragpa Gyaltsen and established his religious authority over Tibet, the Fifth Dalai Lama then moved to establish his political authority. One remaining obstacle in his path to complete supremacy that he perceived lay in control over the power to appoint the Regent, which position had been conferred upon Sonam Rabten by Gushri Khan himself. Gushri Khan and Sonam Rabten died at about the same time and the dispute that ensued amongst the Mongolians as to who would inherit Gushri Khan's authority provided the Dalai Lama with the opportunity he needed to seize the right to appoint the future Regent himself.[64]

In this matter, the main obstacles to the Dalai Lama's attainment of absolute power over Tibet were Norbu and Gona Shagpa (sGo-sna-shag-pa). They were 'matrilineal relations' of the former Regent Sonam Rabten. Although Norbu expected to become Regent after

Sonam Rabten's death, both as a close relative and in view of his career and positions held until then, 'if the fifth Dalai Lama had readily allowed this, it would have been tantamount to endorsing Governor Nor-bu's succession ... in a way over which he had no control, and because the regent's authority had been conferred by Guši Khan, he would have been publicly acknowledging a historical fact that had been beyond his control.'[65] This would have diminished the Dalai Lama's power. Also, by eliminating Norbu he would be getting rid of the one person who could prove that the Fifth Dalai Lama was behind the murder of Tulku Dragpa Gyaltsen.

The Dalai Lama began a ruthless and cynical campaign against these two formerly important figures, until eventually, fearing for their lives, they both took refuge under the protection of Tashi Lhunpo Monastery, the seat of the Panchen Lama. Hearing of this, the Dalai Lama dispatched troops and threatened to attack the monastery. The Panchen Lama, who was the Dalai Lama's own Spiritual Guide, together with the principal lamas of Sera, Drepung and Ganden monasteries, requested that Norbu be forgiven, but the Dalai Lama's response was defiant:

> 'These 130,000 households of Tibet were given only to me by the Upholder of the Teachings and Dharma-King (viz. Guši Khan), and they were not given so that I might share them with those two matrilineal relations.'[66]

In the end, the Dalai Lama's plan of attack was not carried out, but the banishment of the 'two matrilineal relations' secured his sovereign power over all of Tibet. The Panchen Lama, one of the towering spiritual figures in the history of the Gelug tradition, passed away in 1662, but the Fifth Dalai Lama did not even attend the funeral:

> 'The Dalai Lama, now head of state, set out on a trip, claiming that his presence had been requested by the oracle at bSam-yas [Samye] monastery, and he sent only a rather inconspicuous envoy to attend the funeral of the great scholar who had been his teacher. It would appear that the deceased's intercession

> on behalf of the "two matrilineal relations" had considerably angered him.'[67]

In recent years, scholars have begun to investigate the 'myth of the Great Fifth'. For example, Elliot Sperling has remarked:

> 'One may say with confidence that the Fifth Dalai Lama does not fit the standard image that many people today have of a Dalai Lama, particularly not the image of a Nobel Peace Prize laureate.'[68]

An examination of some of the Fifth Dalai Lama's own statements indicates just how far he was willing to go to eliminate those who opposed him. He is reported as telling one of Gushri Khan's officers:

> '... "Relying on that particular virtue which encompasses the bodhisattva—i.e., thinking of oneself and others in an equal manner—has not held back strife. Thus, ... nothing other than shame before others would come of it." '

And also:

> 'Though we might take revenge, I ... the cleric occupying the seat of the omniscient ones, would not appear as a disobedient monk.'[69]

By this the Dalai Lama meant that because of his exalted position the Tibetan people would not find fault in his actions even if the actions were not in accordance with Buddha's teachings.

Shakabpa remarks that 'he could be ruthless in stamping out a rebellion' and quotes him as saying '… no pity should be wasted on a man who had to be executed for his crimes'.[70] During a rebellion of the Karmapas in Tsang, the Dalai Lama issued the following orders:

> '[Of those in] the band of enemies, who have despoiled
> the duties entrusted to them:
> Make the male lines like trees that have had their roots cut;
> Make the female lines like brooks that have dried up in
> winter,
> Make the children and grandchildren like eggs smashed
> against cliffs,

> Make the servants and followers like heaps of grass
> consumed by fire,
> Make their dominion like a lamp whose oil has been
> exhausted,
> In short, annihilate any traces of them, even their names.'[71]

With the Fifth Dalai Lama's sovereignty encompassing all spiritual and temporal authority he became not only an autocrat, but also supreme master over life and death for the masses of ordinary Tibetans. His government would later exploit this position to its maximum. It is significant to note that the present Dalai Lama has often spoken of his close affinity with the Fifth Dalai Lama who as we have seen was so involved in war and political activity. A Tibetan Government official statement issued on 31 May 1996, quotes the Dalai Lama as saying:

> 'I am a successor to the Great Fifth Dalai Lama and, likewise, have a unique karmic relationship with the previous Dalai Lama. I have therefore a duty to carry out the legacy of the Great Fifth and the 13th Dalai Lama.'[72]

The Sixth and Seventh Dalai Lamas

The sequence of events following the death of the Fifth Dalai Lama (in 1682) was most unusual. The Dalai Lama had appointed a young man named Sangye Gyatso as his Regent. Sangye Gyatso had previously been an attendant of the Dalai Lama, and had received a thorough grounding in religious and political matters. But he may have had an even closer relationship to the Dalai Lama: as the Tibetan historian Shakabpa remarks, 'Some scholars have made the statement that Sangye Gyatso was believed to have been the natural son of the fifth Dalai Lama.'[73]

The young Regent concealed the death of the Fifth Dalai Lama for fifteen years, by announcing that he had gone into meditation retreat for an unspecified period of time and could not be disturbed. A monk from Namgyal Dratsang Monastery was ordered to take the Dalai Lama's place by residing in the Potala palace and engaging in the regular routines that the Dalai Lama would have followed. Shakabpa says of this bizarre situation:

> '... the Namgyal Dratsang monk soon tired of his forced imprisonment and made an effort to escape from the duties of impersonation. He had to be beaten sometimes, and at others bribed. Indeed, it could not have been pleasant for him to remain within the walls of the Potala under those conditions for fifteen years.'[74]

Even so, the Namgyal Dratsang monk was relatively fortunate:

> 'In his frenzied determination to maintain the secret, Desi [Regent] Sangyay is said to have murdered both the medium of the Nechung oracle Tsewang Palbar and the latter's mother for getting wind of the secret during Desi's frequent consultation with the oracle in the nerve-wracking suspense of running the Tibetan administrative show without the presence of the Dalai Lama.'[75]

The building of the Potala palace, the supreme symbol of the Dalai Lama's power and of his association with Avalokiteshvara, was finally completed in 1695. Soon afterwards the Regent announced that the Fifth Dalai Lama had in fact died in 1682 and that his reincarnation was already thirteen years old! Regent Sangye Gyatso was later executed by the Mongol leader Lhazang Khan.[76]

Those fifteen years of deception, however, were not as shocking as the behaviour and lifestyle of the Sixth Dalai Lama, **Tsangyang Gyatso**, which nearly destroyed the institution itself:

> 'Because of this one reincarnation [the Sixth Dalai Lama] in the whole chain, there has been some vague scepticism about even the authenticity of this Institution ...
>
> 'Tsangyang Gyatso (1683-1706) lived for only 24 years but even during this short span of life he had created a sensation by the kind of life he led which almost shook the very foundation of this unique system.'[77]

One of the main reforms made by Je Tsongkhapa was strict adherence to the monastic rules set down by Buddha, but the Sixth Dalai Lama rebelled against this very religious tradition he was supposed to uphold. Tsangyang Gyatso favoured a frivolous life of sports, drinking, women and late nights of carousing. As Grunfeld comments:

> 'Tsangyang Gyatso … has come to be known among Tibetans as the "Merry One", and not without just cause, for he devoted himself more to debauchery than to religious pursuits … He is fondly remembered for his poetry, which constitutes almost the entire non-religious literature of Tibet.'[78]

The appeals of his Spiritual Guide, Panchen Lama Losang Yeshe, to focus on religious study and practice were to no avail. The young Dalai Lama, swayed by the pleasures of ordinary life, instead told his Spiritual Guide that he wished to renounce his vows.[79] As had been necessary with the Fifth Dalai Lama, the religious leaders of his time implored him to follow the religious path set forth by Buddha:

> 'The Dalai Lama was … approached by the abbots of the big three monasteries [Drepung, Sera and Ganden], by Desi [Regent] Taktse and by Lhazang Khan, … the grandson of Gushri Khan, all of whom pleaded with the Dalai Lama not to renounce his Getsul [novice monk] vows; but their pleas were of no avail.'[80]

Such behaviour by a senior religious figure was unacceptable, and was far from what his Mongolian patrons expected. When all attempts at persuasion had failed, Lhazang Khan marched into Lhasa and took full political control. He summoned the Dalai Lama to his court and castigated him for his numerous failings. Together with the Manchu Chinese Emperor he decided to depose and exile this disgraceful Dalai Lama, and his military might forced the Dalai Lama to acquiesce. Enroute to his place of exile, the young Tsangyang Gyatso 'mysteriously' died, probably being assassinated.

Lhazang Khan then publicly put forth another monk, Ngawang Yeshe Gyatso, as the true Sixth Dalai Lama and enthroned him at the Potala palace. However, the majority of Tibetans did not support Lhazang Khan's choice. When news arrived that a reincarnation of the late Sixth Dalai Lama had been found in a young child named Kelsang Gyatso, the Manchu Chinese recognised the potential political advantage in controlling this young boy and took him under their protection at Kumbum Monastery. Throughout all this turmoil, the majority of Tibetans still maintained their faith in Tsangyang Gyatso as a most unusual upholder of Je Tsongkhapa's tradition.

As a result of the actions of Regent Sangye Gyatso and the Sixth Dalai Lama, the political power that the Fifth Dalai Lama had so ruthlessly gained was lost, first to the Mongolians and then to the Chinese, through the Manchus. Lhazang Khan soon found himself in conflict with another Mongolian tribe, the Dzungars, who successfully conquered Lhasa and then killed Lhazang Khan himself. Once in control of Lhasa they deposed and imprisoned Lhazang Khan's chosen Dalai Lama, Yeshe Gyatso, and executed many lamas and political officials who had supported Lhazang.

The Tibetans petitioned the Dzungars to bring the true Dalai Lama to Lhasa, but the Manchu Chinese would not release the young **Kelsang Gyatso** (1708-1757) to the Mongol Dzungars. The Regent at that time, Taktse Shabdrung, and a number of Tibetan officials then sent the Manchu Chinese a letter saying that they recognised Kelsang Gyatso as the Dalai Lama. The Manchu Chinese Emperor took this political bait and confirmed that Kelsang Gyatso was the 'Seventh' Dalai Lama. He presented Kelsang Gyatso with a golden seal that read 'Seal of the Sixth Dalai Lama', and thus avoided the question of whether the two previous Sixth Dalai Lamas had been true incarnations or not.[81]

Because of the increasing unpopularity of the Dzungar regime, and frustration with the Dzungars' inability to bring them their Dalai Lama, the Tibetans sided with the Manchu Chinese and forcibly drove out the Dzungars. Thus in 1720 the Manchu Chinese escorted Kelsang Gyatso to Lhasa where at the age of only twelve he was enthroned as the Seventh Dalai Lama, but without temporal power. The Manchu Chinese set up a new form of government in Tibet, with a council of ministers replacing the previously all-powerful Regent.[82]

However, in 1728 one of the newly elected ministers, Pholhanas, violently overpowered his fellow ministers and took full control of Tibet. Three ministers and fourteen of their colleagues were executed just outside the Potala, where their bodies were sliced into small pieces. The father of the Seventh Dalai Lama had been a supporter of the executed ministers, and so he and the Dalai Lama were sent into exile for seven years.[83] Pholhanas ruled Tibet until 1747, while the Dalai Lama remained in the background:

> 'During the nineteen years he had ruled Tibet, there had been uninterrupted peace and prosperity throughout the countryside. He had allied himself firmly with the Manchu Emperors and was able to exert his influence on the Dalai Lama himself.'[84]

Pholhanas was succeeded by his youngest son, Gyemey Namgyal, who sought to re-establish the Dzungar Mongols as allies in order to drive the Manchu Chinese out of Tibet. Learning of his plan, the Manchu Chinese in Lhasa killed him. In 1751 the Dalai Lama himself was given full spiritual and temporal powers over Tibet, but he passed away only shortly thereafter in 1757.[85]

As Shakabpa remarks of the Seventh Dalai Lama's life:

> 'He was a scholarly man. His political life had been marked by difficulties. Only towards the end of his life, did he actually exercise temporal power. Although overshadowed by the political figures of those violent times, the seventh Dalai Lama has been acknowledged superior to the other Dalai Lamas on religious grounds, because of his piety and scholarly achievements.'[86]

THE EIGHTH TO TWELFTH DALAI LAMAS

It is already clear from the foregoing that there was, in fact, no consistent 'God-King' in the lineage of the Dalai Lamas. The first three were pure religious teachers, the Third gaining the admiration of the Mongols and for the first time receiving the title 'Dalai Lama' from the Mongolian ruler Altan Khan. The fourth, Altan Khan's grandson, was in Tibet for only 14 years and died at the relatively young age of 28. These first four Dalai Lamas were not interested in the political affairs of state, but concentrated instead on their main responsibility, which was to uphold and carry on the spiritual legacy of Je Tsongkhapa's tradition.

The Fifth Dalai Lama assumed full control of Tibet by ruthless means, disregarding the advice of his own Spiritual Guide in his ascension to power. In rejecting his monastic vows, the Sixth Dalai Lama also disregarded the advice of his Spiritual Guide, and had very little to do with either spiritual or political matters. The Seventh Dalai Lama, while setting an example of a pure spiritual practitioner, gave little leadership except in the last few years of his life. John Powers writes that after the death of the Seventh Dalai Lama:

> '... Tibet began a period of 130 years during which none of the Dalai Lamas assumed effective control. During this time, the country was ruled by a succession of regents, all of whom were Gélukpa monks. The eighth Dalai Lama, Jambel Gyatso, was uninterested in worldly affairs, and so although he lived to the age of forty-seven, the administration of the country was handled by regents.'[87]

The dominant myth about Tibet that is promulgated in the West is of a peaceful mountain kingdom that has always been led by the human incarnation of Avalokiteshvara, the Buddha of Compassion. On closer scrutiny it can be seen that the institution of the Dalai Lamas, which effectively began with the violent seizure of power by the Fifth Dalai Lama, showed a conspicuous lack of leadership until the twentieth century. In fact:

> 'The Ninth-Twelfth Dalai Lamas played no notable part in the life of Tibet. Their lives are conspicuous for their brevity. Several of them died before they came of age to assume power or write anything.'[88]

There is much speculation about these 'missing' Dalai Lamas. Their premature deaths and the sheer 'greed for power' evident in Lhasa has led many historians '... to suspect foul play in the demise of these Dalai Lamas at such young ages.'[89] What is certain is that for a long period of time the Dalai Lamas played no leading role in Tibetan political or even religious life. This was to change with the next two Dalai Lamas.

THE THIRTEENTH DALAI LAMA

The 'Great Thirteenth' Dalai Lama **Thubten Gyatso** (1876-1933) assumed power in 1895 at the age of nineteen, and was to preside over a period of great political upheaval in Tibet. Sir Charles Bell, a British diplomat and friend and confidant of the Thirteenth Dalai Lama, comments that in the early years of the Dalai Lama's leadership the devotion of his people carried him through internal matters of state:

> 'But in foreign politics he had to stand on his own feet. His ignorance led him astray; and the impetuosity and unyielding will, which were always strong ingredients in his character, pushed him still further on the road that led to disaster.
>
> '... Pathetic indeed was his ignorance as [to] how things were done outside his hermit land.'[90]

Concerned about the Dalai Lama's growing connection with Russia apparent at that time, and interested in expanding their own colonial influence, the British invaded Tibet in 1904. The young Dalai Lama fled the invaders, escaping north into China where he remained in exile for four years.

In Beijing, the Thirteenth Dalai Lama was granted an audience with the Empress Dowager. He was compelled to kneel before her, and he received the humiliating title 'Our Loyal and Submissive Vice-Regent'. As Goldstein comments:

> 'The Chinese had demonstrated clearly to the 13th Dalai Lama that he was subordinate to the emperor and that his position in Tibet was dependent on their goodwill. To the extremely proud Dalai Lama this must have been a very humiliating experience.'[91]

Not trusting him to be either loyal or submissive, China covertly dispatched an army of seven thousand men to march into Tibet, to ensure the Dalai Lama's compliance. After presiding over the Chinese Emperor's funeral, the Dalai Lama returned to Tibet, but this sojourn in his country was brief, for two months after his return the Chinese army entered Lhasa. The Dalai Lama this time fled south to India; and he was deposed by official decree from Beijing a few weeks later.[92]

In India, his former enemies the British treated him kindly but refused him any help to regain independence.[93] So from exile in Kalimpong the Dalai Lama organised a clandestine War Department in Tibet to fight the Chinese. This department reported directly to him in Kalimpong and was responsible for buying arms and recruiting Tibetan soldiers. Even the Tibetan Kashag was left in the dark as to their activities.[94]

Eventually civil war broke out in China and the Chinese army was driven out of Tibet in 1912. The Tibetan historian, K. Dhondup, describes the scene in the 'holy city' of Lhasa at the time:

> 'The monks of the three major monasteries and the local populace, including the fierce Banagshol Khampas joined the Tibetan army and their only weapons were stones, swords and spears … The Lhasa street was strewn with dead bodies of men, dogs, donkeys and horses … Each side displayed the severed head and hands of the other side to discourage each other.'[95]

Those Tibetans who were suspected of having collaborated with the Chinese were given rough treatment, including some members of the Kashag who were shot. The Kashag ceased to exist and the War Department became all-powerful, communicating directly to the Dalai Lama in Darjeeling.[96] Through Sir Charles Bell, the British enjoined the Dalai Lama not to kill the Chinese remaining in Tibet.

> 'At this the Dalai Lama was astounded and angry ... he strongly stated that if the Chinese soldiers could kill to capture Tibet, Tibetans can and must take arms to defend Tibet.'[97]

Writing in 1931 of his return to Lhasa, the Dalai Lama said: 'Religious services were held on behalf of the Faith and secular side of State Affairs. These ensured the full ripening of the evil deeds of the enemies and in consequence, …' referring to the Chinese Revolution, 'internal commotion broke out in their country and the time was changed.'[98] His first tasks upon arriving home were to reward the heroes of the struggle and punish the collaborators. Guilty monks were banished into exile and Tengyeling Monastery, which had been pro-Chinese, was closed forever.[99]

Bell reports that the Dalai Lama received criticism from some Tibetans for this military activity, and he quotes the young prince of Sikkim: 'It is a sin for a Buddhist to take a share in destroying life, a great sin for a lama, and a terribly great sin for the highest of all lamas.'[100] Once again, this shows the nature of the ruling Lama's Policy: the Thirteenth Dalai Lama was an ordained Buddhist monk who had the commitment not to harm others, including not to kill and not to cause people suffering. He therefore acted directly against the spiritual rules of Buddhism. Like the so-called Great Fifth, this is a shameful example in the world of a Buddhist monk who holds the position of high lama, a supposedly holy being.

In the years following this expulsion of the Chinese, the Dalai Lama became increasingly hungry for full Tibetan independence. He modernised certain aspects of Tibetan society, increased army recruitment and imported military equipment from abroad. He made efforts to demonstrate that Tibet was independent from China, and tried to foster relationships with the outside world. However his military aspirations met with considerable resistance, first from the Tibetan aristocracy and later from the monastic establishment. This issue caused a rift between the Dalai Lama and the Panchen Lama, partly because the new Tibetan army was to be funded by estate taxes, and a large portion of this burden fell upon Tashi Lhunpo Monastery, the seat of the Panchen Lama. As a result of this rift, in 1923 the Panchen Lama abruptly left Tibet for China.[101]

Throughout his life, the Thirteenth Dalai Lama followed mistaken advice and predictions from the State Oracle Nechung, (see Chapter 7) including those concerning Dorje Shugden practice. In the period between the death of the Fifth Dalai Lama until the time of the Thirteenth, the practice of Dorje Shugden flourished throughout Tibet; it was popular in monasteries and among lay communities alike. Motivated by jealousy and without giving any valid reasons the spirit medium, Nechung oracle, told the Thirteenth Dalai Lama that Dorje Shugden practice was harmful for the activities of the Tibetan government. Once more, out of mere grasping for the political power of government and without any valid evidence, the spiritual practice of Dorje Shugden was rejected by a Dalai Lama.

During the Thirteenth Dalai Lama's time, Kyabje Je Phabongkhapa was the most famous and influential lama who engaged practically in spreading the doctrine of the Wisdom Buddha Je Tsongkhapa throughout Tibet. It is said that the Thirteenth Dalai Lama told Je Phabongkhapa to stop promoting the practice of Dorje Shugden, but Je Phabongkhapa nevertheless continued to do so. One day, a government minister who was also a disciple of Je Phabongkhapa gave him secret information that the Thirteenth Dalai Lama planned to imprison Je Phabongkhapa if he did not stop spreading the Dorje Shugden practice. To prevent his disciples becoming discouraged, which would happen if he were imprisoned, Je Phabongkhapa went to see the Dalai Lama, verbally apologised in front of him and promised not to spread Dorje Shugden practice any more. From that time until the Thirteenth Dalai Lama's death, all Dorje Shugden practitioners, including Je Phabongkhapa himself, had to keep their practice of Dorje Shugden a secret.

Throughout the time of the Thirteenth Dalai Lama, various foreign journalists, officials and explorers visited Tibet and were astounded by the atrocities that met them in place of their expectations of the supposed 'Shangri-la'. They published accounts of what they saw, and from these works we can gain a more accurate insight into the actual brutality of the theocracy and the Thirteenth Dalai Lama's role in it.

In 1882, on his way to Lhasa, Sarat Chandra Das, an Indian Scholar, observed to his horror 'in the market place of Tashi-Lhunpo, a party of prisoners loaded with chains, pinioned by wooden clogs, and in some cases blinded.'[102]

Sarat Chandra Das' visit to Tibet had been organised by the Sinchen [or Senchen] Lama, who was the governor of Tsang. When it was revealed that Chandra Das was in fact a spy working for the British, his host was held responsible by the Lhasa government even though he had no prior knowledge of this.

> 'Upon the Sinchen Lama they visited their anger in a fearful manner. His servants were taken – all except one – they were beaten, their hands and feet were cut off, their eyes were gouged out, and they were left to die in the streets of Tashi-Lhunpo. ...
>
> 'A message was received from Lhasa to the effect that the Sinchen Lama must commit suicide. This he quietly refused to do. ... This answer produced another peremptory demand that the Lama should lay violent hands upon himself. To this the Lama made no reply at all. ...
>
> 'Thereafter Lhasa grew desperate. They sent a wicked man, a Kashmiri Mohammedan, ... and the Sinchen Lama's head was hacked from his body.
>
> 'Nor was this all. Having destroyed the body, the hierarchy at Lhasa proceeded to annihilate the soul. No further reincarnation of the Sinchen Lama has been recognized from that day.'[103]

During the Thirteenth Dalai Lama's rule such brutality spared no person of any rank, and was extended to innocent family members. Goldstein gives the example of the Regent Demo Rinpoche who was thrown into jail and assassinated by order of the Thirteenth when the Nechung oracle supposedly uncovered a plot by the Regent to regain his former power.[104] How did the Dalai Lama treat the alleged conspirators? Friend and confidant of the Dalai Lama, Sir Charles Bell tells of their fate:

> 'Sharpened bamboos were driven under the finger-nails, a punishment introduced into Tibet by the Manchus. Numerous floggings were inflicted with rods of willow on the bared back and buttocks, each of a hundred lashes or more. ...
>
> 'Various relatives were also punished; among others the wife of Jewel Long Life [Norbu Tsering]. She was a daughter of the noble family of Long Stone ... But in spite of her high birth she was flogged and made to sit every day for a week in one of the main streets of Lhasa with her wrists manacled and a heavy board round her neck. She was afterwards sent into exile.'[105]

No suggestion was ever made that Jewel Long Life's wife had had any part in the alleged conspiracy. But as Bell explains, even a witness would be tortured under the medieval justice system over which the Dalai Lama reigned:

> 'The Tibetan criminal code is drastic. In addition to fines and imprisonment, floggings are frequent, not only of people after they have been convicted of an offence, but also of accused persons, and indeed witnesses, during the course of the trial. For serious offences, use is made of the pillory as well as of the cangue, which latter is a heavy square wooden board round the neck. Iron fetters are fastened on the legs of murderers and inveterate burglars. For very serious or repeated offences, such as murder, violent robbery, repeated thefts, or serious forgery, the hand may be cut off at the wrist, the nose sliced off, or even the eyes gouged out, the last more likely for some heinous political crime. In former days those convicted of murder were put into a leather sack, which was sewn up and thrown into a river.'[106]

As a summary of what he had witnessed, English writer Perceval Landon, who travelled through Tibet in 1903-04, wrote that the Thirteenth Dalai Lama's 'rule was signalised by numerous proscriptions, banishments, imprisonings, and torturings. Neither life nor property was safe for a moment.'[107]

> 'Even an earthly manifestation of Avalokiteswara may carry things too far. Scandals and ill-feeling, however carefully repressed, will at length find a vent ... At Lhasa, under the shadow of the walls of the Palace, people spoke little and with bated breath. But at Tashi-Lhunpo and Shigatse, far from the intrigues of Lhasa and the overwhelming influence of the three great monasteries, there was less reticence, and many tales were told of the overbearing ways and cruel acts of the absent Dalai Lama.'[108]

During his reign the Dalai Lama personally ordered the punishments to be meted out for every serious criminal offence. Sir Charles Bell explains the process by which punishments would be ordered:

> 'Perhaps there is a riot or other disturbance. The Ecclesiastical Court selects an ecclesiastical official, and the Cabinet selects one from the laity; these are to make an inquiry into the reason of the riot, and the punishment that should be inflicted. Their names are sent up to the Dalai Lama for his approval. In their findings they must agree; no divergence of opinion is permitted; the stronger will carries the day. Then they report through the cabinet, who propose different alternative orders, sending their report to the Prime Minister. The Dalai Lama puts his red hand-mark opposite the order he approves.'[109]

It seems fitting that someone with so much blood on his hands should seal others' fate with a red hand-mark.

It is highly inappropriate that any Buddhist monk, and especially one carrying the reputation of being the embodiment of all Buddhas' compassion (Avalokiteshvara), should find torture and execution unavoidable.[110] Bell remarked, 'it must be admitted that the penalties inflicted on the chief offenders were, according to Western ideas, perhaps worse than death'.[111]

In a perverted interpretation of the law of karma (actions and their effects), the Dalai Lama and his officers considered that through administering floggings they avoided the action of killing so long as their victim was still alive when the beating finished, even if the victim would certainly die later. As the Mayor of Lhasa in the 1950s, Gorkar Mebon, told journalist Alan Winnington:

> 'Even when the death sentence was administered ... it was in [a] form that made no person responsible for the death: by hurling the person from a precipice or sewing him in yakskin and throwing him in a river. Lighter sentences were of amputation of a hand, both hands, a leg or both legs, the stumps being sterilised with boiling butter. … "It depends on the situation. That heavy whip, for example: if a person had 300 strokes of it properly applied he would almost certainly die afterwards."
>
> 'Commonest punishments are the whip, the cangue (a portable pillory) and exile.'[112]

As Grunfeld reports;

> 'A British woman who visited Gyantse in 1922 witnessed a public flogging and reported that the victim was then forced to spend the night exposed and tied down on the top of a mountain pass where he froze to death overnight. A British resident of two decades reported seeing countless eye gouging and mutilations, ...'[113]

And as Robert W. Ford, one of the few westerners living in Tibet during the 1940s wrote:

> 'All over Tibet I had seen men who had been deprived of an arm or a leg for theft ... Penal amputations were done without antiseptics or sterile dressings.'[114]

These punishments continued during the 1950s, during the reign of the Fourteenth Dalai Lama: and 'The most graphic evidence readily available of a public torture can be seen in *Life* magazine, with photographs of a whipping (200-250 lashes) that occurred right in the middle of Lhasa [where the Dalai Lama was living] in 1950.'[115] And 'During her travels in Tibet in 1959, American journalist Anna Louise Strong heard one account after another of those who had died shortly after their beatings finished.'[116]

1

© www.dorjeshugden.com

2

© www.dorjeshugden.com

3

1. The first statue of Dorje Shugden, made by the Fifth Dalai Lama with his own hands. The statue is now at Pelgyeling Monastery, in Nepal.
2. Trode Khangsar, the Temple dedicated to Dorje Shugden by the Fifth Dalai Lama.
3. Line drawing of the Fifth Dalai Lama, Ngawang Losang Gyatso, 1617-1682.

4

© Popperfoto/Getty Images

5

Bundesarchiv, Bild 135-S-13-13-14 Foto: Schäfer, Ernst | 1938/1939

6

Bundesarchiv, Bild 135-S-13-13-14 Foto: Schäfer, Ernst | 1938/1939

7

Bundesarchiv, Bild 135-KA-10-072 Foto: Krause, Ernst | 1938/1939

4. The Thirteenth Dalai Lama, Thubten Gyatso, 1876-1933.
5. Yapshi Langdun, a Tibetan minister who Reting regarded as a rival and outmanoeuvered in the search for the new Dalai Lama.
6. Reting Rinpoche with Bruno Beger in 1938, during one of several German SS expeditions to Tibet.
7. An SS expedition to Tibet in 1938. Reting sent them home with a letter to 'King Hitler', praising the Nazi leader and requesting that they strengthen the relationship between the two regimes.[377]

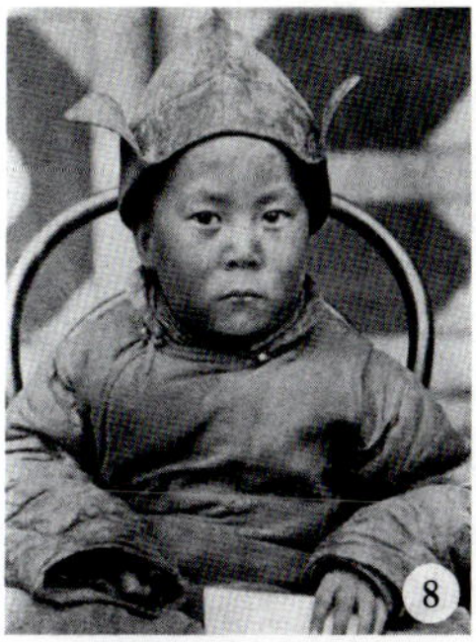

© Popperfoto/Getty Images

© Keystone/Hulton Archive/Getty Images

© Die Welt / Dan Levine / epa / Corbis

© AFP/Getty Images

© AFP/Getty Images

8. Lhamo Dondrub, as a child in the Muslim village of Takster before being brought to Lhasa.
9. Enthroned as the Fourteenth Dalai Lama and given the name Tenzin Gyatso.
10. Nowadays the Dalai Lama lives in exile, but who is the real Dalai Lama behind the mask?
11. The Dalai Lama meeting Chairman Mao in 1955.
12. The Dalai Lama voting at the First National People's Congress, 1954.
13. The Dalai Lama praised Mao as being like a God.

© Bundesarchiv, Bild 135-S-17-14-34 Foto: Shafer, Ernst | 1938/1939

© Bundesarchiv, Bild 135-S-13-13-33 Foto: Shafer, Ernst | 1938/1939

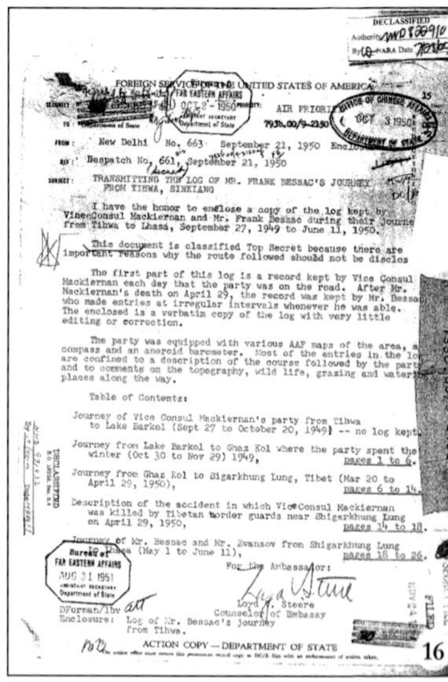

DECLASSIFIED

FOREIGN SERVICE OF THE UNITED STATES OF AMERICA

AIR PRIORITY

TO: Department of State

FROM: New Delhi No. 663 September 21, 1950

REF: Despatch No. 661, September 21, 1950

SUBJECT: TRANSMITTING THE LOG OF MR. FRANK BESSAC'S JOURNEY FROM TIHWA, SINKIANG

I have the honor to enclose a copy of the log kept by Vice Consul Mackiernan and Mr. Frank Bessac during their journe from Tihwa to Lhasa, September 27, 1949 to June 11, 1950.

This document is classified Top Secret because there are important reasons why the route followed should not be disclos

The first part of this log is a record kept by Vice Consul Mackiernan each day that the party was on the road. After Mr. Mackiernan's death on April 29, the record was kept by Mr. Bessac who made entries at irregular intervals whenever he was able. The enclosed is a verbatim copy of the log with very little editing or correction.

The party was equipped with various AAF maps of the area, a compass and an aneroid barometer. Most of the entries in the lo are confined to a description of the course followed by the part and to comments on the topography, wild life, grazing and water places along the way.

Table of Contents:

Journey of Vice Consul Mackiernan's party from Tihwa to Lake Barkol (Sept 27 to October 20, 1949) -- no log kept.

Journey from Lake Barkol to Ghaz Kol where the party spent the winter (Oct 30 to Nov 29) 1949, pages 1 to 6.

Journey from Ghaz Kol to Sigarkhung Lung, Tibet (Mar 20 to April 29, 1950), pages 6 to 14.

Description of the accident in which Vice Consul Mackiernan was killed by Tibetan border guards near Shigarkhung Lung on April 29, 1950, pages 14 to 18.

Journey of Mr. Bessac and Mr. Zvansov from Shigarkhung Lung to Lhasa (May 1 to June 11), pages 18 to 26.

For the Ambassador:

Loyd V. Steere
Counselor of Embassy

DForman/lbv

Enclosure: Log of Mr. Bessac's journey from Tihwa.

ACTION COPY — DEPARTMENT OF STATE

14. A division of the Tibetan army on parade in 1938.
15. Bayonet wielding soldiers on guard at the Norbu Linka, the Dalai Lama's summer palace.
16. This top secret CIA field diary was kept by Douglas MacKiernan and Frank Bessac. It proves that the CIA were in Tibet as early as 1949, before the People's Liberation Army entered Tibet in 1950. CIA covert operations in Tibet continued until the early 1970s. In recent decades the National Endowment for Democracy has continued CIA activities with respect to Tibet. [378]

17

© Popperfoto/Getty Images

18

© Bettmann / Corbis

19

© AFP/Getty Images

20

©LegalEagle/wikimedia

21

© Nicholas Kamm/AFP/Getty Images

22

© Prakash Mathema/ AFP/Getty Images

17. The Dalai Lama with Tibetan Resistance fighters in 1959. According to CIA files, in 1956 the Dalai Lama personally requested the Indian and US governments to support the Tibetan resistance fighters.[379]
18. Monks surrendering the guns and explosives they were using against the Chinese.
19. Gyalo Dondrub, the Dalai Lama's brother, involved - in his own words - in 'very dirty business'.
20. The Dalai Lama inspecting troops at Chakrata. He authorised the Tibetan units of the Indian Special Frontier Force to fight the war in East Pakistan in 1971.
21. John Kenneth Knaus, a CIA operative who was involved with the CIA funded Tibetan guerrillas.
22. Norbu Dorje, a US-trained former Tibetan guerilla.

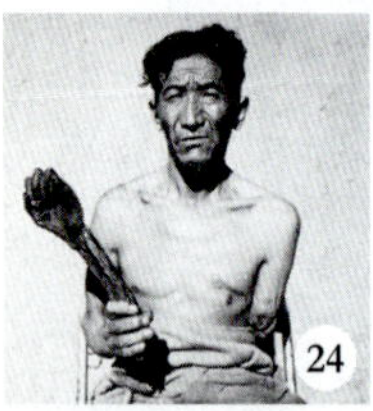

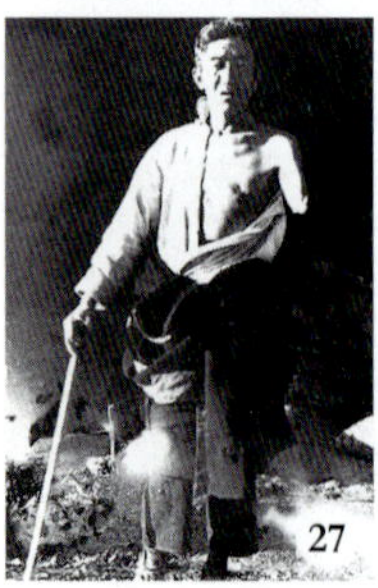

23. Torture implements from the Dalai Lama's era on display in Lhasa. This photo shows tools for gouging out eyes, and crushing fingers.

24. A Tibetan with his severed arm.

25 - 26. Stocks. These were in common use in Shol prison at the base of the Dalai Lama's 1000-room Potala Palace.

27. A Tibetan whose arm was cut off as punishment.

28. A Tibetan whose Achilles tendons were severed as punishment.

29. A Tibetan in leg-irons, left to wander the streets begging for food.

© Stringer/AFP/Getty Images

© Gerald Lehner *

© Boris Roessler/AFP/Getty Images

30. The Dalai Lama with Shoko Asahara, leader of the AUM Cult, who masterminded the sarin gas attack on Tokyo's subway that killed 13 people.
31. The Dalai Lama with Jorg Haider, leader of Austrian extreme rightwing (FPÖ) party.
32.* The Dalai Lama with Bruno Beger, a convicted Nazi war criminal, who conducted experiments on Jews in German concentration camps; 86 of his subjects were murdered.
33. The Dalai Lama with his friend and mentor Heinrich Harrer. Harrer was a Nazi and an SS sergeant. He joined the SA (Sturm-Abteilung) in 1934 when it was illegal in Austria.

* Private Archive Beger/from correspondence with the Austrian journalist Gerald Lehner who investigated the relations between National Socialism and the governments of the Dalai Lamas. Author of *Zwischen Hitler und Himalaya. Die Gedächtnislücken des Heinrich Harrer*, Czernin-Verlag, Wien (Austria) 2007

Image from France 24

© Western Shugden Society

© Western Shugden Society

Image from Bod Gyalo

© Western Shugden Society

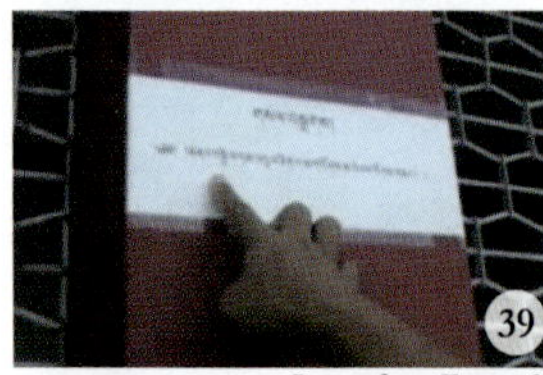

Image from France 24

Image from Bod Gyalo

© Western Shugden Society

34. The Dalai Lama in January 2008: 'These monks must be expelled from all monasteries. If they are not happy, you can tell them that the Dalai Lama himself asked that this be done, and it is very urgent.'[380] Subsequent to this, the persecution, already started in 1996, became more intense.
35. Entry is denied to the monasteries and their facilities.
36. Hundreds of monks are expelled and made homeless. Indian Police provide temporary protection for them.
37. Even children are forced to make public oaths denouncing Dorje Shugden.
38. Wanted posters appear around Dharamsala inciting violence to Dorje Shugden practitioners.
39. Hospitals ban Dorje Shugden worshippers from receiving treatment.
40. The public 'referendum' that forces monks from their monasteries.
41. A wall is built at Ganden Monastery to segregate the Shugden monks from the rest of the monastery.

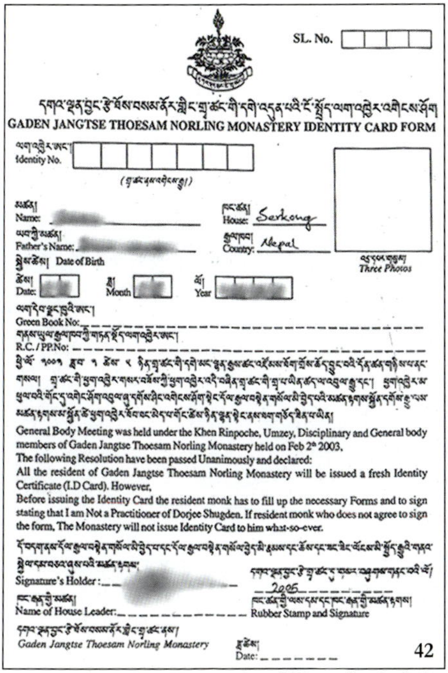

SL. No.

GADEN JANGTSE THOESAM NORLING MONASTERY IDENTITY CARD FORM

Identity No.

Name: [redacted]

House: Serkong

Father's Name: [redacted]

Country: Nepal

Three Photos

Date of Birth

Date: [redacted] Month [redacted] Year [redacted]

Green Book No:

R.C. / PP.No:

General Body Meeting was held under the Khen Rinpoche, Umzey, Disciplinary and General body members of Gaden Jangtse Thoesam Norling Monastery held on Feb 2th 2003.
The following Resolution have been passed Unanimously and declared:
All the resident of Gaden Jangtse Thoesam Norling Monastery will be issued a fresh Identity Certificate (I.D Card). However,
Before issuing the Identity Card the resident monk has to fill up the necessary Forms and to sign stating that I am Not a Practitioner of Dorjee Shugden. If resident monk who does not agree to sign the form, The Monastery will not issue Identity Card to him what-so-ever.

Signature's Holder: [redacted]

2005

Name of House Leader:

Rubber Stamp and Signature

Gaden Jangtse Thoesam Norling Monastery

Date:

© Western Shugden Society

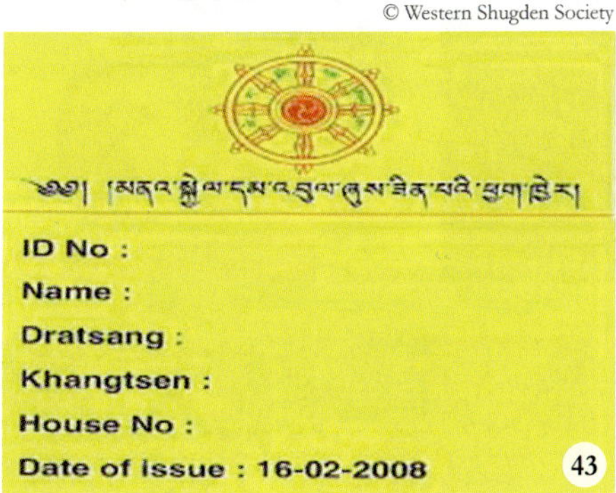

ID No :

Name :

Dratsang :

Khangtsen :

House No :

Date of issue : 16-02-2008

© Western Shugden Society

© Lynn Goldsmith / Corbis

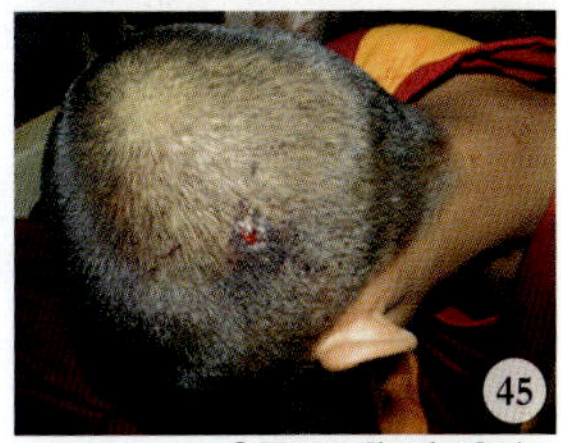

© Western Shugden Society

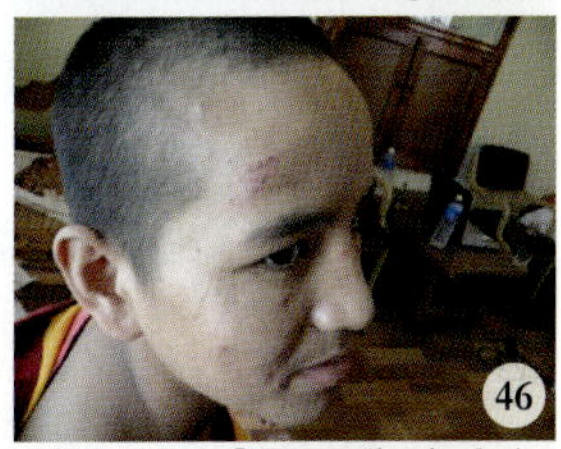

© Western Shugden Society

© Western Shugden Society

42. Application for identity documents require the person to have denounced Dorje Shugden.

43. The Identity card received by those who publically denounce Dorje Shugden; without this there is no access to food and medicine.

44. Samdhong Rinpoche, the Prime Minister of the Tibetan Government in Exile and principally responsible for trying to fulfil the Dalai Lama's wish to 'clean' society of Shugden practitioners.[381]

45 - 47. These young tulkus from Shar Gaden Monastery were beaten up because they worship Dorje Shugden.

DEMONSTRATIONS & PROTEST MARCHS

AUSTRALIA

FRANCE

GERMANY

48 - 59. Demonstrations & Protest Marchs in Australia, France, Germany, India, United Kingdom and the United States against the Dalai Lama's religious persecution.

AGAINST THE DALAI LAMA'S RELIGIOUS PERSECUTION

INDIA

UNITED KINGDOM

UNITED STATES

RADIO CITY, NEW YORK, 2008

© Western Shugden Society (all images)

60-65 Having just received spiritual advice from the Dalai Lama at a talk he gave in Radio City, New York, the attendees left the auditorium and immediately began attacking the peaceful protest being held by members of the Western Shugden Society. The Police called in horse-backed reinforcements and heavily armed riot police; finally they closed down several blocks of Manhattan.

We should remember that the Thirteenth Dalai Lama was a fully ordained Buddhist monk with vows against harming any living creature, let alone killing. Did he struggle with his role as chief judge, commanding such severe punishments and even execution to be inflicted on his people? His friend, Sir Charles Bell, gives the following damning verdict:

> 'He loved the work, ... and he liked the power which the work gave him.'[117]

Writing about the Thirteenth Dalai Lama, Bell says that towards the end of his life he 'became increasingly autocratic' with no one daring to object to his orders. 'The Dalai Lama was indeed an absolute dictator; more so as regards his own country than Herr Hitler and Signor Mussolini in theirs.'[118]

The circumstances around his death are replete with intrigue, superstition and the suspicion of foul play, and also show the malign influence of the Nechung oracle, as described in chapter 7. The Dalai Lama had become seriously ill and had developed a high fever. The Nechung oracle was summoned in a great hurry one night. While in trance:

> '... the Nechung Oracle medium gave the Dalai Lama a powder medicine. As the medium came out [of trance], Jampa-la, the Dalai Lama's regular doctor, pointed out to the Nechung medium that the wrong medicine had been administered. Soon afterwards the Nechung medium gave a second medicine according to the regular doctor's prescription. But both these medicines failed to improve the worsening condition of the Dalai Lama.'[119]

From that point onwards, the fever grew worse; the Dalai Lama became delirious and passed away the next day. Many reports at this time say that he died in anger.[120] Some suspect foul play and the possibility of poisoning, others that the Nechung oracle had made a mistake. All those present, including the medium of the oracle, were interrogated. The oracle was disgraced, and the Dalai Lama's physician was first imprisoned and then banished into exile.[121]

These were the squalid circumstances in which the 'Great Thirteenth' left this world in 1933. Very soon the search would start for his reincarnate successor.

CHAPTER 9

The Fourteenth Dalai Lama

Whereas the Thirteenth Dalai Lama was notorious for his brutality, the Fourteenth will most certainly be remembered for his deception and hypocrisy. There is little doubt that this false Dalai Lama has achieved enormous personal success, establishing a huge reputation and great power; no other figure in modern political history has enjoyed fifty years of uncritical press, had two major biographical motion pictures appear within their lifetime, and been awarded the Nobel Peace Prize. But how has he accomplished this? It is because he wears the robes of an ordained Buddhist monk, and gives teachings taken from his Spiritual Guide, while performing the actions of a politician, hiding his true actions behind a spiritual mask.

What is needed now is an honest evaluation of the man behind this mask, the present Dalai Lama, for he is after all regarded by some to be a key player on the world stage in both political and religious spheres, with the result that his actions have far-reaching effects. There is no reason why the standards by which we hold other world leaders accountable should not also apply to the Fourteenth Dalai Lama.

As Professor Jens-Uwe-Hartmann, Tibetologist at Humboldt University Berlin points out:

> 'The glorification of the Dalai Lama in his function as a political leader does not aid the process of democratisation. A critically differentiating analysis of his political statements must be possible, and it should furthermore not be blocked off by the argument that criticism solely serves the purposes of the Chinese.'[122]

His Early Life and Education

Following the Thirteenth Dalai Lama's death in 1933, the Tibetan authorities immediately made necessary arrangements to maintain the political apparatus of a reincarnate Dalai Lama. The details of the mock search which resulted in the recognition of the present false Dalai Lama have already been given in Chapter 2.

The Fourteenth Dalai Lama had as his Senior and Junior Tutors two of the greatest spiritual masters of our time: Kyabje Ling Rinpoche (1903-1983) and Kyabje Trijang Rinpoche (1901-1981). Trijang Rinpoche and his own principal Spiritual Guide, Kyabje Je Phabongkha Rinpoche, are the two most important figures of the Gelugpa tradition in the twentieth century. It is due primarily to these two spiritual masters that all of the essential Gelugpa lineages have been carried forward, completely pure and unbroken to the present day, including the close lineage of the Dharma Protector, Dorje Shugden.

Trijang Rinpoche, who was considered to be an emanation of Buddha Shakyamuni, Buddha Heruka, Atisha and Je Tsongkhapa, wrote an extensive commentary as well as many special rituals and yogas connected with Dorje Shugden.[123] The present Dalai Lama has referred to Trijang Rinpoche as his root Guru, or principal Spiritual Guide[124]; and Trijang Rinpoche was also the root Guru of many of the senior and junior lamas of the Gelugpa tradition as well as of thousands of other monks, nuns and lay people. He was one of the most respected and loved lamas in the last half of the twentieth century.[125] It is sad to note that the Dalai Lama does not mention these extraordinary qualities of his Spiritual Guide even once in his later autobiography, referring to him in passing only as his Junior Tutor and as a member of his retinue.[126] His earlier autobiography also mentions Trijang Rinpoche, but only as the person who taught him how to read, the principles of grammar and how to spell.[127]

Embracing Communism

In 1949, the new communist Chinese government initially attempted to engage the Tibetan government in peaceful negotiations to resolve their disputes. But when in September 1950 the Tibetans' official representatives failed to arrive for negotiations in the Chinese capital, the People's Liberation Army (PLA) was ordered by Chairman Mao Zedong to enter Chamdo in eastern Tibet. Chinese troops crossed the Yangtse River on 7 October 1950.[128]

The Tibetan forces were poorly led, equipped and organised, and were quickly defeated. Within two weeks the PLA had captured the entire Tibetan army, including the governor-general of the region. Although, with this easy military victory the road to Lhasa was open, the PLA did not advance further; instead they again called on Lhasa to negotiate. Melvyn Goldstein explains:

> 'Mao did not want simply to conquer Tibet, even though it would have been easy to do so. He wanted a political settlement approved by Tibet's leader, the Dalai Lama. He wanted China's claim to Tibet legitimized by having the Dalai Lama accept Chinese sovereignty and work with the PRC [People's Republic of China] gradually to reform Tibet's feudal economy.'[129]

In effect, Mao Zedong was using his military might to force the Tibetans to the negotiating table, for he understood the dangers of a protracted guerrilla war in Tibet's mountainous terrain.[130] With the advent of the Cold War there was also the very real possibility of such a conflict drawing in the United States as part of its worldwide stance against communism.[131]

In Lhasa the news of the Chinese victory brought fear and confusion. High lamas and the traditional oracles were consulted to determine a course of action. It was agreed that the sixteen-year-old Dalai Lama should be 'officially enthroned' and given full powers of government.[132] Shortly afterwards the Dalai Lama and many of the Lhasan nobility fled to the town of Yatung, just north of the Indian frontier, and established a provisional government there.[133]

Before his departure from Lhasa, the Dalai Lama sent a message to the PLA in Chamdo saying that he 'sincerely wanted to restore the friendship' between the Tibetan and Chinese peoples. Moreover, he authorised two delegations to travel to Beijing to begin negotiations with the Chinese, and finally on 23 May 1951, under direct order from the Fourteenth Dalai Lama, the 'Agreement of the Central People's Government and the Local Government of Tibet' was signed, now more commonly known as the 'Seventeen-Point Agreement'.[134] As Goldstein says,

> 'The Seventeen-Point Agreement ushered in a new chapter in Sino-Tibetan relations since it officially ended the conflict over the Tibet Question. Point 1 sets this out clearly: "The Tibetan people shall unite and drive out imperialist forces from Tibet: the Tibet people shall return to the big family of the Motherland—the People's Republic of China." Tibet, for the first time in its 1,300 years of recorded history, had now in a formal written agreement acknowledged Chinese sovereignty.'[135]

The Dalai Lama sent the Chinese leadership a telegram expressing 'unanimous support for the agreement' by the 'local government of Tibet, the monks and the entire Tibetan people'. Whatever his reasons were for sending this message, with his return to Lhasa and ratification of the Seventeen-Point Agreement the political incorporation of Tibet into China was accomplished. Tibet was now formally part of the Chinese state. Mao Zedong had the political agreement he wished for that would lead to the peaceful liberation of feudalistic Tibet, and the Tibetan nobility and clergy had assurances that their positions of power and privilege would continue.[136]

Contrary to popular belief the Chinese invasion of Tibet was peaceful after the initial clash in Chamdo. In some parts of the country the Chinese were even welcomed. Han Chinese soldiers and civilian cadres were authorised to enter central Tibet only after the formal signing of the Seventeen-Point Agreement. They were well-behaved and under strict instructions not to become a burden on the local populace.[137]

The Chinese went to extraordinary efforts to work with the Tibetan elite in a 'united front'. Goldstein writes that:

'... [Mao's] Tibet strategy sought to create cordial relations between Han (ethnic Chinese) and Tibetans, and allay Tibetan anxieties so that Tibet's elite would over time genuinely accept "reintegration" with China and agree to a societal transformation ... Between 1951 and 1959, not only was no aristocratic or monastic property confiscated, but feudal lords were permitted to exercise continued judicial authority over their hereditarily bound peasants. At the heart of this strategy was the Dalai Lama. Mao saw him, in particular, as the vehicle by which the feudal and religious elite (and then the masses) would come to accept their place in China's new multi-ethnic Communist state.'[138]

It is under these circumstances that the Dalai Lama's view of communism evolved. Far from taking a confrontational position as he would have his western audience believe, instead he embraced the communist ideology in general and Chairman Mao in particular.

The first foreigner to interview the Dalai Lama after his signing of the Seventeen-Point Agreement in 1951 was Alan Winnington. In an interview that was obviously warm and respectful, the Tibetan leader shared his convictions with the British journalist, who first asked him what had happened since the signing of the agreement. The Dalai Lama replied:

'Before the agreement ... Tibet could see no way ahead. Since the agreement Tibet has left the old way that led to darkness and has taken a new way leading to a bright future of development.

'... I heard Chairman Mao talk on different matters and I received instruction from him. I have come to the firm conviction that the brilliant prospects for the people of China as a whole are also the prospects for us Tibetan people; the path of our entire country is our path and not any other.'[139]

In 1954 he accepted an invitation to visit Beijing and represent Tibet in the Chinese People's National Assembly. It was the young Dalai Lama's first trip out of Tibet.

> 'It was only when I went to China in 1954-55 that I actually studied Marxist ideology and learned the history of the Chinese revolution. Once I understood Marxism, my attitude changed completely. I was so attracted to Marxism, I even expressed my wish to become a Communist Party member. …
>
> 'I ... went to China to meet Chairman Mao. We had several good meetings.'[140]

While in Beijing the Dalai Lama agreed to be chairman of Mao's proposed Preparatory Committee for the Autonomous Region of Tibet (PCART), whose purpose was to prepare Tibet for regional autonomy under Chinese rule. At the inaugural festivities of the PCART in Lhasa the Dalai Lama praised the Han in Tibet saying they had:

> '... strictly adhered to the policy of freedom of religion, carefully protected the lamaseries and respected the religious beliefs of the Tibetan people. … All this has greatly helped to remove the apprehensions that previously prevailed … as a result of the rumors and instigations made by the agents of the imperialists.'[141]

Right up until the events in 1959 the Dalai Lama was working closely with the Chinese to develop Tibet under communist rule. He expressed 'his most effusive support for China in speeches and articles as late as January 1959 (published in Xizang Ribao)'. He also continued to express admiration for Mao, speaking in 1955, for example, of his joy at meeting him face-to-face'.[142] As Gelder and Gelder have pointed out:

> '… the god-king … in his public statements had proved to be Mao's most valuable ally in Tibet.'[143]

The Myths Surrounding his Escape from Tibet

The release of the Hollywood movie *Kundun* in 1997 sparked fresh interest in the Dalai Lama's escape from Tibet in 1959. Careful investigation into the actual stages of this escape reveal a variety of conflicting versions, which when considered altogether expose one common truth – the Fourteenth Dalai Lama is a shameless liar and master at creating his own deceptive reality in the face of the truth.

Having a leader of the Tibetan people who was a communist sympathiser and admirer of Mao placed those Tibetans rebelling against the Chinese in a very difficult position. For the rebels it became imperative to get him out of Lhasa and to sever his connection with the Chinese.

The image of a beleaguered Dalai Lama as a virtual prisoner, not of the Chinese but of the Tibetan rebels, is reflected in a remarkable series of letters between him and the Chinese General Tan Yuan-san (see Appendix 1). In Lhasa at around 4 p.m. on 17 March 1959, two mortar shells landed harmlessly in a marsh inside the palace grounds. The Tibetans say these were fired from the direction of the Chinese camp, but this has always been open to question. Grunfeld points out that at this time the Dalai Lama:

> '… was writing to General Tan, informing the Chinese of his support and of his plans to move to their camp. Why would the Chinese have fired shots, thereby precipitating a crisis? On the other hand, the rebels, undoubtedly disturbed by the Dalai Lama—Tan correspondence, needed some grand gesture to get the Dalai to finally break with the Chinese. Logically, the mortars could have come from the rebels.'[144]

The mortar shells created panic in the palace and the Dalai Lama turned to his oracle for advice. But which oracle did he consult? There are conflicting accounts; over forty years later the Dalai Lama claims in his most recent autobiography that just before the two mortar shells were fired he consulted the Nechung oracle:

> 'I again sought the counsel of the oracle. To my astonishment, he shouted, "Go! Go! Tonight!" The medium, still in his trance, then staggered forward and, snatching up some paper and pen, wrote down, quite clearly and explicitly, the route that I should take out of the Norbulingka, down to the last Tibetan town on the Indian border. His directions were not what might have

> been expected. That done, the medium, a young monk named Lobsang Jigme, collapsed in a faint, signifying that Dorje Drakden had left his body.'[145]

Eye-witnesses alive today however say that the Dalai Lama did not consult the oracle of Nechung but rather the oracle of Dorje Shugden.[146] In 1998 Swiss National TV interviewed Lobsang Yeshe, the assistant of the previous abbot of Sera Monastery and someone who accompanied the Dalai Lama on his escape from Tibet. Lobsang Yeshe stated that he went to the oracle of Dorje Shugden to request exact instructions about the escape. In the SNTV programme:

> 'Lobsang Yeshe tells us that the oracle gave precise instructions as to how and by which route the escape should take place with the monks as his bodyguard.[147]

Helmut Gassner, for many years the German-language translator for the Dalai Lama, has also pointed out:

> '... the Dalai Lama's Chamberlain, Kungo Phala ... organized His Holiness' escape from the Norbulingka Summer Palace ... The preparations for the escape were made in absolute secrecy and strictly followed instructions received by [the oracle of] Dorje Shugden. I asked him [Phala] what thoughts were on his mind when he had to make his way through the crowds surrounding the Norbulingka with the Dalai Lama, disguised as a servant, just behind him. He said that everything happened exactly as the Dorje Shugden Oracle from Panglung Monastery had predicted ...
>
> 'According to all trustworthy witnesses I know and consulted, the State Oracle [of Nechung] did not provide any help on that occasion. After the Dalai Lama and his retinue had fled, the State Oracle only found out the following day that he had been left behind.'[148]

This last statement is supported by the testimony of the medium of the Nechung oracle himself, except that he says he only found out three days later! In *Exile from the Land of Snows* Lobsang Jigme, the medium of the Nechung oracle, says that he was ill at this time and mentions nothing about the Dalai Lama consulting Nechung or telling him to go that night. After an invocation on March 20th, three days after the Dalai Lama left, Lobsang Jigme and his attendants 'one and all lapsed into silence, pondering Dorje Drakden's [Nechung's] other statement: the stunning news of the Dalai Lama's flight from the Norbulinka … .'[149] This clearly contradicts the Dalai Lama's account.

Also, by revealing that the Nechung oracle, although sick, was obliged to find his own way out of Tibet, this account shows the lower level of respect and importance at which the Nechung oracle was held at that time. It may also help to explain the subsequent resentment of the Nechung oracle towards the Shugden oracle and by extension towards Dorje Shugden.

It is therefore clear that much of what the Dalai Lama has said about his escape from Tibet is untrue. A lot has been written of this dramatic escape – how at any moment the Chinese could have caught up with them, how brave the Tibetan soldiers were and how arduous the journey was. However, two points are now seen to be glaringly omitted from these popular accounts. First of these is that the party was accompanied by a US Central Intelligence Agency (CIA)-trained operative who was in radio contact with the CIA network throughout the escape. As reported in the American *George Magazine*:

> 'Around 3 a.m. on March 18th, they rested for a few hours near the Che-La pass separating Lhasa valley from the Tsangpo valley. It was then that the first coded radio message on the Dalai Lama's progress was broadcast from Tibet to a CIA listening post on Okinawa, Japan. The message was relayed to CIA headquarters near Washington, D.C., where Allen Dulles waited for news of the Dalai Lama's journey. Soon Dulles would brief President Eisenhower. Tibet's war for independence was about to begin.'[150]

The CIA involvement was not just limited to radio operators:

> '… the Dalai Lama was accompanied by a Khampa who had been trained and equipped with a movie camera and

sufficient color film to preserve a visual record of the flight. The Americans used a Lockheed C130 aircraft—modified especially for flight over the thin air of Tibet—to drop food and fodder for the Dalai's party and were able to do so thanks to the training other Khampas had in learning how to place distinctive panels in the snow as targets for the pilots.'[151]

As Grunfeld has quoted,

'… this fantastic escape and its major significance has been buried in the lore of the CIA as one of the successes that are not talked about. The Dalai Lama would never have been saved without the CIA.'[152]

Another feature of this mythical flight that is rarely reported is the Chinese claim to have deliberately let the Dalai Lama go. Two British visitors to Tibet in the early 1960s report that the Dalai Lama's party was followed by observation aircraft, and that no attempt was made to pursue the slowly-moving entourage, which included the Dalai Lama's mother, elderly people and children.[153] Credence is given to this claim by the fact that China announced his arrival in India before anyone else did, causing the Indian government acute embarrassment. The Chinese also state that Mao gave orders to the PLA to allow the Tibetan leader to cross the border. Mao Zedong is reported as telling the Soviet Ambassador in Beijing, 'If we had arrested him, we would have called the population of Tibet into rebellion.'[154]

The western and Indian media reacted immediately and with considerable glee to these dramatic events on the roof of the world. One journalist writing in the *Atlantic* magazine described how:

'Kalimpong became deluged with journalists from around the world, who were inundated with phone calls from frantic editors pleading for colorful, descriptive accounts of burning monasteries. So relentless was this pursuit of "information" that one reporter from a major British newspaper was heard to declare in exasperation, "Fiction is what they want. Pure fiction. Well, by God, fiction is what they are going to get." '[155]

Grunfeld comments that '… fiction is what they got. Stories circulated of two thousand to one hundred thousand Tibetans killed.' The media feeding-frenzy was such that correspondents were filing stories that had not even been witnessed.[156]

The Dalai Lama himself has contributed to the prevailing view of Chinese destruction and mayhem, describing the Norbulingka Palace after the rebellion had been quelled as 'a deserted smoking ruin full of dead'.[157] He wrote in his autobiography:

> 'The shelling had begun at two o'clock in the morning on March twentieth, just over forty-eight hours after I left, and before the Chinese had discovered that I had gone. All that day they shelled the Norbulingka, and then they turned their artillery on the city, the Potala, the temple, and the neighbouring monasteries. Nobody knows how many of the people of Lhasa were killed, but thousands of bodies could be seen inside and outside the Norbulingka. Some of the main buildings within the Norbulingka were practically destroyed, and all the others were damaged in different degrees, … In the great monastery of Sera there was the same useless wanton devastation.'[158]

The Dalai Lama further maintains that the Chinese soldiers searched through the corpses in the Norbulingka looking for him, and that having failed to find him 'either alive or dead they continued to shell the city and monasteries', deliberately killing 'thousands of our people, who were only armed with sticks and knives and a few short range weapons against artillery, … .'[159]

Yet European visitors in Lhasa shortly after this 'wanton destruction' describe little damage to the city, the Potala, the monastery of Sera or the Norbulingka. Indeed, in 1962 the Gelders attended a holiday celebration in the grounds of the Norbulingka and reported no signs of serious damage. The book of their travels includes a photograph of one of them sitting on the steps of the Dalai Lama's favourite residence in the palace, the Chensel Phodrang, with all its contents meticulously preserved.[160]

From this we can see that the Dalai Lama lied repeatedly about the events surrounding his leaving Tibet. These lies have been nurtured ever since by the Tibetan exile government, and perpetuated by the world's media who seems eager to believe whatever the Dalai Lama says and portray him as the wronged 'underdog' in the face of Chinese aggression.

POLITICAL VIEWS AND FAILURES

Since his journey into exile the Fourteenth Dalai Lama has done much to popularise Tibetan Buddhism in the West, even to the extent of becoming a 'Hollywood' icon in the process. He has drawn worldwide attention to Tibet and has amassed hundreds of millions if not billions of dollars for the cause of a free, independent Tibet. But he has completely failed to accomplish the political objective of an independent Tibet upon which his reputation and power have been built. Why? The blatant reason for this is that the Dalai Lama knows that he alone handed Tibet to China on a plate through his own personal desire to embrace communism. How can he possibly undo what he alone started and further consolidated with the Seventeen-Point Agreement?

Such is the perverse nature of Lama Policy: one ruling lama mixes their personal and selfish ambition with their political and spiritual power, resulting in catastrophic life-changing consequences that affect millions but from which the ruling lama alone remains aloof and unscathed. Thus Lama Policy can be seen to be what is commonly referred to as 'dictatorship'.

An assessment of the political views and failures of the Fourteenth Dalai Lama while in exile reveals how his constant public rhetoric for an independent Tibet is a mere front to disguise his actual deceptiveness and ineptitude as a leader of Tibetan people.

To assess the political record of the Dalai Lama, five areas of his international and domestic activity will be examined: (1) the issue of Tibetan independence; (2) negotiations with Beijing; (3) the Panchen Lama affair; (4) the issue of democratization; and (5) how the Dalai Lama's political failures lead to his ban on Dorje Shugden practice.

The Issue of Tibetan Independence

Contrary to the open hand with which the Fourteenth Dalai Lama advocated communism and supported Mao and the Chinese communist government while in Tibet, upon his arrival in India, like a skilled actor, he completely changed roles and began advocating a free, independent Tibet and repeatedly encouraged Tibetans to rise up against China to accomplish this. What could have propelled him to be so blatantly two-faced? Was it a smokescreen to hide the shame of having failed to win the Tibetan populace over to his personal ambition of being leader of a communist Tibet? Or was he daunted by the task of now being under western public scrutiny? Having clearly failed to convert Tibetans to his communist ideology in the confines of Tibet the only way the Dalai Lama could surely maintain his position as a political and spiritual leader in exile was to fulfil the wish of his people – or at least give the impression of striving to do so – and lead them to a free and independent Tibet. Basically, he needed to undo all that his lama policies had created!

Despite now being under the public spotlight in the international arena, the Dalai Lama has not performed the actions of a true leader and worked for the wishes of his people. Although most Tibetans would never dare to question the Dalai Lama directly, it is clear that for them 'the cause of Tibet' is full independence from China, whilst for him it is a partial autonomy within China.

> 'The vast majority of Tibetans, both within Tibet and in exile, favor independence for Tibet.'[161]

Lhasang Tsering, once a member of the Tibetan resistance force based in Mustang, Nepal, writes:

> '… I have no doubt in my mind that our people, even for generations to come, will continue to struggle, to suffer and sacrifice so long as independence remains the goal. However, I cannot expect people to make similar sacrifices for a lesser goal. I, for one, cannot struggle to be in association with China.

> '... so long as we do not recognise China's rule and so long as our goal remains independence, then China's intrusion into Tibet can be seen as a foreign aggression and our struggle will be one of international dimension. But if we change our goal to seeking some kind of accommodation within China, then the issue is entirely different. And, as China always claims, ours would be an "internal" affair and we would have no right to seek international involvement and support.'[162]

Jamyang Norbu, another former Tibetan guerrilla fighter and now a well-known author and playwright, writes:

> '... I am convinced that Tibetans must have independence if only for survival as a people. With every passing year we are getting closer to extinction. ... No autonomy, or any kind of understanding or accommodation with China will prevent it. ... Only full independence holds out some hope for Tibetan survival ...'[163]

Tashi-Topgye Jamyangling, a former official of the Tibetan exile government and member of the Fourteenth Dalai Lama's first fact-finding delegation to China in 1979, writes:

> 'As His Holiness the Dalai Lama always says, the final decision, with respect to the future of Tibet, must be made by the Tibetans themselves. The choice is simple: Is it Independence or is it Extinction?'[164]

However, despite initial rhetoric during the early years of his exile advocating a free, independent Tibet, the independence of Tibet has not been on the Fourteenth Dalai Lama's true political agenda for many years. As early as 1984, in secret meetings in Beijing, independence of the Tibetan State had already been dropped in favour of a Tibetan autonomous region within the sovereignty of China.[165] This decision by the Dalai Lama was taken unilaterally, without any referendum of the people or even consultation with his government.[166]

In April 1988, the Chinese offered to allow the Fourteenth Dalai Lama to return to Tibet on the condition that he would publicly abandon the goal of independence. In the Strasbourg Statement of June 15th 1988, he set forth the conditions for his return, which included, as the Chinese had requested, an acceptance of overall Chinese sovereignty over Tibet, '… a kind of autonomous dominion much as it had been under the Qing dynasty.'[167] In accepting Chinese sovereignty over Tibet, the Dalai Lama lost in one stroke the possibility of an independent Tibet.

The historian Edward Lazar has observed: 'The Strasbourg Statement was a surrender of the most important concerns of the Tibetan people (independence and an end to the Chinese occupation) ...' These two were relinquished before negotiations had even begun. 'It would be hard to recall so much being given up, not for so little, but for nothing, in the annals of diplomacy.'[168]

'Why', asks Lazar, 'do over one hundred countries recognize the PLO [Palestinian Liberation Organization] and not one country in the world recognizes Tibet? A major part of the reason for international tolerance of China's occupation of Tibet is that the Tibetan leadership has maintained a consistent pattern of accommodation with the Chinese occupiers, and that this spirit of accommodation is currently maintained from exile …' 'The official policy of accommodation', Lazar observes, 'translates into a legitimatization of colonial status, a kind of national suicide.'[169]

'The word itself, "independence",' Lazar observes, 'is avoided in official Tibetan pronouncements and is avoided at meetings. "Independence" is not one of the hundreds of index entries in the 14th Dalai Lama's new autobiography. The idea of independence is so dangerous that it is only referred to as the "I" word in some Tibetan circles.'[170]

The Dalai Lama's present policy of accommodation with China is a mere continuation of his own political ideology, first indicated by his ratification of the Seventeen-Point Agreement in 1951.

It is obvious that from the beginning the Dalai Lama strongly favoured communist ideology and the new developments it promised. 'In 1955, after meeting Mao he was quoted as saying, "… from the time I left Lhasa, I had looked forward to our meeting. I was overjoyed to see him [Mao] face to face, and felt he was a dear friend to our people." '[171]

The Fourteenth Dalai Lama's first autobiography *My Land & My People* confirms this enthusiasm. He says that his first meeting with Mao was a 'memorable interview', and describes him as a 'remarkable man'.[172] The Dalai Lama's infatuation with Mao can be seen in a remarkable poem he wrote while on his visit to China in 1954. The following is an extract:

> 'The great national leader of the Central People's Government, Chairman Mao, is a Cakravarti [Universal Ruler] born out of boundless fine merits. For a long time I wished to write a hymn praying for his long life and the success of his work. It happened that the Klatsuang-kergun Lama of Kantsu Monastery in Inner Mongolia wrote me from afar, saluting me and asked me to write a poem. I agreed to do so as this coincides with my own wishes.
>
> The Fourteenth Dalai Lama Dantzen-Jaltso
> at Norbulin-shenfu Palace, 1954.
>
> 'O, the Triratna, (Buddha, Dharma and Sangha) which
> bestow blessings on the world,
> Protect us with your incomparable and blessed light which
> shines for ever.
>
> 'O! Chairman Mao! Your brilliance and deeds are like those
> of Brahma and Mahasammata, creators of the world.
> Only from an infinite number of good deeds can such a
> leader be born, who is like the sun shining over the
> world.
>
> 'Your writings are precious like pearls, abundant and
> powerful as the high tide of the ocean reaching the
> edges of the sky.
> O! most honourable Chairman Mao, may you long live.

'All people look to you as to a kind protecting mother,
they paint pictures of you with hearts full of emotion,
May you live in the world forever and point out to us the
peaceful road!

'Our vast land was burdened with pain, with shackles
and darkness.
You liberated all with your brilliance. People now are
happy, full of blessings!

'Your work for peace is a white jewelled umbrella, giving
shade over heaven and earth and mankind.
Your fame is like golden bells on the umbrella, ringing
and turning forever in the sky!

'Our foe, the bloodthirsty imperialists, are poisonous
snakes, and messengers of the devil furtively crawling,
You are the undaunted roc which conquered the
poisonous serpent. To you be power!

'The cultural and industrial constructions which make
the people prosperous and defeat the enemy's
armed forces are like a vast sea;
These constructions develop continuously until they
shall make this world as full of satisfaction as heaven.

'The perfect religion of Sakyamuni (Buddha) is like a
Moonlight pearl lamp shining bright.
It is like a perfumed pearl ornament which we wear
without prohibition. O! Of this we are proud.

'Your will is like the gathering of clouds, your call
like thunder,
From these comes timely rain to nourish selflessly the earth!

'As the Ganges River rushes precious and to all the earth
The cause of peace and justice will bring to all peoples
boundless joy!

'May our world gradually become as happy as paradise!
May the torch of our great leader, be lit forever.

'May the powers of the benevolent Bodhisattvas,
the resourceful Dharma-Protector and the truthful
words of the Maharishis make these good hopes
true.'[173]

These verses of adulation do not give the impression of someone unhappy with the Chinese presence in Tibet – quite the opposite! The sentiments expressed go far beyond protocol, revealing instead a genuine admiration for Mao and a heartfelt conviction that communism could release his people from their 'shackles and darkness'.

We have seen how, right up until his flight from Tibet in 1959, the Dalai Lama was working closely with the Chinese. The Dalai Lama '... expressed his most effusive support for China in speeches and articles as late as January, 1959, including Learn from the Soviet Union and Construct Our Socialist Fatherland and Strive for a Glorious Leap Forward in Tibet.[174]

Furthermore, many Tibetans can remember that in the 1970s the Dalai Lama attempted to start a Tibetan Communist Party with the intention to spread communism amongst the Tibetans in exile. The Dalai Lama supported this group, which arose at a time when he often spoke sympathetically of communism.[175]

In 1996 the Dalai Lama was reported in the *Times of India* as saying:

'Sometimes I think that, boldly stated, the Marxists' socio-economic theories can be considered Buddhist – a part of Buddhism ... The capitalist West is simply thinking about money and how to make more profit. My main consideration is to find a closer working relation with the Communists.'[176]

In an interview with Pico Iyer that appeared in *Time* magazine in December 1997 the Dalai Lama is reported as referring to himself as 'half Marxist, half Buddhist' and that Mao Zedong was 'remarkable'.[177]

For the Fourteenth Dalai Lama, Marxism has formed his political framework since the 1950s. It is clear that long before the Strasbourg Statement in 1988, indeed throughout all of the years in exile, the Dalai Lama's own political ideology has been the main stumbling block to the Tibetan people achieving their goal of an independent Tibet. As the Dalai Lama said in August 2009 in an exclusive interview with BBC Chinese.com, 'The Chinese Government considers our problem a domestic one. And we also.'[178]

Throughout all of this time there has never been within the Dalai Lama's political outlook a basis for developing a strong commitment to the idea of an independent Tibet. As Lazar points out: '… the goal of Tibet is not defined as independence, with the result that there is not a clear overall strategy for change.'[179]

Negotiations with Beijing

In 1979, First Vice-Premier of the People's Republic of China Deng Xiaoping invited the Dalai Lama to send fact-finding delegations to Tibet and to enter into a dialogue in which, 'apart from the question of total independence all other issues could be discussed and settled.' Beijing accompanied this initiative with two conciliatory gestures, which included allowance for the regeneration of Tibetan culture and religion and measures to increase the standard of living of Tibetans.[180] The Dalai Lama sent three fact-finding delegations to Tibet between 1979-80, and secret talks took place in Beijing in 1982 and 1984. But the talks were fruitless.

With China's sudden ascent as a powerful political and economic player in the international scene in the 1980s, the perceived plight of Tibet (and Taiwan) provided a forum for western powers to attack China. From this point of view the Dalai Lama has become a pawn in the ensuing political struggles between the West and China. With confidence stemming from support received in the U.S. and Europe, in 1987, in speeches in Washington and Strasbourg, the Dalai Lama suddenly began to argue that the Chinese occupation was illegal and that a 'Greater' Tibet should become a self-governing political entity under a 'democratic constitution'.[181]

Encouraged by the Dalai Lama's campaign in the U.S., monks in Lhasa held demonstrations protesting against the Chinese occupation. Several of the monks were arrested, and a full-scale riot ensued. After a series of further demonstrations and riots in 1988 and 1989, Beijing declared martial law and introduced a new hard-line policy limiting religious and cultural expression. It also initiated a programme of rapid economic development in Tibet.[182]

> 'Beijing has, in a sense, turned the tables back on the Dalai Lama, and the triumphs of the Dalai Lama's international campaign look more and more like Pyrrhic victories. The international initiative won significant symbolic gains for the exiles in the West and spurred Tibetans in Tibet to demonstrate their support for the Dalai Lama, but it did not compel China to yield and played a major role in precipitating the new hard-line policy that is changing the nature of Tibet.
>
> 'Beijing now has little interest in discussions with the Dalai Lama. It feels he is not serious about making the kind of political compromises they could agree to ….'[183]

The unexpected death of the Panchen Lama in Tibet in January 1989 produced another Chinese initiative, an invitation to the Dalai Lama to attend memorial services in Beijing during which time informal talks could take place.

> 'The Dalai Lama had suddenly been offered an exceptional opportunity to visit China without having to sort out complicated political protocol issues.
>
> '... The Dalai Lama and his officials, however, were reluctant to accept the invitation. … with events apparently going well from their perspective, the exile leadership persuaded the Dalai Lama to take the safe course and decline the invitation ... Many look back at this as one of the most important lost opportunities in the post-1978 era.'[184]

In recent times the Dalai Lama has flipped back and forth, one day adopting a conciliatory tone towards the Chinese[185] and offering ever increasing concessions[186], and the next accusing them of 'cultural genocide'[187], of turning Tibet into 'a living hell'[188] and comparing the Chinese Government to the Nazis.[189]

Since 2002, eight rounds of talks have been held between the Dalai Lama's representatives and the Chinese government. The Dalai Lama says 'the talks did not yield any tangible result'[190]. By the Dalai Lama's own admission, therefore, in 30 years of negotiating with Beijing, he has achieved nothing for his people.

The reason for this, according to the Chinese side, is the Dalai Lama's lack of sincerity. Chinese Foreign Ministry spokesperson Jiang Yu said in April 2008:

> 'The Central Government has exerted great sincerity and patience with regard to its dialogue with Dalai. However, the Dalai side failed to respond to our position in a positive and comprehensive manner. The door for dialogue is open, but Dalai is the one to make the difference by exerting sincerity for dialogue, particularly in his concrete actions. As we said on many times, we are ready to continue contacts with Dalai, provided that he gives up separatist activities against the motherland, disruptive activities against the Beijing Olympic Games and incitement of violent activities.'[191]

The following day in Ann Arbor, Michigan, the Dalai Lama held a press conference and said:

> 'From the very beginning I have supported the Olympics. We must support China's desires. Even after this sad situation in Tibet, today I support the Olympics.'[192]

And previously, in March 2008, in his 'An Appeal to the Chinese People' the Dalai Lama had said:

> 'Similarly, despite my repeated support for the Beijing Olympics, the Chinese authorities, with the intention of creating a rift between the Chinese people and myself, the Chinese authorities assert that I am trying to sabotage the games.'[193]

However, on 18 January 2008, (the UK) ITV news together with the London-based 'Free Tibet' conducted an interview with the

Dalai Lama. ITV News published a piece entitled 'Dalai Lama calls for Olympic Protests' and broadcast excerpts of the interview.[194]

Perhaps realizing the Dalai Lama had let his guard down and strayed from his public message, the Department of Information and International Relations of the Tibetan exile government issued a press release saying the Dalai Lama had been misquoted and that he fully supported the Beijing Olympics.[195]

Free Tibet, however, had already printed a partial transcript of the interview:

> 'Asked by ITV's China correspondent, John Ray, whether supporters of Tibet "should be allowed to express, in China, at the time of the Olympics, in a peaceful way, their support for the people of Tibet" the Dalai Lama responded that peaceful protests would be justified in order to bring the Tibetan issue to the attention of the Chinese public:
>
> ' "It is worthwhile to remind. I think the (Chinese) government knows that, but the Chinese people sometimes may not realize the problem. So I think it is worthwhile. So in the eyes of millions of Chinese I think worthwhile to remind them there's a problem. That I think is very important."
>
> 'Asked if now was the best time for peaceful protest, the Dalai Lama responded: "I think so." '[196]

Throughout the build up to the Beijing Olympics, particularly during the Olympic Torch relay, violent protests were organised by Tibet Support Groups.[197] The action plan for these protests were drawn up at the Fifth International Conference of Tibet Support Groups held in May 2007 in Brussels. This international gathering was convened by the Department of Information and International Relations of the Central Tibetan Administration [the Tibetan exile government].[198]

The conference was addressed by Samdhong Rinpoche, the Prime Minister of the Tibetan exile government, and Lodi Gyari, the Dalai Lama's representative in negotiations with China,[199] the two Tibetan politicians most closely linked with the Dalai Lama.

On the steering committee of the conference was Dr. B. Tsering Yeshi, the President of the Tibetan Woman's Association.[200] Dr

Tsering is also on the organizing committee of the 'Tibetan People's Uprising Movement'[201] that are accused of directly organising the riots in Lhasa in March 2008.[202]

At its inception in January 2008, the Movement issued the following declaration:

> 'Through unified and strategic campaigns we will seize the Olympic spotlight and shine it on China's shameful repression inside Tibet, thereby denying China the international acceptance and approval it so fervently desires.
>
> 'We call on Tibetans inside Tibet to continue to fight Chinese domination and we pledge our unwavering support for your continued courageous resistance. We call on Tibetans in exile and supporters in the free world to take every opportunity to protest China's Olympic Games and support the Tibetan people's struggle for freedom.'[203]

And in a press release in February 2008, the group declared:

> 'We will bring about another uprising that will shake China's control in Tibet and mark the beginning of the end of China's occupation of Tibet.'[204]

Other press releases claimed that the Tibetan People's Uprising Movement 'will launch an all-out struggle on a war-front scale'.[205]

Of the five principal groups that established the 'Tibetan People's Uprising Movement': two were founded directly by the Dalai Lama, one was founded at his request, and another was founded under the auspices of organisations funded by his government.[206] The Tibetan Youth Congress in particular has as its primary aim:

> 'To dedicate oneself to the task of serving one's country and people under the guidance of His Holiness the Dalai Lama, the Spiritual and Temporal Ruler of Tibet.'[207]

Despite these groups' sworn allegiance to him, and the fact that they carry out all their activities in explicit support of the Dalai Lama, he himself claims to have neither involvement in their activities nor power to influence them. At a meeting with the media on Sunday

16 March 2008, at the time of the riots in Lhasa, the Dalai Lama was asked if he could stop the protests. The Dalai Lama replied swiftly: 'I have no such power.'[208]

Furthermore, as the *New York Times* reported in an article entitled 'Dalai Lama won't stop Tibet protests' the Dalai Lama revealed that he is in direct personal contact with those involved in the rioting in Tibet.

> 'He said he had received a call on Saturday from Tibet. "Please don't ask us to stop," was the caller's request. The Dalai Lama promised he would not.'[209]

It should be noted that during the Lhasa riots many Han Chinese and Hui Muslims in Lhasa were attacked, beaten, stabbed and killed. Many shops were looted and destroyed and then set alight – those trapped inside were left to burn to death.[210] Since the Dalai Lama would not ask his supporters in Tibet to stop, could their actions be consistent with his idea of 'non-violent protest'?

Dawa Tsering, the head of the Chinese Affairs Ministry of the Tibetan exile government was interviewed by Radio France International at the time of the riots. He displayed a chilling lack of compassion for the victims, and exhibited the twisted Tibetan exile government's understanding of 'non-violence':

> 'First of all, I must make it clear that the Tibetan [rioters] have been non-violent throughout [the incident]. From Tibetans' perspective, violence means harming life. From the video recordings you can see that the Tibetans rioters were beating Han Chinese, but only beating took place. After the beating the Han Chinese were free to flee. Therefore [there was] only beating, no life was harmed. Those who were killed were all results of accidents. From recordings shown by the Chinese Communist government, we can clearly see that when Tibetan [rioters] were beating on their doors, the Han Chinese all went into hiding upstairs. When the Tibetan [rioters] set fire to the buildings, the Han Chinese remained in hiding instead of escaping, the result is that these Han Chinese were all accidentally burnt to death. Those who set

and spread the fire, on the other hand, had no idea whatsoever that there were Han Chinese hiding upstairs. Therefore not only were Han Chinese burnt to death, some Tibetans were burnt to death too. Therefore all these incidents were accidents, not murder.'[211]

In an interview back in 1997, Samdhong Rinpoche, the Prime Minister of the Tibetan exile government, spoke about the inserting agents into Tibet to engage in direct action:

> ' "Many think this plan is nothing but a suicidal effort, but we thought it worth trying. At the moment we are training the people who might take part, though it's a difficult thing to accept that you might be imprisoned or even shot." He adds: "Whatever may come, they will be dedicated non-violent activists. If we are going to disappear, let it be with some positive resistance. If we keep quiet it would amount to an acceptance and we, too, would be guilty." '[212]

How can we reconcile these words of the Tibetan Prime Minister, conjoined with the special Tibetan understanding of what non-violent activists can do (as revealed by Dawa Tsering above) with the Dalai Lama's statement to the Chinese people:

> 'It is unfortunate that despite my sincere efforts not to separate Tibet from China, the leaders of the PRC continue to accuse me of being a "separatist". Similarly, when Tibetans in Lhasa and many other areas spontaneously protested to express their deep-rooted resentment, the Chinese authorities immediately accused me of having orchestrated their demonstrations.'[213]

The Dalai Lama portrays himself in the western media as untainted by any protest against the Olympics or any unrest in Tibet, and yet behind the scenes organisations established by him and dedicated to fulfilling his wishes carry out his 'dirty work' for him. Is it any wonder that despite his declarations of sincerity the Chinese government have little confidence in negotiations with him?

It is also of interest that many of the groups involved in the Tibetan People's Uprising Movement are supported by the U.S. organization

'National Endowment for Democracy' (NED). Hundreds of thousands of dollars have been poured into these groups over the last few years as part of the NED's efforts to undermine Communist China and support the US government's strategic interests.[214]

What exactly is the National Endowment for Democracy and who are they? A brief history of how the NED was established has been given by the South Asia Analysis Group:

> 'After his election in November, 1980, and before his taking-over as the President in January, 1981, Mr. Reagan appointed a transition group headed by the late William Casey, an attorney and one of his campaign managers, who was to later take over as the CIA Director, to recommend measures for strengthening the USA's intelligence capability abroad.
>
> 'One of its recommendations was to revive covert political activities. Since there might have been opposition from the Congress and public opinion to this task being re-entrusted to the CIA, it suggested that this be given to an NGO with no ostensible links with the CIA.
>
> 'The matter was further examined in 1981-82 by the American Political Foundation's Democracy Programme Study and Research Group and, finally, the National Endowment for Democracy (NED) was born under a Congressional enactment of 1983 as a "non-profit, non-governmental, bipartisan, grant-making organisation to help strengthen democratic institutions around the world."
>
> 'Though it is projected as an NGO, it is actually a quasi-governmental organisation because till 1994 it was run exclusively from funds voted by the Congress (average of about US $16 million per annum in the 1980s and now about US $30 million) as part of the budget of the US Information Agency (USIA). Since 1994, it has been accepting contributions from the private sector too to supplement the congressional appropriations.'[215]

The *New York Times* exposed the secret side of the National Endowment for Democracy:

> 'Project Democracy, began as the secret side of an otherwise open, well-publicized initiative that started life under the same name. Project Democracy's covert side was intended to carry out foreign policy tasks that other Government agencies were unable or unwilling to pursue, the officials said.
>
> 'Although the public arm of Project Democracy, now known as the National Endowment for Democracy, openly gave Federal money to democratic institutions abroad and received wide bipartisan support, officials said the project's secret arm took an entirely different direction ...
>
> 'Project Democracy grew into a parallel foreign policy apparatus – complete with its own communications systems, secret envoys, leased ships and airplanes, offshore bank accounts and corporations.
>
> 'It operated outside the established Government decision-making process and beyond the purview of Congress and was, officials said, an expression of the Administration's deep frustration that it could not push the foreign policy bureacracy or Congress to embrace what Administration officials described as the '"Reagan doctrine"' of supporting anti-Communist insurgencies.'[216]

In an interview with the Washington Post in 1991, Allen Weinstein (Programme Director of American Political Foundation's 'Democracy Programme' which led to the establishment of the NED) said: 'A lot of what we do today was done covertly 25 years ago by the CIA.'[217]

As has been widely reported by both the American operatives and the Tibetan fighters involved, from the 1950s through to the 1970s, the Dalai Lama and his government were involved with the CIA's secret war in Tibet.[218] Throughout that time the Dalai Lama presented himself as a champion of non-violence and denied any involvement with the CIA.[219]

Today the Dalai Lama again has groups working for him – supported by a shady CIA-like American NGO – creating violent unrest against Communist China, and yet in the media he presents himself with the opposite image. The Dalai Lama was dubbed in *Newsweek* as 'the Teflon Lama'[220], and while he usually succeeds in mesmerising the western media, in the all-important matter of negotiations with Beijing it is clear that his duplicity has brought no result for the Tibetan people.

The Panchen Lama Affair

The Panchen Lama is considered to be the second highest ranking incarnate Lama after the Dalai Lama in the Gelugpa tradition of Tibetan Buddhism. The successive Panchen Lamas form a tulku reincarnation lineage who are said to be incarnations of Buddha Amitabha.[221]

After the death of the Panchen Lama in 1989, the Chinese government agreed to permit the selection of a new Panchen Lama and in 1993 the Fourteenth Dalai Lama was invited to cooperate in the selection process. At the end of 1994, Chadrel Rinpoche, the head of the search team, indicated that, of the twenty-five candidates, Gendun Choekyi Nyima was the true reincarnation of the Panchen Lama. 'By early February the Dalai Lama got a message back to Chadrel Rinpoche stating that he had done divination that confirmed Gendun Choekyi Nyima.'[222]

Having obtained the Dalai Lama's confirmation, Chadrel Rinpoche tried to secure Chinese approval of the boy, but '… the [Chinese] government asked Chadrel to submit three to five names for the golden urn drawing.'[223] The 'golden urn drawing' is a traditional divination lottery in which the reincarnation is determined by selecting or 'drawing' one name from a golden urn containing the names of all the short-listed candidates. In mid-May, before the Chinese government had completed the arrangements for the golden urn drawing , the Dalai Lama suddenly announced to the world that he recognised Gendun Choekyi Nyima as the new Panchen Lama. He 'asserted that the Chinese government had no authority over this selection by saying, "The search and recognition of Panchen Rimpoche's reincarnation is a religious matter and not political." '[224]

'This announcement, of course, embarrassed and infuriated the Chinese government.

'... Chadrel was sentenced to six years in prison ... Beijing ... disqualified Gendun Choekyi Nyima and used the golden urn lottery to select a different boy, whom the Chinese government formally confirmed in November 1995.'[225]

The Dalai Lama's premature announcement of his choice of the Panchen Lama was a disaster, both politically and for those personally involved. Melvyn Goldstein writes:

' the Dalai Lama's decision to pre-emptively announce the new Panchen Lama was, to say the least, politically inastute. ... To be sure, it made Tibetans and their Western supporters feel good to see the Dalai Lama exert his authority over the issue, but the price he paid was substantial and the gains were minuscule. In practical terms, ... he has in effect relegated the boy he chose to a life of house arrest.

'... Moreover, his announcement has badly undermined the credibility of the more moderate Chinese officials who sold the State Council on the idea that the ethnically sensitive selection process would be in China's best interests. It has therefore reinforced the hard-liners' contention that China cannot trust or work with the Dalai Lama and has set back chances that China will agree to renew talks with him.'[226]

The Issue of Democratization

The Dalai Lama's proposal of a Western-style democracy, put forward in the 1988 Strasbourg Statement and repeated since, is designed to gain Western support, but does not reflect the Dalai Lama's actual intention. This can be understood from several different points of view. Throughout the history of the Dalai Lamas, as shown above (chapter 8), there has never been any interest in democracy on their part. The Tibetan government, with the Dalai Lama as its head, has always been, and continues to be, a feudal theocracy.

The Dalai Lama's system of government did not arise from the wishes and aspirations of the Tibetan people; it did not arise through an electoral process or referendum. It was imposed ruthlessly and even violently through a series of military campaigns and political intrigues that in the end established the Fifth Dalai Lama's absolute political and religious supremacy over all of Tibet.

The continuing lack of interest in democracy shown by the present Dalai Lama's government is also evident in the fact that even after fifty years in exile within the democratic state of India, the Tibetan exile government is still undemocratic; the Dalai Lama retains total authority and control. No decision of the Tibetan exile parliament has ever gone against his wishes, and it is inconceivable that this could ever happen. As the Tibetan writer and former editor of *Tibetan Review*, Dawa Norbu, has commented:

> 'It is unfortunate but equally true that the Dalai Lama in exile has tended to discourage the emergence of alternative leaders, unless officially approved by him.'[227]

And as Dr. Ursula Bernis has pointed out:

> 'The effort to democratize has not extended to separating the domains of religion and politics. Since the Tibetan exile government in Dharamsala is not legitimately a government by legal and international standards, it is difficult to analyze this problematic [sic] in an easy or straightforward way. Democratic it is not. The Tibetan people have never been asked to vote on any of the major political decisions concerning the future of their country either inside or outside Tibet.
>
> 'Often not even the Assembly and Cabinet (Kashag) are asked. Even more basic, freedom of speech, the very foundation of democratic striving, is woefully absent among exile Tibetans. Criticism of official exile government business is usually dismissed as being of Chinese origin.'[228]

In 1963 a draft Constitution for a free Tibet was laid down by the Dalai Lama with the help of an Indian lawyer. Under this constitution the Dalai Lama retained supreme authority, and as Grunfeld points out: 'If that statement [within the Foreword of the Constitution, that the Constitution "takes into consideration the doctrines enunciated by Lord Buddha"] is to be accepted at face value, then the Dalai Lama can never be deprived of his powers—spiritual or temporal—unless he abdicates.'[229]

In the Tibetan Constitution adopted on 14 June 1991, Article 19 on Executive Power reads:

> 'The executive power of the Tibetan Administration shall be vested in His Holiness the Dalai Lama, and shall be exercised by Him, either directly or through officers subordinate to Him, in accordance with the provisions of this Charter. In particular, His Holiness the Dalai Lama shall be empowered to execute the following executive powers as the chief executive of the Tibetan people.
>
> '(a) approve and promulgate bills and regulations prescribed by the Tibetan Assembly;
> (b) promulgate acts and ordinances that have the force of law;
> (c) confer honors and patents of merit;
> (d) summon, adjourn, postpone and prolong the Tibetan Assembly;
> (e) send messages and addresses to the Tibetan Assembly whenever necessary;
> (f) dissolve or suspend the Tibetan Assembly;
> (g) dissolve the Kashag or remove a Kalon or Kalons;
> (h) summon emergency and special meetings of major significance; and
> (j) authorize referendums in cases involving major issues in accordance with this Charter.'

And Article 20 on the Kashag (elected Cabinet) and the Chief Kalon (Chief Minister) specifically states:

> 'There shall be a Kashag and a Chief Kalon primarily responsible for exercising executive powers of the Tibetan Administration subordinate to His Holiness the Dalai Lama.'[230]

Despite the appearance of attempting to separate the powers of 'church' and 'state', they still converge in the person of the Dalai Lama, which results in a passive and powerless National Assembly and a political system that follows advice received by its leader, the Dalai Lama, from a spirit medium, the Nechung oracle.

As already quoted, in his autobiography *Freedom in Exile* the Dalai Lama states:

> 'I seek his [the Nechung oracle's] advice in the same way as I seek the opinion of my Cabinet and just as I seek the opinion of my own conscience. I consider the gods to be my "upper house". The Kashag constitutes my lower house. Like any other leader, I consult both before making a decision on affairs of state.'

Not content with comparing unelected 'gods', to whom only he has access, with a cabinet of ministers elected by the Tibetan people, the Dalai Lama continues:

> '… my relationship with Nechung is that of commander to lieutenant; I never bow down to him. It is for Nechung to bow to the Dalai Lama.'[231]

With this attitude it seems highly unlikely that the Dalai Lama will ever bow down to the will of the people, a fundamental principle of democratic government.

In 1998 Swiss National TV (SNTV) reported that the Tibetan National Assembly had never in its history made a decision against the wishes of the Dalai Lama. The Swiss journalist Beat Regli asked the Vice-President of the Assembly if this could ever happen. The Vice-President smiled benignly and responded with a chilling, 'No … No'.[232]

As the unelected political and spiritual leader of the Tibetan people, the Dalai Lama's influence over his government, executive and people is all-pervasive. Because of the exalted position he enjoys his decisions are beyond reproach or even serious debate. Indeed the vast majority of Tibetans 'are overawed [into silence] by the mere mention of the name of their religious and temporal head'.[233] So powerful is this control that almost no Tibetan will dare criticise the Dalai Lama's activities for fear of the swift retribution that they know would follow. Nowhere is this seen more clearly than in the repression of freedom of speech in the Tibetan exile community.

An advertisement published in both the *Times of Tibet* and the magazine *Sheja* (Knowledge), and which was widely circulated in Tibetan communities, reads:

> 'Anyone who is against the Dalai Lama must be opposed without hesitation with men, money and possession. This is to say with any means, including violence.'[234]

SNTV introduces Tashi Angdu as, 'the general secretary of the society that published the advertisement demanding ruthless action against all critics of the Dalai Lama. He is a well known politician and president of the Tibetan regional council.' Willingly he confirmed to SNTV earlier in 1998, '… their society also threatens to use violence against those Dalai Lama critics who won't listen to them'.[235]

Shortly after expressing concern about the Dalai Lama's ban on Dorje Shugden, in June 1996 a retired government minister was stabbed and badly wounded; he barely survived.[236]

A free press is a sign of a healthy democracy, giving avenues of expression and allowing views other than the official to be heard. There is no independent press within the Tibetan exile community in India. The only independent newspaper in Dharamsala, *Democracy* (Mang-Tso), stopped publishing in March 1996 under pressure from the Tibetan government. Palden Gyal, writing in Tibetan News, explained that the newspaper *Mang-Tso* '… was started in 1990 by a group of Tibetan intellectuals with the aim of providing international and Tibetan news. It also hoped to educate young Tibetans about democracy.' It was popular and influential and had a healthy circulation. He continues:

> 'The newspaper has always dabbled with criticisms of government ministers and open discussion of their policies. Then, in May 1995, it published a piece about Shoko Asahara, the Japanese cult leader, highlighting the fact that he had been

> friends with the Dalai Lama before being accused of killing eleven people in a nerve gas attack on the Tokyo subway. The article suggested that perhaps the government should be careful about who it conducted relations with in the future. Not long after that, in March 1996, the newspaper ceased publication.'[237]

Among the reasons given by the publishers for shutting down was, 'subjective antipathies towards the publishers which had made publication difficult.' As Palden Gyal says, 'Even running news stories about the Dalai Lama, if they do not reflect on him well, can provoke anger among Tibetans.' He also quotes Robbie Barnett of Tibetan Information Network concerning the pressures that are brought to bear on publications that do not toe the party line, '… antipathy towards the publishers usually comes in the form of anything from death threats to ostracisation to whisper campaigns.'[238] In short the paper had dared to question the activities of the Tibetan leader and paid the ultimate price.

As Jamyang Norbu, a leading Tibetan intellectual writing in 1996 says:

> '… not only is there no encouragement and support for a free Tibetan press, there is instead a near extinguishing of freedom of expression in Tibetan exile society … Samdong Rinpoche, the Speaker of the Tibetan Parliament in exile, … declared … that the Tibetan Parliament should find new ways to control the Tibetan press.'[239]

This profound intolerance of criticism pervades all avenues of expression. As the well-known Tibetologist Heather Stoddard has written:

> '... [a] considerable number of new books written in Tibetan ... have been censored or banned from publication [by the Tibetan exile government] because they do not conform to the desired image of traditional Tibetan society. Any serious discussion of history and of possible shortcomings in the society before 1959 is taboo.'[240]

In the foreword to a collection of essays by Jamyang Norbu, Lhasang Tsering, formerly twice president of the Tibetan Youth Congress, writes,

> 'The ban on books for the simple reason that the writers had expressed ideas that do not conform to the official line of thinking – be it on history or politics – has been among the biggest blots against our exile government.'[241]

It is deeply ironic that the leader and government of a people who have been treated so badly by a totalitarian regime that brooks no criticism, cannot tolerate the slightest criticism themselves. On this core issue of freedom of expression not much has changed since the exodus from Tibet, despite some fifty years of open contact with democratic societies.

As expressed in his remarks to *The Times of India* in May 1996, the political-ideological attitude of the Dalai Lama is Marxist-Socialist, which he considers 'a part of Buddhism'; it is not Western-style democracy, and he dismisses the West as '... simply thinking about money and how to make more profit.'[242] Even after the numerous atrocities committed in the cause of Marxism within the former Soviet Union and throughout Eastern Europe, China and Tibet, the Dalai Lama's political views still remain unchanged.

The Dalai Lama has many faces, including a democratic face for westerners and a communist face in the hope of influencing the Chinese. But the face the Dalai Lama shows to westerners is false. Although he has been in the West for fifty years he has made no real efforts to establish true democracy within the exile Tibetan community, and although for many westerners he is the figurehead for Tibetan freedom he has never really worked for Tibetan independence, and has long accepted that Tibet will remain under Chinese rule.[243] Even though he spoke in Strasbourg in 1988 of Tibetan autonomy under the sovereignty of China, the Dalai Lama continues to perpetuate the illusion among Tibetans and within the popular culture of the West that he is still working for a free, independent Tibet. Is it any wonder that he cannot be trusted?

For years the Dalai Lama maintained a high level of expectation within the Tibetan exile settlements that a return to a free Tibet was imminent. Living within a closed society with no voice allowed to his people – no freedom of speech, no freedom of press – the Dalai Lama has managed to maintain the myth of promoting an independent Tibet as 'the Tibetan Cause', even though he already abandoned that as a political objective many years ago.

These factors need to be taken into consideration in any assessment of the Dalai Lama's statements on democracy. The political views he expresses to western audiences in the U.S. and Europe are not the same as those he expresses in Asia. The Dalai Lama's advocacy of a western-style democracy for a future free Tibet is strictly for western consumption. The type of government over which he would actually preside if Tibet were ever to regain its independence would be far from democratic.

How the Dalai Lama's Political Failures Led to His Ban on Dorje Shugden Practice

In March 1996, the Dalai Lama shocked the Tibetan communities and the wider international Buddhist community by taking the unprecedented step of imposing a ban on the practice of Dorje Shugden, blaming this very popular, centuries-old religious practice for his failure to achieve political independence for Tibet, but without giving any valid reasons. He was acting, he said, on the advice of the Nechung oracle, the spirit medium that regularly advises him on matters of state, and in letters sent by his Private Office in March 1996 to the abbots of the Tibetan monasteries in South India, the Dalai Lama gave two reasons for imposing the ban:

> '... government oracles point towards there being a danger to the health of His Holiness the Dalai Lama, as well as to the cause of Tibet, due to the worship of Shugden. Banning this is also the conclusion reached by His Holiness after years of observation.'[244]

Then, as Dr. Ursula Bernis reported: 'Immediately government offices promulgated this advice, stated in no uncertain terms by the Dalai Lama, and turned it into a full-fledged ban.'[245] Shortly afterwards the Kashag formalised the ban in a written statement:

> 'The essence of His Holiness' advice is this: "Propitiating Dolgyal does great harm to the cause of Tibet. It also imperils the life of the Dalai Lama. Therefore, it is totally inappropriate for the great monasteries of the Gelug tradition, the Upper and Lower Tantric Monasteries and all other affiliated monasteries which are national institutions ever to propitiate Dolgyal ...'[246]

In this way, the Dalai Lama singled out practitioners of Dorje Shugden as state enemies accounting for the failure of his policy to achieve an independent Tibet, and as targets for the wave of frustration and disillusionment arising from the catastrophic collapse of popular hope in 'the cause of Tibet' that he had artificially maintained for years. From this point of view, the ban against the practice of Dorje Shugden is a smokescreen to obscure the Dalai Lama's own political failure; a device designed to divert the anger of the Tibetan people at being no nearer returning to Tibet after 50 years, by creating an 'enemy within' against whom this anger can be directed.

In 2009, the Tibetan exile government began saying that the Dorje Shugden issue is not even religious, but entirely political. Samdhong Tulku is quoted as saying: '... it is not a question of religion; it falls under the situation of politics only', claiming that Shugden practitioners are tools being used by the Chinese government.[247]

For centuries Buddhists have viewed Dorje Shugden as an enlightened being who functions as one of the principal protectors of the Gelugpa tradition. How the practice of Dorje Shugden could have the remotest connection to the achievement of Tibetan independence or to the state of the Dalai Lama's health has never been explained. Nevertheless, as there is no objective closer to the heart of the vast majority of Tibetans than 'the cause of Tibet' (equated in their minds with a free, independent Tibet) and because of the careful nurturing of the Dalai Lama's image as the focus of the Tibetan people's aspirations, the new ban was vigorously implemented. In the McCarthyite witch-hunt that followed and which continues to the present day, Tibetan society has been divided against itself at every level.

CHAPTER 10

The Implementation, Effects and Alleged Reasons for the Ban on the Practice of Dorje Shugden

In March 1996, in an aggressive and threatening manner, the Dalai Lama stated that there would be a forceful implementation of the ban against those who persisted in the practice of Dorje Shugden. In the following months, and over the years since then, at empowerments, in speeches, in interviews and through government decrees, the Dalai Lama has made clear his views and intentions in imposing the ban. A number of these statements against Dorje Shugden practice and practitioners, as well as evidence of the persecution of Dorje Shugden practitioners, can be seen in Chapter 5.

The Dalai Lama's words shocked and wounded millions of Dorje Shugden practitioners around the world, and sent waves of confusion, resentment and fear sweeping through the Tibetan communities. In the months following the Dalai Lama's ban, a transformation took place within the Tibetan community. The relative peace, joy and internal harmony normally enjoyed within the Tibetan settlements were destroyed by threats and acts of terrorism against a steadily marginalised and isolated minority of Dorje Shugden practitioners.

Vigilante mobs of fanatical followers of the Dalai Lama, acting in the spirit of his public pronouncements, stormed into temples and private homes, seizing and destroying pictures and statues of Dorje Shugden – even taking them from shrines. Mobs attacked Dorje Shugden practitioners and their homes with stones and petrol bombs, destroying their possessions and threatening their lives. There were beatings, stabbings and even killings.

People lost their jobs, children were expelled from schools, and monks were expelled from monasteries; foreign travel permits and visas were denied; refugee aid, monastic stipends and allowances were cut off; and forced signature campaigns were undertaken. In these and many other ways that made Tibetans outcasts from their own already exiled community, the Dalai Lama, in the guise of his government, ministers and associated organisations, introduced a reign of terror against tens of thousands of his own people, making restrictions similar to those imposed on the Jewish people in Germany in the early years of Hitler's rule.[248]

This persecution has been enforced since 1996 and still continues. The international news and current affairs television channel *France 24* reported:

> 'Photos of Shugden leaders are posted on city walls, branding them as traitors. Signs at the entrance of stores and hospitals forbid Shugden followers from entry …
>
> 'Our reporters followed an ostracised Buddhist monk as he tried to confront the fellow villagers who have banned him. "We're not violating Buddha's teachings, and we're excluded from everywhere just because of our religion" he complains … "It's apartheid, in a Buddhist land." '[249]

On a separate occasion in 2008 the international television channel *Al Jazeera* also visited the south of India and followed Delek Tong, a monk who practices Dorje Shugden, through the streets of his Tibetan refugee settlement:

> '[Delek Tong] Pointing at a poster on the wall, "Look at this, it says: 'No Shugden worshippers allowed.' "
>
> ' "Hi, I worship Shugden, can I come in?"
>
> '[Shopkeeper] "No, I am sorry, I don't want you or any Shugdens in my shop."
>
> '[Reporter] The Dalai Lama has asked the Tibetan community to stop the worship of the 400 year old Deity Shugden.
>
> '[Delek Tong] "When you followed the Dalai Lama's advice, did you not forget that us Shugdens are also Tibetans like you?"

> '[Reporter] What this means in practice is that Delek Tong cannot walk into this shop because of his religious beliefs.
>
> '[Shopkeeper] "I have taken an oath and I won't have anything to do with the Shugden people." '[250]

To maintain the pretence of a democratic referendum on the issue of Dorje Shugden, the Dalai Lama has carried out forced signature campaigns within the lay and monastic Tibetan communities worldwide. The first were introduced in 1996, but these did not bring about the Dalai Lama's desired goal of completely marginalising Shugden practitioners. Frustrated by this failure, he initiated another such forced signature campaign in January 2008.

As a direct result of the Dalai Lama's second campaign, 900 monks were driven out of their monasteries on 8 February 2008.

On 14 February 2008 in Bangalore, Samdhong Rinpoche (Prime Minister of the Tibetan exile government) made a statement reminiscent of words used by Hitler:

> 'If the monasteries are completely cleansed, the campaign of taking the oath not to practise Shugden and not to share material and religious resources with Shugden devotees will be initiated throughout India, Nepal and Bhutan, then abroad and gradually in Tibet.'[251]

Becoming aware of the international public horror at these violations, the Tibetan Prime Minister and other officials of the Tibetan exile government attempt to distance the Dalai Lama from responsibility for this referendum.

On 22 April 2008 at Colgate University (New York State, USA) a public demonstration was held outside a public talk given by the Dalai Lama, protesting against his religious persecution. Tashi Wangdu, the Dalai Lama's Representative and former Cabinet Minister, after being asked repeatedly for a public statement, was obliged to respond and said to gathered reporters:

> 'I think there is a lot of misunderstanding. I was trying to explain that there is no ban.'[252]

And, as thousands of members of the Western Shugden Society engaged in a series of demonstrations around the world to expose the shameful facts of the Dalai Lama's ban and his dictatorial behaviour, in an interview on BBC News 27 May 2008 the Dalai Lama himself could only resort to a direct lie to his audience, saying that '… he had not advocated a ban ... .'[253]

In the West the Dalai Lama's representatives try to maintain the fiction that there is not a ban and that the Dalai Lama has only 'advised' people not to practise Dorje Shugden. However, it is clear from the statements made by the Dalai Lama himself and by his Private Office as shown in chapter 5 that there is a very real ban and it is vigorously applied. The Tibetan words 'kagdom' (bkag.sdom), 'damdrag' (dam.bsgrag) and other expressions that are frequently used clearly indicate this.

Through the Tibetan Kashag (Cabinet), the Dalai Lama originally gave two reasons for imposing the ban. They claimed that the practice of Dorje Shugden: (1) '... does great harm to the cause of Tibet' (that is, Tibetan independence); and (2) 'It also imperils the life of the Dalai Lama.'[254] The Dalai Lama has been asked repeatedly to give valid reasons to prove these assertions, but none have been forthcoming. However, saying that Shugden practice harms the Dalai Lama is as senseless as saying that one person taking medicine causes another person to get sick. How can others' practice of Dorje Shugden harm the Dalai Lama? It is a ridiculous assertion.

Subsequently, the Dalai Lama and his government fabricated a third reason for the ban: the bogey of sectarianism. This third reason has been variously expressed in public statements made by the Dalai Lama, and in documents issued by the exile government. For example, on 16 July 1996 on *The World Tonight*, BBC Radio 4, the Dalai Lama said:

> 'It is well known that the worshipper of that spirit, usual approach a little bit sectarian. So that does not go well with my approach.'

And in 1998 on the Tibetan exile government website, 'Shugden Versus Pluralism and National Unity' said:

> 'Propitiation of Shugden has taken on the characteristics of a fanatical cult, in which there is no place for the views or practices of other schools of Tibetan Buddhism, particularly those of the ancient Nyingma tradition founded by Padmasambhava. Naturally, such divisiveness does not sit well with Tibetans' need to unite and withstand external threats to their very identity.'[255]

On 27 August 1998 at the annual convention of the Tibetan Youth Congress in Dharamsala, the Dalai Lama said in his opening address:

> 'I have imposed this ban for three reasons: (1) Throughout history this worship has been at odds with the Ganden Phodrang ruling government of Tibet, (2) Buddhism, which is very profound, is in danger of degenerating into spirit worship, and (3) worship of Dholgyal (Shugden) creates sectarianism. For these three reasons I have imposed the ban.'[256]

More recently in 2009, as mentioned above, the Tibetan exile government has said that the issue is entirely political and not religious[257], thus undermining the Dalai Lama's original 'religious' reasons for the ban. But if we look at these 'reasons' in turn, it is, as we have seen, the Ganden Phodrang system of government of mixing religion and politics that is the source of the many problems that have afflicted the Tibetan people for generations. And it is the Dalai Lama through his reliance on spirit-oracles who is degenerating Buddhism. In saying that Dorje Shugden practitioners are worshippers of an evil spirit he is deliberately manipulating the superstitious fears of many ordinary Tibetans. Instead of promoting Buddhism as a religion chiefly concerned with developing inner qualities such as love and compassion, it is the Dalai Lama who is causing it to degenerate through his portrayal of Buddhists seemingly in a state of constant warfare against invisible spirits. In this he is going against even his own teachings:

> 'If … one … always puts the blame on external harmful spirits and thinks of them as one's own enemies, this is actually quite contradictory to the practice of bodhichitta [the compassionate wish to attain enlightenment for the benefit of others]. If I were a harmful spirit and someone pointed his finger at me and said, "You are a harmful spirit," I would be happy because that shows that my accuser has not been able to identify his own enemy, and hence is vulnerable to my harms. If one actually practices bodhichitta properly and views all beings as friends, then harmful spirits will not harm one, for one will be invincible.'[258]

As for the charge that Shugden practice causes sectarianism, in reality every Tibetan knows there were no problems of disharmony between Nyingmapas and Gelugpas before the ban was imposed. There is not a single instance of disagreement between Nyingmapas and Gelugpas; although there have been disagreements historically between Gelugpas and Kagyupas, such as those at the time of the Fifth Dalai Lama coming to power. Nyingmapas practised Nyingma teachings purely and Gelugpas practised Gelug teachings purely without any problem. The problem was created only by the Dalai Lama himself in saying such things as: 'Say I want to practise Nyingma. They say this Protector will harm me. Now, that's an obstacle to religious freedom'. Within the Tibetan community no one has the opportunity, power or confidence to say such a thing to the Dalai Lama; and even if someone had said something like this to him it doesn't prove that 'Shugden people' say this. There is no reason for him to be angry with innocent Shugden people in general just because of one person's view; any individual can say anything, this is their personal choice.

Division and sectarianism within Tibetan society has been caused only by the ban imposed by the Dalai Lama himself. Of course, the Dalai Lama has freedom to choose his own practice. If he wants to stop practising Dorje Shugden and choose another practice, following indications in his personal dreams and so forth, then he is free to do so, but he should not interfere with the freedom of others who wish to worship as they choose in accordance with their individual human right of religious freedom.

In reality, Dorje Shugden practitioners are seeking religious freedom from the Dalai Lama's dictatorial behaviour, and it is the Dalai Lama who is maintaining a sectarian attitude of religious intolerance, destroying people's happiness and resulting in other serious consequences. Geshe Kelsang Gyatso explains:

> 'For instance, although Sera, Ganden and Drepung (in Tibet) were Gelug monasteries, many Nyingmapa and Bön practitioners joined to study the philosophical teachings. In my class in Sera-Jey [Monastery] I had some friends from a Nyingma monastery in eastern Tibet. Their daily practice was Nyingma, and no one was unhappy about this. They had complete freedom. We never had any problems because the Abbot gave complete freedom for individual practice.
>
> 'Although most of my family are Gelugpas who rely on Dorje Shugden, some of them are Nyingmapas. My younger sister married a Nyingmapa Lama from western Tibet from a renowned lineage; he was called Ngora Lama. They had many children and I visited them frequently, sometimes he and I would do puja together. I would do Dorje Shugden puja and he would do his own practice. We had a very good relationship until his death in Mussoorie, India.
>
> 'When I lived in Mussoorie I had many good friends from the Nyingma tradition, one of whom in particular was called Ngachang Lama. He was an old man, a lay practitioner; one winter he and I did retreat in the same house. In between sessions we talked Dharma, each talking about our experiences. His oldest son would often invite me to his house to do puja. Also, I was often invited to do puja at houses of other Nyingma families. I was so surprised to hear the Dalai Lama and others saying that Dorje Shugden practitioners and Nyingmapa practitioners are like fire and water!'[259]

This attitude of following one tradition but being open to and accepting of other traditions was widely prevalent in Tibet and is confirmed by many other contemporary accounts. For example Khyongla Rato writes:

> '… although my grandparents and parents had quite different attitudes towards religion, there was never any discord between them or disagreement in the matter of belief. My grandparents had been initiated, at one time or another, into all four of the main Buddhist sects of Tibet … and had found in them no real conflict.
>
> 'My mother and father, on the other hand, unlike my father's parents, belonged only to the orthodox Gelugpa "Yellow Hat" sect, and it would never have occurred to them to accept initiation from any other. Yet they respected all, and had friends from all.'[260]

Because of the present Dalai Lama's view, this attitude of following one tradition but respecting others is now regarded as a sectarian crime. However, many respected masters from all traditions of Tibetan Buddhism have spoken of the importance of maintaining each tradition. For example, the late highly respected Kagyu teacher Kalu Rinpoche was quoted as saying:

> 'In general, to have faith in all the traditions is a sign of a profound understanding of the teachings. However, it is absolutely necessary to engage in one given tradition, to receive detailed instructions in it, and to be introduced to its essential practices; and then, it is proper to practice mainly those teachings.'[261]

In an interview with Professor Donald Lopez in *Tricycle Magazine*, Geshe Kelsang Gyatso stated very clearly his own completely non-sectarian attitude toward other traditions:

> 'Of course! Of course we believe that every Nyingmapa and Kagyupa have their complete path. Not only Gelugpa. I believe that Nyingmapas have a complete path. Of course Kagyupas are very special. We very much appreciate the example of Marpa and Milarepa [in the Kagyu lineage]. Milarepa showed the best example of guru devotion. Of

> course the Kagyupas, as well as the Nyingmapas and the Sakyapas, have a complete path to enlightenment. Many Nyingmapas and Kagyupas practice very sincerely and are not just studying intellectually. I think that some Gelugpa practitioners need to follow their practical example. But we don't need to mix our traditions. Each tradition has its own uncommon good qualities, and it is important not to lose these. We should concentrate on our own tradition and maintain the good qualities of our tradition, but we should always keep good relations with each other and never argue or criticise each other. What I would like to request is that we should improve our own traditions while maintaining good relations with each other.'[262]

The Dalai Lama has made public statements about why he has imposed this ban but as we have seen they are completely flawed and have no valid basis. So what are the real reasons? One is the influence of the spirit Nechung, the protector of the Dalai Lama. The spirit-medium of Nechung has wanted predominant power to advise the Dalai Lama for many years, and has consequently developed jealousy towards the practice of Dorje Shugden, which was and still is very popular among many lamas, including the tutors and root Gurus of the Dalai Lama, many scholars and millions of other practitioners. There are also the factors of ignorance and superstition, because as the Dalai Lama publicly admits, he has based all of his decisions for the implementation of this ban on divinations, oracles and dreams. He has affirmed this in many discourses, including the one in July 1978 when he first spoke out in public against the practice of Dorje Shugden.

When asked what he thought was the main reason for the Dalai Lama's ban, Kundeling Rinpoche explained:

> 'All of the different traditions of Tibet have their own unique protectors. So why is Dorje Shugden being singled out as the big enemy of unity and being singled out as the main object of sectarianism? That is absolutely not true that Dorje Shugden is an enemy of unity and a cause of sectarianism. It's a big lie.

> 'Actually, the main reason behind the ban on Dorje Shugden is because Dorje Shugden has been very, very popular. You see, Gelugpas have been a majority in Tibet. They happen to be a majority also in exile. Dorje Shugden worship is very, very popular amongst the Gelugpas. It's also very popular amongst the Sakyapas. So I think this popularity may have caused some constraint and jealousy with Nechung oracle. Now jealousy and competition, in connection to growing popularity, is a common occurrence in Tibetan history. There have always been some minor quarrels and disagreements and arguments over fame, popularity, patrons, property, disciples. These are typical human feelings, human problems. They have nothing to do with the protectors of Gelugpas such as Dorje Shugden.'[263]

In *The Dalai Lama: A Report on the Dalai Lama's Abuses of Human Rights and Religious Freedom* James Belither notes:

> 'Many people believe the real reason why the Dalai Lama has banned the worship of Dorje Shugden is because he wants to integrate all the four schools of Tibetan Buddhism into one. The leaders of the other traditions will gradually disappear leaving him as the sole head of Tibetan Buddhism. In this way he will be able to control all aspects of Tibetan Buddhism, thereby consolidating his own power. By destroying the practice of Dorje Shugden, a popular practice within the Gelug tradition, he is trying to change, and thereby weaken, the Gelug tradition itself. By weakening the Gelugpas, relatively the most powerful of the four schools, the Dalai Lama has cleverly gained the support of the other schools. His next step will be to integrate them all into one.'[264]

And this is exactly what the Dalai Lama is doing as confirmed in his own words:

> '... what I say [is] – "We should try to practice all the four traditions in a complete form within one single physical basis." '[265]

As Kundeling Rinpoche points out, the ban and the wish to integrate the four traditions relates to the Dalai Lama's hidden political agenda (see Chapter 9):

> 'The Dalai Lama's other reason for the ban, that Dorje Shugden is an obstacle to the unity of all the Tibetan traditions, is definitely not true. You see, there was no such problem before this ban. When the Dalai Lama talks about bringing unity, he means making one tradition out of all the existing traditions of Tibet ... What the Dalai Lama is talking about is unifying all of the different practices to make one tradition.
>
> 'Now if you ask, who's going to be the head of this new, one tradition, of course it's the Dalai Lama himself who is going to be the head. It is very clear in the Dalai Lama's mind that when he goes back to Tibet, he's never going to be the temporal leader. That's very clear. Since he's opted for autonomy, he's not going to be a temporal leader anymore. So the only option left for him is to be a spiritual leader. To be spiritual leader of the Gelugpas alone means his power is marginalised, is reduced. Therefore, in order to be the common spiritual leader of all Tibetans, he is trying to create one tradition here in exile. He believes that when he goes back to Tibet he will be able to exercise power over all the traditions by having created this one tradition in which he is the supreme leader. So this is also a power struggle. This is also a power game. So this is the Dalai Lama's hidden political agenda.'[266]

Although the Dalai Lama clearly has a political motive in imposing the ban on Dorje Shugden practice, he is acting against the basic principles of Mahayana Buddhism. With this ban he has totally rejected the view of his Spiritual Guide, Kyabje Trijang Rinpoche, his 'root Spiritual Guide'[267], thus breaking the commitment to rely upon the Spiritual Guide, the cornerstone of Mahayana Buddhist practice.

CHAPTER 11

Open Secrets concerning the Fourteenth Dalai Lama

What emerges from our analysis of the Dalai Lama so far is a portrait of someone who has the external appearance of a spiritual personality, a holy being, but in truth is ordinary, self-centred and ruthless. As the following chapter reveals, behind the mask of Avalokiteshvara hides an ordinary person, engaged in the same kinds of unsavoury actions and with the same kind of motivation that we associate with corrupt politicians.

THE RECOGNITION OF THE FOURTEENTH DALAI LAMA

As explained in Chapter 2, fundamental questions are now being asked publicly about the veracity of many aspects of the selection process by which the current Dalai Lama was identified, and therefore about the true identity of the Fourteenth Dalai Lama himself.

THE ILLUSION OF GOVERNMENT

Gradually over the years since the Dalai Lama left his homeland, 145,000 Tibetans have moved from Tibet and made settlements in India, Nepal and Bhutan or settled further afield in exile communities throughout the world.[268]

The Dalai Lama himself, together with many of his closest followers, eventually settled in the old British hill station of McLeod Ganj, near the small Indian town of Dharamsala in northern India.

The Tibetan town that has grown up around him there is now the principal Tibetan refugee community.

At enormous expense an administration was established in Dharamsala to maintain effective control over the widely-spread refugee population.[269] This administration has become known as 'The Government of Tibet in Exile' though it has no legal status either within or outside India and is not officially recognised by any country, least of all by India.[270]

An official statement, published by the Department of Information of the Tibetan government in exile, reads:

> 'In exile, the Tibetan Government has been reorganized according to modern democratic principles. It administers all matters pertaining to Tibetans in exile, including the restoration, preservation and development of Tibetan culture and education, and leads the struggle for the restoration of Tibet's freedom.'[271]

There is a Tibetan National Assembly of People's Deputies (usually simply called the 'National Assembly'), which consists of forty-six representatives. However, of these representatives only thirty are directly elected by the Tibetan people. The five major religious traditions (Gelug, Kagyu, Sakya, Nyingma and Bön) elect two representatives each, and the remaining six are direct appointees of the Dalai Lama. This in itself represents a breach of democratic principles, since only two-thirds of the delegates are directly elected by the people. The National Assembly nominally appoints the members of the Cabinet ('Kashag' in Tibetan), but in practice these are often directly appointed by the Dalai Lama. And for a time in the early 1980s the Dalai Lama even took it upon himself to appoint unilaterally all delegates of the National Assembly.[272]

Tsering Wangyal writing in the *Tibetan Review* in 1979 pointed out that 'every important office-bearer in Dharamsala has to be approved by the Dalai Lama before formally taking his office.'[273] In the same article he continued:

> 'Despite the introduction in 1963 of some of its external paraphernalia, Tibetan democracy is yet to come of age. The

> Commission of Tibetan People's Deputies (The National Assembly), the most consciously democratic institution in the exiled Tibetan community, has at its last public appearance failed to alter its image of being an impotent body – subservient for all practical purposes to the dictates of the government (the Dalai Lama). … The experience so far has shown that the old-world values and ideas continue to dominate the positions of power in the Tibetan community …'

In the last fifty years, the Tibetan exile government functioning in Dharamsala has never faced an opposition party, nor even an individual who could be called an opposition member. It has never taken a decision contrary to the Dalai Lama's position, and such an event is even considered to be inconceivable. With all authority (executive, legislative, judicial and religious) invested solely in the person of the Dalai Lama, this government has ceased to uphold any pretence of constitutional democracy.

The Tibetan government is the Dalai Lama, and the Dalai Lama is the Tibetan government. Behind the trappings of government with its illusion of democracy, the Dalai Lama's position, with its central tenet, 'L'etat, c'est moi' ('I am the State'), extends its domain of authority over all aspects of policy and decision-making. There is no decision of government that is not the Dalai Lama's decision.

Because the Dalai Lama is commonly held to be an infallible being, the embodiment of a Buddha, it is not only inconceivable but would also be heretical to formulate a policy or make a decision contrary to his wishes. Furthermore, because it would again be an act of heresy to criticise the policy or decision of a supposedly enlightened being, all criticism and blame for the Dalai Lama's mistakes are directed at the Tibetan government, which has no means of redress.

In this way, the so-called Tibetan government is blamed for all of the Dalai Lama's mistakes, and the untarnished image of the Dalai Lama is maintained. This very convenient system has enabled the Dalai Lama, through the illusion of government, to destroy the reputation and activities of others, to intimidate and persecute them, and to instigate violence against them, all while maintaining a faultless public image, and knowing full well that all subsequent blame will be carried by his 'government'.

In September 1995, an unprecedented 'open letter' from the Tibetan people to the Dalai Lama was given anonymously to an English woman travelling in Nepal. Called the 'Mongoose-Canine Letter' (see Appendix 2), it revealed to Westerners for the first time another side of the Dalai Lama, one which was already an open secret within the Tibetan community. For the first time ever, the Dalai Lama and his government were publicly accused of such things as illegal international trading in arms, persecution and assassination; and of creating schism and disharmony within the Tibetan spiritual traditions and community.

THE DALAI LAMA'S BROTHER, GYALO DONDRUB

According to Tibetan sources, an older brother of the Dalai Lama called Gyalo Dondrub has taken advantage of the exile situation to gain increasing personal influence.

> 'In Tibet, the family of the Dalai Lama was respected, but had no political power. Gyalo Dondrub, however, has used the changed situation in exile to gain a powerful influence over Tibetan politics.'[274]

Various established Tibetan 'noble families' such as Phala, Surkhang and Yuthog actively used their influence to achieve great benefits for the Tibetan exile community.

> 'In old Tibet, political matters were in the hands of the nobility. After the successful escape from Tibet, it was these families in particular who established settlements, schools and political representation in foreign countries.
>
> 'They however stood in the way of Gyalo's ambition. In the mid-1960s he succeeded in setting public opinion against Surkhang and Yuthog, who were thus forced to leave India and move to Taiwan. Phala was assigned as representative in Switzerland and thereby lost his direct influence in India.'[275]

To this day Gyalo Dondrub remains one of the most powerful figures in the Tibetan government and community.

> 'He [Gyalo] is continuously occupied with 'secret' business behind the scenes, and although he maintains contact with the CIA, he is the only direct contact the Dalai Lama has with the communist leadership in Beijing. He is regarded as the 'secret boss', and his role, as well as his goals are unclear.'[276]

In a speech given in Taiwan on 29 October 1967 by a former minister of the Tibetan exile government, Yuthok Tashi Dhundup:

> 'Yuthok criticized many of Gyalo's activities, for example, (1) Gyalo dominates DL [Dalai Lama] and controls TGE [Tibetan government in exile] through his brother; (2) Gyalo embezzles TGE's budget and invests it into his own business; (3) Gyalo embezzles the donations intended for the Tibetan guerrilla force; (4) Gyalo controls TGE by tactics involving bribery and boycott against its officials. This talk reveals not only Gyalo's growing influence in TGE, but also the discord between him and officials such as Yuthok.'[277]

A picture begins to emerge of a government dominated and controlled by the Dalai Lama and his family.

> 'In Tibet, a family member of a Dalai Lama was legally barred from holding office, something that changed in exile, where Gyalo Thondup [or Dondrub] and others later became ministers. Much controversy surrounds Gyalo Thondup whom Tibetans believe to be the main architect of the Dalai Lama's plan to integrate Tibet into China under increased cultural autonomy.
>
> 'Recently, another brother of the Dalai Lama has claimed that today only three families, including his, run the exile government … "the Tibetan exile government is run by three families, one of which is mine' [that is, the Dalai Lama's family, or Yapshi Taklha family] … the old Gelugpa elite in the exile government had largely been replaced in the 1960s. The family

> of the Dalai Lama, [admits] to running the government from behind the scenes for decades …" '[278]

And as Michael Backman reports in his article *Behind the Dalai Lama's holy cloak*:

> 'Like many Asian politicians, the Dalai Lama has been remarkably nepotistic, appointing members of his family to many positions of prominence. In recent years, three of the six members of the Kashag, or cabinet, the highest executive branch of the Tibetan government-in-exile, have been close relatives of the Dalai Lama.
>
> 'An older brother served as chairman of the Kashag and as the minister of security. He also headed the CIA-backed Tibetan contra movement in the 1960s.
>
> 'A sister-in-law served as head of the government-in-exile's planning council and its Department of Health.
>
> 'A younger sister served as health and education minister and her husband served as head of the government-in-exile's Department of Information and International Relations.
>
> 'Their daughter was made a member of the Tibetan parliament in exile. A younger brother has served as a senior member of the private office of the Dalai Lama and his wife has served as education minister.
>
> 'The second wife of a brother-in-law serves as the representative of the Tibetan government-in-exile for northern Europe and head of international relations for the government-in-exile. All these positions give the Dalai Lama's family access to millions of dollars collected on behalf of the government-in-exile.'[279]

It is not only Gyalo Dondrub's position on Tibetan independence that has attracted the most censure from Tibetans, but also the way in which he has manipulated his position as the Dalai Lama's older brother and thus the secular head of the Yapshi Taklha family, the Dalai Lama's family, which has been automatically co-opted into the Tibetan aristocratic system.

As it is clear that the source of Gyalo Dondrub's power lies in his closeness to the Dalai Lama, and that the Dalai Lama has done nothing to restrain his brother, it is the Dalai Lama who must take responsibility for his brother's bullying and destructive actions.

The Dudjom Rinpoche Affair

Dudjom Rinpoche was one of the important modern masters of the Nyingma tradition, and a great spiritual teacher. Shortly after his arrival from Tibet, in the early 1960s, he gave extensive teachings in Kalimpong and Darjeeling. These were very popular and he became famous throughout the Tibetan community. But suddenly Dudjom Rinpoche was arrested and jailed in Siliguri, falsely accused by the Dalai Lama's exile government of being a Chinese spy. As Kundeling Rinpoche notes:

> 'This is the favourite accusation of the Tibetan government in exile made against anyone who they perceive as posing a threat to the absolute authority of the Dalai Lama.
>
> 'Dudjom Rinpoche became very popular; he became very famous and that posed a threat to their absolute authority. That is basically what an autocratic system is all about. Except for the leader, nobody can be smarter or more famous or more good looking or more prosperous than that particular person. You can't outshine your ruler. If you do, you have to be cut down to size.'[280]

It may also be that Dudjom Rinpoche was not interested in the Dalai Lama's desire for a union of all Tibetan traditions. In replying to the question 'If some people have been practising according to one lineage, is it necessary for them to change lineages in order to create unity in the community?' Dudjom Rinpoche replied:

> 'Certainly not. Whatever practice a person is well-grounded in is what he should continue. Part of our purpose is to preserve all lineages as methods for attaining enlightenment. … as practitioners we should sustain our own tradition

while respecting and rejoicing in the virtue of other traditions.'[281]

The Assassination of Gungtang Tsultrim

Gungtang Tsultrim was the leader of an organisation known as the 'Thirteen Settlements' or 'Thirteen Groups of Tibetans'. This organisation consisted of thirteen (later fourteen) Tibetan exile groups and settlements that wished to establish themselves under Indian law, independent of the jurisdiction of the Dalai Lama's exile government. Although this organization had its origins in a grassroots movement in Tibet, the principal impetus for its formation in India occurred shortly after the Dalai Lama's arrival in Dharamsala.

When the Dalai Lama first arrived in Dharamsala, he held a series of meetings with other senior leaders from all the traditions. The purpose of these meetings was for the Dalai Lama to introduce a proposal for the integration of all four schools of Tibetan Buddhism into one. At the time the Gelugpa did not reject the Dalai Lama's ideas directly because of their close relationship with the institution of the Dalai Lama; they remained neutral. But the proposal was rejected by the Sakya, Nyingma and Kagyu lamas. Practitioners of these other traditions were extremely worried about this proposal, fearing that their traditions would soon be destroyed. In response to the proposal, and against the Dalai Lama's wishes, they organised thirteen groups which then associated to form the 'Thirteen Settlements'.

Over the years many conflicts developed between the Dalai Lama and these thirteen settlements, until in 1976 their secular leader Gungtang Tsultrim was murdered. Without the strong leadership of Gungtang Tsultrim, and with no other leader of his capacity to replace him, the coalition disintegrated. This had been the motive for the assassination.

A website dealing mainly with controversies regarding the Karmapa adds:

> 'In 1964, the government-in-exile of the Dalai Lama wanted to introduce social, economic and religious reforms to the recently evicted Tibetans. Gyalo Thondrub, the Dalai Lama's audacious brother, decided that the best answer to Mao's invasion and destruction of their country was to adapt Tibet and Tibetan policy in exile to the new Communist realities. He boldly proposed to abolish the old Buddhist schools, to do away with the rich, religious show, and thus bring the high lamas to the ground. "No more thrones, rituals, or gold brocades," he was rumoured to have uttered. The spiritual hierarchies of the Nyingma, Kagyu, Sakya and the corollary sub-orders fell victim to slander and reproach. His words struck fear into the lamas' hearts. As more details of the elaborate plan began to emerge, it became clear that a coup against three of the schools was being hatched. The new religious body that would replace the traditional lineages was to be controlled by the Gelugpa hierarchy. The worried lamas rushed to Karmapa for help.
>
> 'When in 1976, Gungthang Tsultrim, the political head of the alliance, was murdered, the assassin confessed to operate on orders from the Tibetan cabinet. Hired for the job, he was paid rupees three hundred thousand by the Tibetan government-in-exile in Dharamsala. The Tibetan government-in-exile had also offered him more money for eliminating the 16th Karmapa, he confessed.'[282]

THE KARMAPA AFFAIR

The Sixteenth Karmapa, the head of the Karma Kagyu tradition, was one of the most famous and highly-revered spiritual masters within the Tibetan community in India, and gradually his reputation also spread throughout the West. He was regarded as one of the greatest spiritual masters of the twentieth century. He had a strong following throughout the Himalayan region including India, Nepal, Bhutan and Sikkim, and a growing discipleship in the West. The Thirteen Settlements had wished to make the Karmapa their spiritual head. The Dalai Lama's government therefore tried directly and indirectly to eclipse the popularity and fame of the Karmapa. It is well known that the Dalai Lama and the Karmapa were in open conflict in the last years of the Karmapa's life.

In an interview the Dalai Lama has talked of his relationship with the Sixteenth Karmapa:

> ' "On a personal level, still old friends; no problem. But as to the Tibetan community and the politics, a little bit of doubt, a little distance ..." The Karmapa, he went on, had refused to contribute to the booklet for independence. "And later, I heard that in talking to some of his centres in Europe and America he said the Tibetan freedom struggle is politics, and that as spiritual practitioners they should not be involved."
>
> ' "... So Karmapa Rinpoche, I think perhaps he misled people a little bit, and that made me a little sad ..." '[283]

The Karmapa was here actually exposing the truth about the Dalai Lama's use of 'Lama Policy', so in light of the Dalai Lama's views on the union of religion and politics, and his identification of the Tibetan state under his control with the continued development of Buddhism, it is unlikely that the Dalai Lama's reaction was merely one of sadness.

After the Sixteenth Karmapa passed away, the Dalai Lama took the unprecedented step of using his own power to force the selection of the Karmapa's reincarnation. This was entirely unwarranted because historically the selection has always been an internal matter solely under the jurisdiction of the Kagyu spiritual tradition itself. There were two candidates: one born in Chinese-occupied Tibet, the candidate officially recognised by the Chinese authorities; and the other born in India and recognised by the great Kagyu spiritual master Shamar Rinpoche. Shamar Rinpoche's lineage has been closely connected with the Karmapa lineage since the 13th century, and he has been considered second only to the Karmapa himself within the Kagyu tradition. The Dalai Lama sided with the Chinese and 'officially' recognised their candidate, a decision that caused chaos within the Kagyu tradition, producing a deep schism between those who follow the Dalai Lama and those who follow Shamar Rinpoche.

This schism has divided this spiritual tradition against itself, and at times has led to violence.

As an article in the Indian *Sunday* magazine commented:

> 'The Dalai Lamas have never held any right over the confirmation, let alone recognition, of a Karmapa at any time throughout history. In fact, the Karmapa line precedes that of the Dalai Lamas by over three hundred years and their lineages are and always have been entirely separate.
>
> 'The Dalai Lama does not have historic or religious authority to approve Karmapa reincarnations, or head lamas for any school of Tibetan Buddhism besides his own Gelugpa lineage. This point may be confusing to non-Tibetans because, as head of the Tibetan government-in-exile, the Dalai Lama has a claim on the political loyalty of many Tibetans. Yet, his political role does not give the Dalai Lama spiritual authority to validate the head lamas of Buddhist schools outside his own. The four Buddhist schools of Tibet have always had separate administrations and have chosen their own head lamas, much as Protestants and Catholics choose their own leaders. So, just as the Pope has no role in choosing the Protestant Archbishop of Canterbury, so the Dalai Lama is not authorized to recognize the Karmapa, who is the leader of the Karma Kagyu school. Only the administration of the late 16th Karmapa is authorized to validate its own chief lama's reincarnation.'[284]

In a letter to the Dalai Lama in February 1997, Shamar Rinpoche stated clearly that the Dalai Lama has no authority in confirming a Karmapa reincarnation and no business throwing his 'weight' at the Kagyu lineage:

> 'This amounts to a medieval dictatorial command and I understand that this is the approach that you desire. But it is completely unacceptable to me ... Therefore, my final request to the Private Office of the Dalai Lama is that [it] does not involve His Holiness's name in this problematic issue ... with

> respect to our lineage it is up to us, who are part of that lineage, to achieve its aims ... you ought to be cautious in your undertakings!'[285]

As a consequence of his outspoken criticism of the Dalai Lama on this issue, the Tibetan government has done everything possible to turn this lama into a pariah within Tibetan society.

As the Mongoose-Canine Letter addressed to the Dalai Lama says:

> '… when in the 1960's you tried to get rid of the influence of one great Lama's power, such as Dujom Rinpoche and Karmapa, the side-effect was felt by many Tibetan Lamas, and you caused them to unite in opposition. You could not leave it lightly and you had to do something that caused a split within Tibetan society ... Your ministers will have told you that a Karmapa established in the Himalayas will affect the name and power of the Dalai Lama as before since he is very popular in the Himalayas. If the Tibetan exile government of Dalai Lama is really for the independence of Tibet, how can a private organisation like that of the Karmapa, affect your government?
>
> '... When your Holiness Dalai Lama gave support for this (backed by the Chinese candidate) how badly will this harm Tibet's future? You think that if within your life you cannot be the leader of the Tibetans in Tibet, at least you must keep your position as leader of Tibet in India by using Dharma and politics. For that you calculate that it does not matter what happens for the future of Tibet after your life, as long as you can keep your power now. It is really sad.' (see Appendix 2)

In an interview in 1994, Jigme Rinpoche, a leading Kagyu lama, made the following comments on the Karmapa situation:

> '... in my opinion a mistake was made right at the beginning, there were miscalculations, control was lost and it was necessary to go that way … The mistakes were not just made now but centuries ago, and led to the loss of the country. Many

people in the West think that everybody in Tibet was wise, and they wonder why Tibetans lost Tibet. But when one looks objectively one finds that mistakes like those led to the loss of Tibet and will lead to the loss of the freedom of Tibet in the future. ...

'If this continues, Tibet has only [a] few years left ... The 16th Karmapa said something like that to Gendun Rinpoche. He said, "You should go to Europe and establish the Dharma." Gendun Rinpoche asked Karmapa what will happen in Tibet and Asia, and Karmapa said, "Only the outer form of Dharma will continue to exist there, and it will be very difficult in the future to maintain its essence." '[286]

When other Tibetans achieve fame or influence the Dalai Lama destroys their reputations, their security and even sometimes their lives, acting with political motivations of jealousy and clinging to power. This is what he did to the Panchen Lama, to Dudjom Rinpoche, to Guntang Tsultrim, even to his own Spiritual Guide Trijang Rinpoche, and his Spiritual Guide Je Phabongkha Rinpoche. This is what he did to the Karmapa and what he is trying to do to the few holy spiritual masters who are left within the Gelugpa Tradition today.

THE POLITICS OF THE KALACHAKRA INITIATIONS

On this subject the Mongoose-Canine Letter says:

'Normally the Kalachakra initiation is not given in public. Then you [Dalai Lama] started to use it continuously in a big way for your politics ... Nowadays you have given the Kalachakra initiation so many times you have made the Tibetan people into donkeys. You can force them to go here and there as you like.' (See Appendix 2)

When people receive a Tantric Buddhist initiation or empowerment they are encouraged to establish a close connection with the person giving the initiation. It has been said that the main reason for the Dalai Lama giving so many Kalachakra initiations in the West is to create many Western disciples as a powerful basis of support for his political actions – such as the ban on the practice of Dorje Shugden.

According to some sources, in the past Kalachakra initiations were mainly given by those holding the Panchen Lama's position, and that this is because of a special connection, the Panchen Lama being a manifestation of Shambhala's god-king. Gradually the Fourteenth Dalai Lama has taken over this position, until finally now no other lama has the opportunity to give the Kalachakra initiation in public. For the Dalai Lama, giving the Kalachakra empowerment is the best method to make money, to control people through spiritual devotion, and to spread his reputation. In this way he can use people's religious faith to fulfil his political aims. It is shameful that Buddha's precious teachings of Highest Yoga Tantra are being used for such worldly achievements.

DEFAMATION OF JE PHABONGKHAPA

Je Phabongkhapa, or Phabongkha Rinpoche, (1878-1941) 'was one of the great lamas of the twentieth century. He attained his geshe degree at Sera Monastic University, Lhasa, and became a highly influential teacher in Tibet. He was the root Guru of both tutors of the present Dalai Lama, and the teacher of many of the other Gelug lamas who have been bringing the Dharma to the West since they fled Tibet in 1959.'[287]

But the Fourteenth Dalai Lama now defames this great Teacher. As recently as 27 March 2006 the Dalai Lama implied that Je Phabongkhapa developed a sectarian bias due to his association with Dorje Shugden:

> 'In the case of Kyabje Pabongkha Rinpoche, he was, in the earlier part of his life, a practitioner of ecumenical faith. Gradually, he developed a relationship with Dholgyal. Need I say more?'[288]

But the Dalai Lama gives no evidence for saying that Je Phabongkhapa was sectarian later in his life.

On another occasion the Dalai Lama said that although 'Kyabje Phabongkha Rinpoche was really an incredibly great master. ... virtually the supreme holder of the Stages of the Path (Lam rim) and Mind Training (Lo jong) traditions' and 'was a highly realized being', that nevertheless 'with regard to Dholgyal [Dorje Shugden] he seems to have made mistakes.'[289]

The following account illustrates the low esteem in which Je Phabongkhapa is held within certain sections of the Gelugpa Tradition as a result of the Dalai Lama's defamation. In August 2009 there was a Rigchung degree ceremony (for those who have successfully completed their study of the *Perfection of Wisdom Sutra*) held at Sera-Mey Monastery in South India. During the ceremony for a monk from the Gungru Khamtsen section of the monastery, the disciplinarian of the monastery Geshe Ngawang Yonten publicly read out the 'refuge letter' (in which a patron writes the names of his family and spiritual masters for blessing by the assembled monks). The refuge letter included the names of Kyabje Phabongkha Rinpoche and Drana Rinpoche (another prominent Dorje Shugden practitioner).

After the ceremony the disciplinarian received phone calls from monks complaining about his reading out the names of these two Lamas. The next day in the assembly hall, the disciplinarian apologised: 'I didn't get any prior notice before reading the letter. The person who wrote the names has accumulated negativity, as I did for reading it [the letter]. Therefore we should purify our sin by offering katag [traditional Tibetan offering scarf] to the Protector Thawo. These Lamas did not sign and pledge that they will never worship Shugden, and we will never share material and religious ties with Shugden followers.'

During the Thirteenth Dalai Lama's time, Je Phabongkhapa was the most famous and influential Lama who engaged practically in spreading the doctrine of Je Tsongkhapa throughout Tibet. He was greatly influential in reviving the Gelug Tradition at this time, emphasising the practical application of Buddha's teachings instead of just scholastic knowledge, and he was the lama most involved in promoting the practice of Dorje Shugden. Because of this, detractors of this practice such as the present Dalai Lama have tried either to maintain that Je Phabongkhapa rejected the practice of Dorje Shugden towards the end of his life, or to smear him with the accusation of being sectarian and of promoting Dorje Shugden practice as a way of damaging other Buddhist traditions.

There may be another reason for the present Dalai Lama's defamation of Je Phabongkhapa. As Goldstein says 'Phabongka was famous for his view that lamas should not become involved in politics ...'[290], which is not an attitude the Dalai Lama can accept, especially from such an important figure within the Gelug Tradition.

With regard to the many rumours being circulated about Je Phabongkhapa, someone once asked Geshe Kelsang Gyatso, 'Is it true what some people say about Je Phabongkhapa rejecting the Nyingma Tradition?' Geshe Kelsang Gyatso replied:

> 'This is a hundred-per-cent not true. Through careful investigation I came to understand that when Je Phabongkhapa visited the Kham area in eastern Tibet he gave extensive teachings everywhere. Many thousands of people gathered for his teachings. People of Kham deeply respected him and were devoted to him. At that time, some people, due to jealousy and in order to destroy Je Phabongkhapa's reputation, circulated false information saying "Phabongkhapa is evil, he rejects the Nyingma tradition and he destroyed statues of Padmasambhava". Gradually this false information spread throughout Tibet, but I clearly understand that these people lied.'[291]

There are a number of personal accounts of Je Phabongkhapa that testify to his enormous spiritual power and his ability to turn people's minds towards spiritual practice. Geshe Lobsang Tharchin, who was for fifteen years abbot of Rashi Gempil Ling, a Kalmuck Mongolian temple in New Jersey, USA, and founder of the Mahayana Sutra and Tantra Centers, recalls attending Lamrim teachings given by Je Phabongkhapa:

> 'Like so many others in the audience, I was stunned by the power of his teaching. Most of it I had heard before, but the way in which he taught it and, I felt, the blessing I had received from him made it suddenly strike home for me. Here I was, living the short precious life of a human, and fortunate enough to be a student at one of the greatest Buddhist monasteries in the world. Why was I wasting my time? What would happen if I suddenly died?'

Geshe Tharchin remembers a Tibetan nobleman who held a 'powerful position equivalent to Minister of Defense' attending Je Phabongkhapa's teachings, showing up in his:

> '... best finery ... decked out in silk, his long hair flowing ... A great ceremonial sword hung from his belt, clanging importantly as he swaggered in. ... By the end of the first section of the teaching he was seen leaving the hall quietly, deep in thought—he had wrapped his weapon of war in a cloth to hide it, and was taking it home. ... finally one day he threw himself before the Rinpoche and asked to be granted the special lifetime religious vows for laymen. Thereafter he always followed Pabongka Rinpoche around, to every public teaching he gave.'[292]

In his autobiography Khyongla Rato, founder of the Tibet Center in New York, writes that Tibetans referred to Khangser Rinpoche and Phabongka Rinpoche respectively as 'the Sun' and 'the Moon'. He also writes of the tremendous power of Je Phabongkhapa's teachings:

> 'During that summer session several traders and at least two high government officials found their lives transformed by his eloquence: they forsook their jobs to study religion and to give themselves to meditation.'

Khyongla Rato requested and received full ordination from Je Phabongkhapa and would often pray '... that like Pabongka Rinpoche, I might learn to help people by teaching, writing, and discussion.'[293]

In a short account about his life, Rilbur Rinpoche says:

> 'That was the time of the great lama Pabongka Dorje Chang, who was the most outstanding unsurpassable lama of that time. It was him and nobody else. I'm not saying there weren't any lamas except Pabongka – there were Kyabje Kangsar Rinpoche, Tatra Rinpoche, and many other great lamas – but he became the principal teacher, the one who was giving continuous teachings.'[294]

And:

> 'I have had some success as a scholar, and as a lama I am somebody, but these things are not important. The only thing that matters to me is that I was a disciple of Pabongka Rinpoche.'[295]

None of these highly-respected teachers who knew Je Phabongkhapa personally make mention of any sectarian bias whatsoever. In an interview given in the FPMT *Mandala* magazine, Mogchok Rinpoche, shortly after being appointed resident teacher of the FPMT centre in Lavaur, France, said that his previous incarnation had first belonged to the Shangpa Kagyu tradition:

> 'In my past life, Mogchok Rinpoche was a student of Kyabje Pabongka Rinpoche; it was then that he changed to the Gelug tradition. He received many initiations and teachings from Kyabje Pabongka Rinpoche.'

However, it is clear that Je Phabongkhapa did not put any sectarian pressure on his new disciple. As the interview continues:

> 'Q: Do you know why he chose to change tradition?
>
> 'A: I think he found that the Gelugpa tradition contained a lot of wisdom. But the previous Mogchok Rinpoche didn't abandon Shangpa Kagyu completely, he practiced according to that tradition as well.'[296]

Je Phabongkha's spiritual influence – over government ministers and even lamas from other traditions – was undoubtedly a source of jealousy. As a Gelugpa lama he was responsible for promoting the pure teachings of Je Tsongkhapa, but there is no evidence of him acting out of sectarianism, or in any way that was damaging to other traditions. The claims made by the present Dalai Lama are completely false.

THE DALAI LAMA'S INVOLVEMENT WITH THE CIA AND THE TIBETAN GUERRILLAS

Of all the lies that surround the Dalai Lama, surely the greatest is that he is a champion of non-violence. This aspect of the image that he likes to portray of himself and with which he has mesmerised the media and much of the world is actually just another part of the myth.

The truth of the matter is that from the mid-1950s through to the mid-1970s there was an active and violent Tibetan resistance movement that was funded by the CIA.[297] Even the Dalai Lama's notorious brother Gyalo Dondrup, who was the principal link between the Tibetan guerrillas and the CIA, called this 'a very dirty business'.[298] The question is, how involved was the Dalai Lama in this 'very dirty business'?

In 1974, the Dalai Lama claimed: 'The accusation of CIA aid has no truth behind it'.[299] But gradually as more and more US State Department documents have been declassified he has been forced to admit the truth.

In 1999, discussing the early CIA operations involving his people, he said: 'They gave the impression that once I arrived in India, great support would come from the United States.'[300] The CIA provided $1.7 million dollars annually to train and support the guerrillas, including setting up training camps in the US (Camp Hale, Colorado) and elsewhere, flying the guerrillas there and parachuting them back into Tibet, and providing weapons, equipment and intelligence.[301] The Dalai Lama himself received $180,000 annually to maintain himself in India, a grant for which he did not have to account.[302]

The reason for the Dalai Lama's expectations could well be the letter sent to him by the United States ambassador to India, Loy Henderson, in 1951. Henderson was passing on a message from the State department that said, amongst other things:

> 'The United States ... is prepared to support resistance now and in the future against Communist aggression in Tibet, and to provide such material aid as may be feasible.'[303]

Indeed, as CIA documents uncovered under the Freedom of Information Act reveal, when the Dalai Lama did finally flee Tibet one of the first messages sent to Americans demanded an air-drop of substantial quantities of weapons:

> 'Please inform the world about the suffering of the Tibetan people. To make us free from the misery of the Chinese Communist operations [you] must help us as soon as possible and send us weapons for 30,000 men by airplane.'[304]

The Dalai Lama has tried to conceal the level of the CIA's involvement in Tibet and his own involvement with the CIA. Thomas Laird recounts how the Dalai Lama was apprehensive when he explained that he was to publish a book revealing when CIA activity began in Tibet.

> 'The Dalai Lama worried aloud to me when I interviewed him for this book. He wondered if revealing the covert American presence in Tibet in 1950 would give the Chinese some excuse for their invasion. After all, when China invaded Tibet in 1950 it said its motivating reason was to halt the imperialist plots of American agents in Tibet. At the time, America denied that there were any American agents in Tibet prior to the invasion. Until now that denial has stood unchallenged. This book proves, for the first time, not only that there were Americans in Tibet, but that several agents, in and out of Tibet, worked actively to send military aid to the Tibetans prior to the Chinese invasion. It proves that the highest levels of the US government were involved in that planning – despite government denials ever since.'[305]

The Dalai Lama's military intrigues are not limited to the CIA. In 1962, some of the Tibetan guerrillas became part of the Indian Army's Special Frontier Forces with the intention that they would be dropped into Tibet to fight the Chinese. However the Indian Army instead deployed them to fight the war in East Pakistan. As the official website of the Tibetan guerrillas declares:

> 'The SFF never had a chance of being used in operations against its intended enemy, Red China, but it was used against East Pakistan with the consent of His Holiness the Dalai Lama in 1971.'[306]

Having been forced out of Tibet, the guerrillas set themselves up in Mustang, across the border in Nepal. For some time the Nepalese tolerated them 'because it was the wish of the Dalai Lama'.[307] But the guerrillas' continued attacks on the Chinese army put greater and greater strain on the Nepalese government's relationship with China, and eventually the Nepalese government decided to wipe out the guerrillas. Finally, in 1974, the Dalai Lama sent a recorded message to the guerrillas instructing them to surrender to the Nepalese.[308]

The CIA had previously ordered the guerrillas to stop their offensives against the Chinese, but they had ignored their US commanders.[309] However, as soon as the Dalai Lama gave them the order, all but a handful handed over their weapons.[310] If the Dalai Lama really wanted non-violent resistance, why did he wait until 1974 to give his message to the guerrillas – after nearly two decades of fighting during which thousands of Tibetans and Chinese had died in violent combat?

THE ATTEMPTED COUP IN BHUTAN

A serious problem (not mentioned in the Mongoose-Canine Letter) that emerged in the early 1970s was the 'so-called Tibetan conspiracy organised by the Dalai Lama's brother' [Gyalo Dondrub or Thondup] to overthrow the government of Bhutan.[311]

Between four and six thousand Tibetan refugees chose to settle in this tiny country, which is geographically similar and ethnically and culturally related to Tibet. At first these Tibetans were warmly received, but in 1973 more than thirty people, twenty-two of them prominent Tibetan refugees, were arrested by the Bhutanese authorities in response to an alleged plot to assassinate the young Bhutanese king, just months before his official coronation. Among those arrested was the Dalai Lama's personal representative in Bhutan, Lhading.[312]

Derek Davies, reporting in the *Far Eastern Economic Review*, writes that behind the group that planned the assassination:

> ' …is alleged to be the sinister figure of the Dalai Lama's brother, Gyalo Thondup, who runs a well-funded Tibetan refugee group in Darjeeling, India. It is reliably reported that the group mounts raids across the Himalayan valleys via Sikkim into the Chinese province of Tibet.'[313]

With the involvement of both Gyalo Dondrub and the Dalai Lama's own personal representative in this attempted coup, is it not reasonable to ask what role did the Dalai Lama himself play in it?

THE TIBETAN ARMS TRADE

Other problems mentioned in the Mongoose-Canine Letter include the Tibetan government dividing the Tibetan guerrilla fighters in Mustang against themselves, which ultimately led to their destruction; and the role played by the Dalai Lama's brother, Gyalo Dondrub, in illegal arms trading carried on by exile Tibetans between Taiwan, Pakistan and Burma. It is said that Losang Gyatso, the senior lama of the three monks who were murdered in Dharamsala in February 1997, had just returned from Taiwan carrying a very large amount of cash from one such arms sale, and that this money was a possible motive for the murders.

THE HYPOCRISY OVER TAIWAN

After the People's Liberation Army of communist China entered Tibet and the Dalai Lama made his journey into exile in 1959, any Tibetan having ties with China was considered a traitor.[314] This view was not confined only to those who dealt with the People's Republic of China ('PRC') but even to those who had association with the Republic of China ('ROC', that is, Taiwan).[315]

The Dalai Lama banned Tibetans from travelling to Taiwan. Those who wished to take up opportunities to study or work in Taiwan therefore had to circumvent this ban. Some obtained forged passports through Nepal, putting themselves at great personal risk and becoming illegal citizens abroad.[316] But the ROC (Taiwan) was itself in conflict with the PRC, so why did the Dalai Lama adopt this extreme view in the first place?

Not only was the ROC the sworn enemy of the PRC, but it was actively involved in supporting the Tibetan guerrillas in their fight against the PRC, supplying them with weapons and providing training.[317] The Dalai Lama's brother Gyalo Dondrub – the so-called 'spymaster of Lhasa'[318] – was good friends with General Chiang Kai-Shek[319], the first leader of the ROC, and had married a daughter of one of Chiang Kai-Shek's senior generals[320]. Given that they were allies with close connections at the highest levels of government, why were ordinary Tibetans not allowed to associate with the ROC in Taiwan?

A clue may come from the Dalai Lama's own official visits to Taiwan. According to reports the Dalai Lama's visit in 1997 raised NT$17 million (New Taiwan dollars) in donations, and his next visit a further NT$15 million.[321] Who knows how much money had previously reached the Dalai Lama's coffers from this wealthy nation? With no competition to their fundraising efforts, for years the vast wealth of the ROC in Taiwan could be exclusively tapped by the Dalai Lama's family. No other Tibetan could gain access to this wealth without having their reputation destroyed by the Tibetan exile government.

THE DALAI LAMA'S FASCINATION WITH WAR AND NAZISM

Renowned as a champion of non-violence, the Dalai Lama revealed a shocking side to himself in an interview with the *New York Times* in 1993:

> 'Dalai Lama: War – without an army, killing as few people as possible – is acceptable ...
>
> 'New York Times: Did you say that killing sometimes is acceptable?
>
> 'Dalai Lama: Comparatively.'[322]

Later in the interview, he is asked what he does to relax. The reply is astonishing.

> 'Dalai Lama: I am fond of looking at picture books of the Second World War. I own some, which I believe are produced by *Time-Life*. I've just ordered a new set. Thirty books. ... I find many of the machines of violence very attractive. Tanks, airplanes, warships, especially aircraft carriers. And the German U-boats, submarines. . . .'[323]

The Dalai Lama had plenty of opportunity to find out about the military machinery of the Nazi regime; as a child he was under the tutelage of Heinrich Harrer – a former sergeant in the SS, Hitler's most loyal soldiers – who for some years in Tibet before the Chinese occupation taught the young Dalai Lama about the outside world.[324] Heinrich Harrer enjoyed the fame his book *Seven Years in Tibet* gave him but concealed his Nazi past. When Disney made a film version of the book, journalists uncovered his dark secrets. Harrer played down his role in the SS, but Gerald Lehner's book *Between Hitler and the Himalayas: Heinrich Harrer's Memory Lapses* provides a much more complete version of events.[325]

Indeed throughout his life the Dalai Lama has had close associations with many Nazis, including Bruno Beger, who was convicted for his 'scientific research' at Auschwitz[326]; and Miguel Serrano, head of the Nazi Party in Chile and the author of several books that elevate Hitler to a god-like status[327].

Despite his supposed omniscience, the Dalai Lama could be forgiven for not knowing the perverted views of these people when he first met them, as each tried to hide their dark pasts. But even once they had been exposed, the Dalai Lama didn't distance himself from them or their views.

For example, while working as a Chilean ambassador, Miguel Serrano kept silent about his view of Hitler as a god on earth, but even after he published books expounding his views in 1978, the Dalai Lama maintained a close personal friendship, having private meetings with him in 1984 and 1992.[328]

In 2006 and 2007, the Dalai Lama publicly gave Jorg Haider his blessings with a ceremonial white scarf (Katag). Haider had been the leader of the Far-Right Austrian Freedom Party (FPÖ), and known for publicly airing his appreciation of the policies of Nazi Germany. So much so that when his party was brought in to form a coalition government in Austria the European Union imposed a diplomatic boycott on Austria because of the FPÖ's extreme views.[329]

So, how deep does the Dalai Lama's appreciation of the Nazi regime go? The German *Stern* magazine reports some comments he made at a teaching in Nuremberg (the site of the major Nazi party rallies in the 1930s) in 2008:

> 'The Dalai Lama greeted the crowds with his lovely child-like waving of hands. But his speech in the town hall made people gasp, ...
>
> 'He recalled seeing Nuremberg on photographs when he was still a child. "Very attractive" with "generals and weapons" and with "Adolf Hitler and Hermann Goering".
>
> 'Some of the listeners seemed to be embarrassed, some were "alienated for a second". Nuremberg's chief mayor Ulrich Maly called it a "moment of shock".'[330]

Stern reflected that:

> '... the Tibetan court used to have close ties with the Nazi regime, SS-expeditions were welcomed to Lhasa with full mark of respect. To this day, His Holiness has never distanced himself from these inglorious relationships.'[331]

The Friendship with Shoko Asahara

Shoko Asahara, the leader of the Japanese AUM Cult, claimed to have attained enlightenment in the Himalayas in 1986. In the following year he visited the Dalai Lama in Dharamsala, the first of at least five such meetings.[332] Russell Skelton reporting in the *Sydney Morning Herald* writes that:

> '... [Asahara] repeatedly claimed the Dalai Lama gave him a divine mission to spread "real Buddhism" in Japan. He said the Tibetan leader had told him he was ideal for the mission because he had the "mind of a Buddha".'[333]

According to the Dalai Lama's representative in Japan, Karma Gelek Yuthok, Asahara made financial donations to the Dalai Lama from 1988 onwards. Over the next four years these were to amount to over $2 million, in an attempt to win over the Dalai Lama's 'favor and endorsement'.[334]

It is clear that Asahara's financial largesse to the Tibetan cause was successful. The Dalai Lama helped Asahara by writing letters of 'recommendation guaranteeing that Aum Shinrikyo was a sect that raised public awareness through religion and social activity and promoted social kindness through religious teaching and yoga exercises.' As the German magazine *Focus* also comments, the Dalai Lama 'served as Shoko's guarantor for tax-exemption while Shoko used tax-exempt funds to produce lethal gases'.[335]

Russell Skelton also says, 'Posters depicting Asahara and the Dalai Lama and carrying the Tibetan leader's endorsement were used extensively in cult promotions.'[336] It is also clear that in the minds of many Japanese the Dalai Lama's endorsement was a powerful incentive to believe in Asahara.

The Dalai Lama visited Tokyo a month after the cult released lethal gas into the city's subway system. Shoko Asahara was standing trial for the attack that killed eleven people and left nearly 4,000 suffering the effects of sarin nerve gas. He was also facing seventeen further charges of murder, attempted murder, abduction and the production of illegal chemical and biological weapons. At that time the Dalai Lama said of Asahara, 'I consider him as my friend, but not necessarily a perfect one.'[337]

As mentioned earlier, Palden Gyal writing in Tibetan News spoke of this scandal in relation to freedom of the press within the Tibetan community:

> 'In May 1995, [the only independent Tibetan newspaper, *Democracy*] published a piece about Shoko Asahara, the Japanese cult leader, highlighting the fact that he had been friends with the Dalai Lama before being accused of killing eleven people in a nerve gas attack on the Tokyo Subway. The article suggested that perhaps the government should be careful about who it conducted relations with in the future. Not long after that, in March 1996, the newspaper ceased publication.'[338]

Incitements to Murder

In August 1996, a group calling itself 'The Secret Society of Eliminators of the External and Internal Enemies of Tibet' made public its death threats against the two young incarnations of highly realized Tibetan masters:

> 'Anyone who goes against the policy of the government must be singled out, opposed and given the death penalty ... As for the reincarnations of Trijang [the Dalai Lama's own Spiritual Guide] and Zong Rinpoche [another great Tibetan spiritual master of the Gelug Tradition], if they do not stop practising Dolgyal and continue to contradict the word of H.H. the Dalai Lama, not only will we not be able to respect them, but their life activities will suffer destruction. This is our first warning.'[339]

These two young incarnate lamas were subsequently forced into hiding.

In an interview with the Dalai Lama appearing in the November 1997 issue of the American magazine *Mother Jones*, Robert Thurman asked the Dalai Lama:

> 'The loss of your own nation to China has been used as an example of the futility of non-violence and tolerance. When is something worth fighting for?'

In his reply the Dalai Lama said:

> '... if the situation was such that there was only one learned lama or genuine practitioner alive, a person whose death would cause the whole of Tibet to lose all hope of keeping its Buddhist way of life, then it is conceivable that in order to protect that one person it might be justified for one or ten enemies to be eliminated—if there was no other way.'[340]

Following the Dalai Lama's words 'for one or ten enemies to be eliminated', and mistakenly believing that Shugden practitioners worked with the Chinese authorities, in February 1998 posters of the 'Ten Most Hated Enemies of the Dalai Lama and Tibet' were circulated throughout Tibetan settlements in India and Nepal. Prepared by the Research and Analysis Wing of the Department of Security of the Tibetan exile government, they were complete with photographs and biographical information, and encouraged Tibetan people to kill these ten innocent Dorje Shugden practitioners. Since first published, this list has been distributed to Tibetan communities throughout the world.

The ten individuals listed included highly respected spiritual masters, both in the Tibetan settlements and in the West, and they had been so identified only because they openly encourage the practice of Dorje Shugden.[341]

The individuals identified in the posters were listed in the following order:

> 1. Geshe Kelsang Gyatso Rinpoche [Founder and Spiritual Director of the New Kadampa Tradition – International Kadampa Buddhist Union], which has over 1,100 Buddhist Centres and branches worldwide. He is the author of twenty authoritative and highly acclaimed books on Buddhism covering every aspect of the path to enlightenment.]

2. Geshe Dragpa Gyaltsen (Chime Tsering) [General Secretary of the Dorje Shugden Society in Delhi, India].
3. Lama Gangchen Tulku Trinlay Yorphel Rinpoche [Spiritual Director of Gangchen Kunphen Ling Buddhist centres throughout the world].
4. Gen Chatring Jampel Yeshe [President of the Dorje Shugden Society in Delhi, India].
5. Lama Serkong Tritul Rinpoche [Abbot of the Gelugpa Buddhist Centre in Singapore and of the Chinese Gelugpa Society in Taiwan].
6. Tseten Gyurme [a well known supporter of Dorje Shugden practitioners].
7. Tenzin Chodak [a Dorje Shugden practitioner living in the UK, who spoke out against the ban at demonstrations in London in 1996].
8. Dr. Losang Thubten [a scholar who advises the Dorje Shugden Society, and who had already been attacked and severely injured, on November 7th 1996].
9. Geshe Konchog Gyaltsen [Vice-President of the Dorje Shugden Society in Delhi, India].
10. Kundeling Lama Losang Yeshe Rinpoche [Abbot and Founder of Atisha Charitable Trust and Monastery in Bangalore, India and Spiritual Director of Buddhist centres in Italy and the Netherlands].

With regard to this issue, the Western Shugden Society holds that by publishing this list the Dalai Lama and his ministers have given explicit encouragement to Tibetan people to kill the 'one or ten enemies' listed; and declares that if in the future any of these ten people is killed then the Western Shugden Society will automatically recognize the principal perpetrator to be the Dalai Lama himself and will pursue necessary investigative and legal action to ensure his eventual conviction under criminal law.

HOW DID THE DALAI LAMA ACHIEVE THE NOBEL PEACE PRIZE?

In December 1989 the Fourteenth Dalai Lama was awarded the Nobel Peace Prize. Having been awarded to terrorists and war-makers before, the Nobel Peace Prize is no stranger to controversy – even Hitler, Mussolini and Stalin are among previous nominees for the prize![342] In his presentation speech to the Fourteenth Dalai Lama, Egil Aarvik said:

> 'This year's Nobel Peace Prize has been awarded ... first and foremost for his consistent resistance to the use of violence in his people's struggle to regain their liberty. ...
>
> 'This is by no means the first community of exiles in the world, but it is assuredly the first and only one that has not set up any militant liberation movement.'[343]

Was he unaware that the Dalai Lama had spoken since 1961 of the Tibetan guerrillas that were waging war on the People's Liberation Army?[344] Had he not read any of the accounts of the Tibetan guerrilla war that were in wide circulation, such as Jamyang Norbu's *Warriors of Tibet* – a book commissioned by the Tibetan exile government itself?[345]

Given that Tibetan 'non-violence' is merely a facade, why was the Dalai Lama awarded the prize? Tom Grunfeld says:

> 'Everything having to do with Tibet is subject to mythologizing. That the Dalai Lama was awarded the Nobel Peace Prize for his efforts on behalf of Tibetan independence is one of these myths.'[346]

According to the *New York Times*, the prize was awarded to the Dalai Lama 'largely because of the brutal suppression of the democracy movement in China and the international outrage that followed.'[347] A source close to the Norwegian Nobel Committee revealed:

> 'the choice of the Dalai Lama, was an attempt both to influence events in China and to recognize the efforts of student

> leaders of the [Chinese] democracy movement, which was crushed by Chinese troops in June.'[348]

In addition to criticising the Chinese by implication, awarding the prize to the Dalai Lama was an explicit attempt by the committee to atone for what is widely considered to be its greatest embarrassment: failing to award Mahatma Gandhi the Nobel Peace Prize, despite his having been nominated five times![349] As Egil Aarvik said in the presentation speech:

> 'The Dalai Lama likes to consider himself one of Gandhi's successors. People have occasionally wondered why Gandhi himself was never awarded the Nobel Peace Prize, and the present Nobel Committee can with impunity share this surprise, while regarding this year's award of the prize as in part a tribute to the memory of Mahatma Gandhi.'[350]

The Nobel Peace Prize is considered by some to be the easiest Nobel Prize to win because no actual achievement needs to be demonstrated. What the Dalai Lama has clearly achieved, though, is to deceive the world utterly as to his real nature and intentions. By awarding him the Peace Prize the Nobel Committee has helped him to continue to dupe the world.

CHAPTER 12

Judging the Dalai Lama by his Actions

WHAT HAS THE DALAI LAMA ACHIEVED?

The Fourteenth Dalai Lama moves with impunity through his many roles as politician and religious leader. When he does something wrong as a politician, he is excused as a religious leader; and when he does something wrong as a religious leader, he is excused as needing to act as a politician. It seems that no one can 'pin him down'; no one can blame him for anything and he is able to get away with whatever he likes.

With a role for every occasion – holy man, politician, international statesman, simple monk, pop icon, Buddhist Pope, socialist, movie star, autocrat, democrat, Marxist, humanitarian, environmentalist, Nobel Peace prize winner, nationalist, Buddha of Compassion, communist, God-King – the Dalai Lama weaves a complex web of religion and politics that entraps his audiences wherever he goes. Nobody has ever seen anything like it. People are easily swayed by the historical mystique of Tibet and its 'God-King', and feel captivated and convinced by his charm.

Wearing the robes of a monk and using the Buddha's profound words, the Dalai Lama has presumed to teach the world how to accomplish all of the things that he has in fact failed to achieve himself. Through words alone, and a vast and very expensive publicity machine, the Dalai Lama has established for himself the position of a 'God-King' in the minds of most people of the world. But behind the rhetoric, the public image and the charisma that has dazzled the world is someone who has failed repeatedly.

> 'It's not clear what practical benefit Tibetans in Tibet have received from the Dalai Lama's activities abroad, though. Arguably, they have made their plight worse. The Dalai Lama's main achievement has been to turn himself into an international celebrity, a status that ironically is dependent on the continued subjugation of Tibet.'[351]

If we look behind the charisma, the antics and charm of the Dalai Lama, behind the illusion and the calculated deception that he has been working all these years for an independent Tibet, and we ask, 'What has the Dalai Lama actually done for Tibet?', the answer is 'Nothing'. Actually it is worse than nothing, because he has given up Tibet, he has lost Tibet totally.

If we ask, 'What has the Dalai Lama done for world peace, for the environment, for human rights and religious freedom?', the things he constantly talks about, the answer is again 'Nothing'. We cannot point to an acre of earth anywhere in the world that the Dalai Lama has rescued from deforestation, strip-mining, exhaustive agriculture or contamination. The Dalai Lama talks about world peace, human rights and religious freedom, but except for the prizes and awards he personally has received, we cannot point to a single achievement in any of these areas that has been accomplished through his own efforts. In fact, through his violation and abuse of human rights and religious freedom he contributes directly to conflict and disharmony in the world.

If we look behind the Dalai Lama's attacks against so-called 'fundamentalists' and 'sectarians' we find to the contrary that he himself is in fact destroying the peace, harmony and happiness of his own faithful community, and of other Buddhist practitioners around the world. If we look behind the Dalai Lama's call for harmony and unity among the four Tibetan Buddhist traditions, we find a plan through which he is actually destroying the four traditions, thus securing for himself a position of prime power and influence in the event of his return to Tibet.

After so many years in exile, the Dalai Lama stands in the wake of a series of international and domestic political failures that has produced deep crisis and division within the Tibetan exile community and now threatens the Buddhist community worldwide. He has created nothing but problems for the Tibetan people he claims to represent including vicious discrimination against innocent religious practitioners. In the international sphere, we see a political leader who has been overwhelmed and marginalised, not so much by the course of history but as a result of his own political views, misjudgements and mistakes.

The Dalai Lama has not been able to do anything to reverse Beijing's integrationist policy in Tibet, the prospects for the exiled Tibetans' return to Tibet are as remote as ever, negotiations with the Chinese are in deadlock, and there is no inclination amongst the world's governments to recognise Tibet as an independent state. The Dalai Lama has become a world-famous figure, but has failed to gain anything concrete for his people.

The Dalai Lama's endorsement of Marxist ideas and praise of Mao Zedong's activities clearly shows that he does not like democracy or wish to share his power with other people. On the other hand he does not like the present Chinese government. In his own newspaper *Sheja* he is always criticising the Chinese government, calling them 'ten-dra China', or 'China, enemy of Buddha's doctrine'.

The main reason why he continually criticises the Chinese is that at present Tibet is controlled by the Chinese, and he wants to take back the power and control for himself. For this reason he devised a scheme: to regain his power and position he told the Chinese that though he accepted the loss of Tibetan independence he nevertheless wanted autonomy, which would give him alone sole control of Tibet.

He applied effort to achieve this for many years, but when he finally realized that his scheme was not working and that the Chinese would not fulfil his wishes he became frustrated and began organising international demonstrations whose violent nature disturbed people in many countries. Through this we can see the Dalai Lama's hypocritical behaviour and selfish nature: he is not concerned with the future of Tibet but only with his own position and power. He received the Nobel Peace Prize, apparently indicating that he is a peacemaker, but in truth he is a troublemaker who has destroyed the hitherto unquestioned trust, peace and harmony within Tibetan communities throughout the world.

As a direct result of the Dalai Lama's disastrous domestic policies and inflammatory speech, the Tibetan community is deeply and even violently divided against itself on an increasing number of critical issues. These include: (1) the Dalai Lama's unilateral decision to drop the aim of Tibetan independence, without consultation with government or the Tibetan people; (2) his failure to fulfil his avowed commitment to democratise the Tibetan government; (3) his acquiescence in, or even instigation of, press censorship and the repression of freedom of expression; (4) his ruthless suppression of freedom of religion through banning the practice of Dorje Shugden; and (5) his sanctioning or instigation of many violations and abuses of human rights, including threats, coercion, intimidation, excommunication, physical violence and even murder.

There are many causes of the Dalai Lama's failures to achieve anything substantial for the Tibetan people, including his own political-ideological views and attitudes, his incompetence as 'head of state', the dubious role played by the Nechung oracle and the participation of the Dalai Lama's immediate family in the generation and execution of government policy.

But the fundamental factor underlying the present crisis lies within the very nature and function of the Dalai Lama's Tibetan government as a feudal theocratic system – with its endemic mixing of religion and politics, its translation of religious ideas into government policy, its deep confusion over the roles of religious leader and head of state, and its retrogressive view of the position of the Dalai Lama as the 'God-King' of Tibet.

After fifty years, we do not see in this Dalai Lama a 'God-King', a saviour, or even a wise statesman skilfully shaping the destiny of his country and its people through a difficult time. What we see instead is a desperate and cynically self-seeking man who has precipitated the greatest catastrophe in Tibetan history.

With these points in mind, we should note John Goetz's remark in the conclusion of his article, 'On the Outs with the Dalai Lama':

> 'The tragedy of Tibet is not only the brutal Chinese occupation but also the desperation that has led so many to believe that return to the Dalai Lama is the only alternative.'[352]

'FREE TIBET' - WHERE HAS ALL THE MONEY GONE?

For decades, support groups and organisations throughout the West have been raising funds for a 'Free Tibet'. From government donations to sale of buttons, bumper-stickers, bags and hats through organising concerts, dinners and exhibitions; and through every other imaginable fund-raising device, these organisations continue to raise a vast amount of money for what most western benefactors believe is the goal of a free, independent Tibet.

In his article *Selling Tibet to the World* printed on 5 June 2008, Michael Backman reported:

> 'GUCCI, iPod, Facebook, Tibet – these are among the world's hot brands, for which brand integrity is everything.
>
> 'Tibet, as a brand, works particularly well. It brings in millions, and Hollywood A-listers queue to endorse it. What's more, they do it for free. Creative director and brand chief executive, the Dalai Lama, will visit Australia again next week. He will preside over a five-day Tibetan prayer instruction course in Sydney. A company has been set up to handle the visit – Dalai Lama in Australia Limited.
>
> 'Tickets for the event can be bought online even from *The Age*'s own Box Office website along with tickets for Bjorn Again and The Pink Floyd Experience. But few are as expensive as the Dalai Lama experience, with tickets ranging from $800 for front seats to $450 for seats at the back. Tickets for good seats for the Sunday session alone are $248. Lunch is extra – between $18 and $27 for a pre-ordered lunch box. A clothing range has even been created. There are polo shirts, baseball caps - even men's muscle tees emblazoned with the endless Buddhist knot. From street chic to urban cool, baby, this monk has funk.

> 'Saving Tibet, like Saving Private Ryan, is a good earner. Everyone's into it, even China. Back in April, a factory in China's Guangdong province was exposed as one of the manufacturers of the Free Tibet flags so prominent in the anti-Olympic torch protests in Britain, France and the US. The factory workers claimed they had no idea what the colourful flags represented. Blame China's state-controlled media for that.'[353]

In addition, every Tibetan, whether male or female, infant, infirm or old, and whether living in the East or West, is expected to pay an 'independence-tax' to the Tibetan exile government. A record of these payments is kept in the 'Green Book' that every Tibetan is expected to carry. This book is essential for Tibetans in India wanting a permit for travel outside India; and those who do not pay lose benefits and services, and are often ostracised, risking persecution and exile from their own community.[354] The Dalai Lama's government also receives large donations from other sources including national governments, private individuals of many countries, philanthropic institutions, businesses and many other types of organizations (including the Japanese Aum cult, as already documented).

The funds collected from the 'independence-tax' and all these other fund-raising activities are not used for the support or relief of the Tibetan community. Most of the funds for the relief of refugees, for the orphaned, for education, for medical care and hospitals, are obtained directly from the Indian government, from the major worldwide relief agencies, western governments and private charitable trusts.[355] This funding includes $1.7 million a year from the United States CIA.[356]

In this regard Grunfeld says:

> 'One of the major sources of political power for the Dalai Lama is his ability to control relief funds, educational scholarships, and the hiring of Tibetan teachers and bureaucrats. These powers only continue as long as there are many stateless refugees. Consequently, it is to the benefit of the leadership to

> keep Tibetans in children's homes, transit camps and temporary facilities—not unlike the situation among the Palestinian refugees.'[357]

There has been widespread corruption and mismanagement of relief funds by the Tibetan administration.[358] A case in point is the nursery administered by the Dalai Lama's late sister, Tsering Dolma. Grunfeld notes:

> '...while the children in her care were frequently on the verge of starvation, she was noted for her formal twelve-course luncheons. Meanwhile, in bitterly cold weather the children were clad in thin, sleeveless cotton frocks—though when VIPs visit the Upper Nursery, every child there is dressed warmly in tweeds, wool, heavy socks, and strong boots.'[359]

The amount of money raised for the Tibetan causes over the last few decades – which most contributors in the West have been led to believe is for a free Tibet – probably runs into hundreds of millions, if not billions, of dollars. If these funds are not being used in the support or relief of the exiled Tibetan community, or for a free, independent Tibet (because the Dalai Lama stopped aiming for this as early as the 1980s), then what is this money being collected for? How much money has been collected? And where is all this money being kept? These are questions to which many benefactors, including national governments around the world, should demand answers.

The author, Michael Backman did ask these questions, and reported:

> 'Little is known about the government-in-exile's finances. I did contact its Department of Finance in Dharamsala with a series of questions about how it funds itself and expenditure. I was sent a series of spreadsheets in reply.
>
> 'The government-in-exile claims that its total budget for 2002-03 amounted to the equivalent of US$22.028 million. The budget was spent on various programs such as health, education, religion and culture. The biggest item was for

> "political-related expenditure" at US$7 million. The next biggest was administration, which runs to US$4.5 million. Around US$1.8 million was allocated to running the government-in-exile's offices of Tibet overseas.
>
> 'For all that the government-in-exile claims to do, these sums appear too low. Nor is it clear how donations enter its budgeting. These are likely to run to many millions but there is no explicit acknowledgment of them or their sources.'[360]

After making this report Michael Backman received anonymous death threats.[361]

WHO IS THE REAL DALAI LAMA?

Who, after all, is the Dalai Lama, the mythical 'God-King of Shangri-la'? In the 1920s after her fifteen-year sojourn in Tibet, the writer and explorer Alexandra 'David-Néel' wrote:

> '… these writers, men who not only had never set foot on Tibetan soil but who possessed no reliable information as to its inhabitants, have indulged in fables utterly without foundation. Some represented the Dalai Lama as one who understood and spoke every language on earth. Others peremptorily asserted that he was the 'pope' of all Buddhists. Others again, spoke of him as a magician usually engaged in working miracles of the most fantastic nature, while some imagined his palace of Potala to be a kind of 'holy of holies', inaccessible to the profane and peopled with supermen, hierophants, guardians of dreaded mysteries. All of this is pure fancy. The Dalai Lama is pre-eminently a temporal sovereign: the autocrat-monarch of Tibet.'[362]

And as a journalist recently reported, the same fantastic notions of the Dalai Lama still exist:

> 'The state of denial in the West about some of the Dalai Lama's alleged power-tripping, or at least the unquestioning attitude

> towards the Dalai Lama and everything that he does, highlights the role that he plays for many Western celebs, commentators and politicians today: he's a cartoon 'good guy', giggling, pure and righteous, who apparently should be unconditionally applauded for standing up to the 'Evil Chinese'. All of the Dalai Lama's bad points – his origins in the stifling medievalism of 1930s Tibet; his archaic practices; his disregard for 'concepts like democracy and freedom of religion'; his backing from the CIA in its Cold War with the Chinese – are simply ignored, as His Holiness is invited to guest-edit French *Vogue*, attend charity auctions with Sharon Stone, and rub shoulders with Richard Gere. Pema shows me the *Independent on Sunday*, published the day before we met, which has a feature about the Dalai Lama 'charming the West'. There are around 12 photos showing him meeting celebrities and other do-gooders. Yet in two of the photos, it isn't the Dalai Lama at all; it's a different Lama. Maybe these Tibetans all look the same to British picture editors.
>
> ' "He's just a photograph and a symbol to many people in the West", says Pema.'[363]

For over 360 years, it has not been really certain which or for that matter whether any of the occupants of the Potala, was a real Dalai Lama, a real reincarnation of Gendun Drub, including the present Dalai Lama. But whether or not the present Dalai Lama is the real Dalai Lama – a true embodiment of Buddha's compassion – should be judged not on the Dalai Lama's words or on the mystique surrounding his position, but by his actions. And on the evidence presented in this book the Dalai Lama's actions have fallen short of even ordinary standards of decent behaviour let alone the enlightened actions of a Buddha.

Broadly speaking, this book has considered three kinds of actions of the current Dalai Lama: (1) deceptive actions; (2) unethical or non-virtuous actions; and (3) actions of violence and persecution.

Many of these actions constitute major or minor transgressions of the Dalai Lama's three sets of Buddhist vows (Pratimoksha, Bodhisattva and Tantric). Because he has incurred root downfalls in all three sets, he has lost all three levels of ordination. As he has broken his monastic vows, the Dalai Lama is actually no longer a monk, although he continues to dress like one.

Examples of some of the Dalai Lama's direct and indirect actions are summarised below to illustrate each of the categories and sub-categories.

Deceptive actions:

1. Advocating human rights and religious freedom, while engaged in systematic violation and abuse of human rights and religious freedom.
2. Advocating democratic government, values and principles, while operating a repressive autocratic theocracy in Dharamsala and holding a Marxist-communist ideology.
3. Deceiving Tibetan communities into thinking that he is working for a return to a free, independent Tibet, and collecting an 'independence-tax' from every Tibetan for decades for the purpose, having already unilaterally abandoned the idea of Tibetan independence over fifteen years ago.
4. Deceiving the West into thinking that he is working for Tibetan independence, and collecting vast sums of money through 'Free Tibet' concerts, banquets and other fund-raising sources for this purpose.
5. Including deceptions and lies within his writings such as his autobiography and the biographical film on his life, *Kundun* (in which he played a major role in directing), specifically concerning:
    i. The nature of the Tibetan Rebellion as a popular reaction of the masses against atrocities of the Chinese;
    ii. His commitment to working with the Chinese in the development of Tibet under communism, and the extent of his support and advocacy of Chinese communism;
    iii. The extent of the killing of Tibetans by the Chinese, and of their destruction of the Norbulingka Palace; Potala and city of Lhasa at the time of his escape;

   iv. The nature and organization of the escape to India, including which oracle was consulted before his escape to India.
6. Lying and deceiving others as to the reasons for banning the practice of Dorje Shugden, through numerous Tibetan exile government statements, and for orchestrating a campaign of propaganda and slander against Dorje Shugden practitioners.
7. Denying having imposed a ban on Dorje Shugden practice, while at the same time ruthlessly implementing such a ban in the lay and monastic Tibetan communities worldwide.
8. Claiming to be creating harmony, unity and non-sectarianism within the four Tibetan Buddhist traditions, while actually dividing Tibetan society, creating deep schisms within the four traditions and systematically trying to destroy them.
9. Claiming to be the Fourteenth Dalai Lama and to be within the lineage of the Fifth and Thirteen Dalai Lamas when actually he is not.

Unethical or non-virtuous actions

1. Complicity in actions of violence, slander, coercion and intimidation.
2. Complicity in illegal arms trading; and in a conspiracy to overthrow the government of Bhutan, that would have involved assassination.

Actions of Violence and Persecution

The Fourteenth Dalai Lama's activities of physical, verbal, social and religious violence and persecution, carried out directly and indirectly, by edict, threat, coercion and blackmail, by slander and propaganda, by excommunication and banishment, have been well documented above. Many of these actions, in addition to being the most serious transgressions of the moral discipline of an ordained person, also involve civil and constitutional illegalities. Most of them are also gross abuses of human rights and religious freedom.

In these and many other ways, the Fourteenth Dalai Lama has been deceiving the world, and causing suffering and problems.

In democratic countries, Presidents and Prime Ministers are held accountable for the actions of their ministers, their governments and the politicians and political parties that support them. In the same way the Dalai Lama bears direct or indirect responsibility for all of these actions because they were carried out by him personally or on his behalf. He, and he alone, should be held to account for these actions and for their consequences.

APPENDIX 1

1959 Correspondence between the Dalai Lama and General Tan Kuan-san

The release of the Hollywood movie Kundun in 1997 sparked fresh interest in the uprising of March 1959 and the Dalai Lama's epic escape from Tibet. Speaking of these events, an article in *George Magazine* says:

> 'The operation was guided by CIA director Allen Dulles, whose wartime experience with anti-Nazi resistance movements inspired the Tibetan covert war. But the mission's success hinged upon a case officer ... [who] was still in his 30s when he and Gyalo Thondup, one of the Dalai Lama's brothers, planned the spiritual leader's flight.'[364]

To rally the people of Lhasa around the rebels, a rumour was deliberately circulated that the Chinese were about to kidnap or even kill their precious leader. The perfect opportunity to promote the rumour arose because the Dalai Lama agreed to attend a theatrical performance at the camp of the Chinese Military Command on a specified date. Grunfeld comments on this invitation:

> 'China ... emphatically denies that the Dalai Lama was coerced in any way to set that date. Beijing has maintained, in fact, that it was the Dalai [sic] who set the date and, indeed, had done so *one month earlier* [italics by Grunfeld]. For years this claim was roundly ridiculed as "communist lies and propaganda" until Dawa Norbu publicly acknowledged that a former Tibetan official had confided in him that the Chinese account was correct. When confronted with this contradiction in 1981

> the Dalai Lama admitted that his original story was incorrect, agreeing that he had selected the date several weeks prior to the event.'[365]

At the time, the rumour that the Dalai Lama's life was threatened spread like wildfire. On 10 March 1959, between ten and thirty thousand Tibetans, together with the entire Tibetan army, converged on the Norbulingka – the 300-year-old summer palace where the Dalai Lama was residing.[366]

The atmosphere was highly charged as the people assembled to thwart the feared Chinese plot. A Tibetan monastic official who arrived at the palace to defuse the situation was stoned to death. After reassurances from the Dalai Lama that he would not visit the camp of the PLA (People's Liberation Army) the crowd partially dispersed. However, that evening a meeting of rebel leaders and seventy members of the Tibetan government was held outside the palace to support a resolution declaring that Tibet no longer recognized China's authority, thus repudiating the 'Seventeen-Point Agreement', and calling for the expulsion of the Chinese from Tibet.[367]

The rebels posted guards around the palace and told ministers they would not be allowed to leave. They also erected barricades north of Lhasa on the main road to China. Realizing the incendiary nature of their proclamation the Dalai Lama called a meeting with the seventy rebel members of his government.[368]

> 'He told them that General Tan had not compelled him to accept his invitation [to the theatrical performance]. He had in fact been consulted and given his consent before the invitation was formally issued. He assured them he was in no personal danger from the Chinese. They agreed it was impossible to disobey his orders but ignored them just the same.'[369]

The image of a beleaguered Dalai Lama, a virtual prisoner of the rebels, is reflected in a remarkable series of letters between him and the Chinese General Tan Kuan-san. At first it was assumed that the letters:

'... could not be anything but the cleverest of forgeries. This rush to judgment caused considerable embarrassment when China published photocopies of the letters, half of them in the Dalai's [sic] handwriting, whereupon the cleric was obliged to verify their authenticity.[370]

After hearing that the Dalai Lama could not leave the Norbulingka to attend the theatrical performance in the Chinese camp, the Chinese commander wrote to him that day, March 10th:

'Respected Dalai Lama,

'It is very good indeed that you wanted to come to the Military Area Command. You are heartily welcome. But since the intrigues and provocations of the reactionaries have caused you very great difficulties, it may be advisable that for the time being you do not come.

'Salutations and best regards,

'Tan Kuan-san'[371]

The Dalai Lama replied on March 11th:

'Dear Comrade Political Commissar Tan,

'I intended to go to the Military Area Command to see the theatrical performance yesterday, but I was unable to do so, because of obstruction by people, lamas and laymen, who were instigated by a few evil elements and who did not know the facts; this has put me to indescribable shame. I am greatly upset and worried and at a loss what to do. I was immediately greatly delighted when your letter appeared before me—you do not mind at all.

'Reactionary, evil elements are carrying out activities endangering me under the pretext of ensuring my safety. I am taking measures to calm things down. In a few days, when the situation becomes stable, I will certainly meet you. If you have any internal directives for me, please communicate them to me frankly through this messenger.

'The Dalai Lama,

'written by my own hand.'[372]

In response to the rebels putting up fortifications and posting large numbers of guerrillas with machine guns along the national highway, General Tan wrote to the Dalai Lama later that day, March 11th, explaining that the Chinese forces had asked the rebels to withdraw from the highway immediately or face the consequences.[373]

In his reply dated March 12th the Dalai Lama wrote:

> '... The unlawful activities of the reactionary clique cause me endless worry and sorrow. Yesterday I told the kasa [Kashag, or Tibetan Cabinet] to order the immediate dissolution of the illegal conference [of the underground Tibetan resistance movement] and the immediate withdrawal of the reactionaries who arrogantly moved into the Norbulingka under the pretext of protecting me. As to the incidents of yesterday and the day before, which were brought about under the pretext of ensuring my safety and have seriously estranged relations between the Central People's Government and the Local Government, I am making every possible effort to deal with them.'[374]

In his reply on March 15th General Tan wrote:

> '... We are very much concerned about your present situation and safety. If you think it necessary and possible to extricate yourself from your present dangerous position of being held by the traitors, we cordially welcome you and your entourage to come and stay for a short time in the Military Area Command. We are willing to assume full responsibility for your safety. As to what is the best course to follow, it is entirely up to you to decide.'[375]

On March 16th the Dalai Lama wrote his third and last letter to the General:

> 'Dear Comrade Political Commissar Tan,
>
> 'Your letter dated the 15th has just been received at three o'clock. I am very glad that you are so concerned about my safety and hereby express my thanks.

'The day before yesterday, the fifth day of the second month according to the Tibetan calendar, I made a speech to more than seventy representatives of the government officials, instructing them from various angles, calling on them to consider present and long-term interests and to calm down, otherwise my life would be in danger. After these severe reproaches, things took a slight turn for the better. Though the conditions here and outside are still very difficult to handle at present, I am trying tactfully to draw a line separating the progressive people among the government officials from those opposing the revolution. In a few days from now, when there are enough forces I can trust, I shall make my way to the Military Area Command. When that time comes, I shall first send you a letter. I request you to adopt reliable measures. What are your views? Please write me often.

'The Dalai Lama'[376]

APPENDIX 2

The Mongoose-Canine Letter

This anonymous letter was given by Tibetan people to an English woman now living in Italy while she was travelling in Nepal in September 1995. Much of this information is widely known within the Tibetan Community in India and Nepal.

This is a letter called the 'Mongoose-Canine' sent to H.H. Dalai Lama

'Your Holiness, in 1959 your country was invaded by the communist Chinese army. You and about 90,000 Tibetans had to flee to India, Nepal and Bhutan. At that time you began to take the main responsibility for Tibet. Looking at what happened from then until now, Tibetan refugees have received aid from the Red Cross and India. They were given land to settle down. The Tibetans have survived and they have managed to become quite well off and have a comfortable life.

'Your Holiness, you are the one who established the exile government. Therefore, I want to mention what has been going on under your rule:

'1. The problem of Dujom Rinpoche (the spiritual leader of the Nyingma tradition) caused by the jealousy of your government: your government made the Indian government accuse Dujom Rinpoche of being a Chinese spy and have him arrested in 1963 in Siliguri, after he had given an impressive religious teaching in Kalimpong.

'2. The problem of thirteen Tibetan settlements uniting against your exile government: In connection with the events regarding Dujom Rinpoche and others, thirteen Tibetan settlements united against your exile government in Dharamsala from 1964 until 1981.

'3. The problem of your government splitting the Tibetan guerrilla fighters in Mustang. In fact, they were originally organised by your government with the help of the CIA. In 1969, as a consequence of Nixon's policy with China, you provoked a fight among the Tibetan guerrillas over their weapons. This fight finally destroyed them.

'4. The problem of Mr. Alo Choedzoe connected with your economics minister. Your government cheated Mr. Choedzoe's factory.

'5. The problem of your government assassinating (Mr.) Gongtang (Tsultrim) in 1975. He was the leader of the thirteen groups.

'6. The problem regarding the late Gyalwa Karmapa Rigpay Dorje (the spiritual leader of the Kagyu tradition) because of his influence and the fact that the thirteen groups had appointed him as their spiritual leader.

'7. The problem regarding the misunderstanding between you and your tutor Yongdzin Trijang Rinpoche (one of the principal Spiritual Guides of the Gelug tradition) because of your brother's slandering.

'8. The problem with the Tibetan-Mongolian Association in Taiwan. You were making money by sending your brother Mr. Dondrub to Taiwan to trade arms between Taiwan, Pakistan and Burma. Because of the danger of this information leaking out to the public, you claimed that Taiwan goes along with China in the Tibet issue. Therefore, in order to keep Tibetans from going to Taiwan, you accused everyone travelling to Taiwan, even those engaged in private business only, of siding with China.

'9. The problem of Kunzang Lama pointing out faults in your government. In 1989 Mr. Kunzang Lama found out that your government had received large amounts of money from the Tibetan-Mongolian Association in Taiwan and for this reason he accused your government.

'10. The current problem of the issue of the reincarnation of the Karmapa. You back up the candidate established by communist China; this causes tremendous harm within Tibetan politics.

'11. The problem of Chu Shi Gang Druk ['Four Rivers, Six Mountains' Khampa Organisation'] finding another way for the future of Eastern Tibet. You made a secret deal with communist

China offering them the area of Kham in favour of your personal benefit. Chu Shi Gang Druk found out about this and the result has been continual heavy fighting.

'During the last forty years your exile government has created problems non-stop. As for you, Your Holiness, what have you been doing during this time? You have treated your own Tibetan people as your enemies and, rather than working for Tibetan democracy, you have thoroughly challenged them as your main responsibility. If you had focused on making a proper democracy and thus had given up any concern for protecting your own power in religion and politics, these problems would not have had ground in which to grow. Even if these kinds of problem had occurred, they would not have been connected with your government and they would not have kept recurring. How has this happened? If Your Holiness had really tried to be like Mahatma Gandhi, as you yourself repeatedly mentioned, all these matters would be problems of your children and not of you, the father. These problems arose not from the efforts of working for the freedom of Tibet, but from your trying to protect your own power.

'Here I would like to comment a little further on what actually happened. First Your Holiness had good intentions. In 1959 you were young and it was a period of many great people, such as Mahatma Gandhi, Johala Nehru, J.F. Kennedy. Your Holiness had a hard and painful time being the leader of Tibet, but you were also dynamic. That is why you were able to challenge the power of Red China. You had joy in committing and dedicating yourself in being the number one leader of Tibet. Your plan was to make Tibet into a modern and democratic country as many other countries in the world. However, you still remained orthodox and hung onto your position as being the boss over religion.

'In the beginning you expelled the hierarchical officials who accompanied you from Tibet. This was because it was clear that those who hold such positions could not sacrifice their prestige. They would not have accepted democracy and modernisation but would instead have objected to any reform. You also strongly went against re-establishing in exile the orthodox system of big monastic institutions with hundreds of monks. However, you did not succeed and what was the real cause for that? The cause is the invisible disease which is still there and which develops immediately if met with various conditions. And what is this disease? It is the clinging to your own power. It is a fact that even at that time if someone would have used democracy on you, you would not have been able to accept it. The habit of being the powerful boss of the Potala palace woke up and showed its ugly face.

'Look at the example of the great Mahatma Gandhi who served his country selflessly and managed to establish pure democracy in the great land of India. The secret behind his success was that he realised from the beginning that one must sever all ties and attachments to one's own life and welfare thoroughly. If only a little self-concern is still there it can break out at any time and destroy everything, just as a small match can cause a whole forest to burn.

'Look at Stalin and Chairman Mao on the other hand. They did not know that the ego has to be removed in order to serve the nation properly. When they reached the peak of their power they were so concerned about holding onto it that they became paranoid. To eliminate what they saw as dangerous threats to their power, they had to kill the people who had worked with them from the beginning. Then those people who know about this killing had to be killed as well. So it went on and on and on until hundreds, thousands, and even millions of people had to be killed.

'The Buddha said that one needs "right view", "right meditation", and "right conduct". To fulfil this, one has to truly commit and dedicate oneself with a pure mind; a mind of a Bodhisattva. The result, good or bad, of one's work, whether religious or political, depends upon the degree of one's dedication. Your Holiness, you wish to be a great leader, but you do not know that in order to fulfil this wish, a "political Bodhisattva vow" is required. So you entered instead the wrong "political path of accumulation" (tsog lam) and that has led you on a continuously wrong path. You believed that in order to be a great leader you had to secure your own position first of all, and whenever any opposition against you arose you had to defend yourself, and this has become contagious.

'When I talk about the consequences of your work, I am not calculating the personal victories you have gained for your own fame. I am calculating how much benefit the Tibetan people have gained for their future aims. For example, when in the 1960's you tried to get rid of the influence of one great Lama's power, such as Dujom Rinpoche and Karmapa, the side-effect was felt by many Tibetan lamas, and you caused them to unite in opposition. You could not leave it lightly and you had to do something that caused a split within Tibetan society. Moreover, to challenge lamas you have used religion for your aim. To that purpose you had to develop the Tibetan people's blind faith. In the end you adopted the same activity that you yourself had pointed out was mistaken in other lamas. For instance, you started the politics of public Kalachakra initiations. Normally the Kalachakra initiation is not given in public. Then you started to use it continuously in a big way for your politics. The result is that now the Tibetan people have turned to exactly the same muddy and dirty mixing of politics and religion of lamas which you yourself had so precisely criticised in earlier times. The current event in relation to the controversy about the Karmapa reincarnation is one such instance. Your ministers will have told you that a Karmapa established in the Himalayas will affect the name and power of the Dalai Lama as before, since he is very popular in the Himalayas. If the Tibetan exile government of Dalai Lama is really for the independence of Tibet, for the democracy of Tibet, and for the civilisation of Tibet, how can a private organisation, like that of the Karmapa, affect your government? There is no connection and no relevance. Or did the communist Chinese devise a deeply political game by establishing a Karmapa in Tibet? When your Holiness Dalai Lama gave support for this (backed the Chinese candidate) how badly will this harm Tibet's future? You think that if within your life you cannot be the leader of the Tibetans in Tibet, at least you must keep your position as leader of Tibet in India by using Dharma and politics. For that you calculate that it does not matter what happens for the future of Tibet after your life, as long as you can keep your power now. It is really sad.

'Seen from another angle. In 1985-86 the Nyingma Shingchong Tulku of Karok Monastery, Dzongnang Tulku of Clementown, Dehradun, and Mr. Lingtsang Gyalsaw went to Tibet as guests of the communist Chinese government. At that time your exile government commanded us Tibetans to revolt against them because they were siding with the Chinese and we made a thorough attack on them. Today the Situ and Gyaltsab Rinpoches of the Kagyupa do everything with regard to the Karmapa reincarnation in favour of the politics of communist China. Instead of objecting your Holiness is giving them your full support. Isn't this surprising? This is what I meant when I mentioned above that you always give priority to your own well-being and power, even at the cost of Tibet's future. I am not trying to tell you that you should be concerned with the future Dalai Lamas regarding them being leaders of Tibet. I am telling you that you are not working for the future progress and democracy of the Tibetan people in Tibet. Also, I am telling you that you are extremely dishonest and hypocritical.

'When Katok Shingchong Rinpoche and the others went to Tibet and proclaimed that they will get the Kham autonomous region from China, your exile government told us to challenge them and we did very well. Nowadays you yourself have accepted both secretly and openly that the Tibet Autonomous Region and Kham is under China. Whenever you give objections, be it to Katok Shingchong Tulku earlier on or to the Chu Shi Gang Druk nowadays, you do it only for yourself and solely out of jealousy and for power. It is very sad. Nowadays you have given the Kalachakra initiation so many times you have made the Tibetan people into donkeys. You can force them to go here and there as you like. In your words you always say that you want to be Gandhi but in your action you are like a religious fundamentalist who uses religious faith for political purposes. Your image is the Dalai Lama, your mouth is Mahatma Gandhi and your heart is like that of a religious dictator. You [are] a deceiver and it is very sad that on top of the suffering that they already have, the Tibetan people have a leader like you. Tibetans have become fanatics. They say that the Dalai Lama's name is more important than the principle of Tibet. You have achieved your goal.

In brief, if somebody like Mr. Dawa Norbu who is totally dedicated to Tibetan politics and society says something very important for the Tibetan cause, but his talk might affect your power, you send your men secretly to encourage the public of fanatic devotees to protest and to spread the wrong information that Mr. Dawa Norbu is against the Dalai Lama and so on. Simultaneously you appear publicly and praise this man. Due to this double game, not one dedicated person can appear to do something for the good of Tibet. You are already so confident that you can use the Kalachakra initiation for repairing everything you might have done wrong, and, as a matter of fact, it works, because the situation of Tibet nowadays is based on blind faith and continual talking.

'I request you with my eyes filled with tears, 'Please, if you feel like being like Gandhi, do not turn the Tibetan situation into the church dominated style of 17th Century Europe.'

REFERENCES

Abbreviations:

Bell refers to Charles Bell, *A Portrait of a Dalai Lama: The Life and Times of the Great Thirteenth* (London: Wisdom Publications, 1987).

Dhondup refers to K. Dhondup, *The Water-bird and Other Years: A History of the Thirteenth Dalai Lama and After* (New Delhi: Rangwang Publishers, 1986).

Gelder refers to Gelder and Gelder, *The Timely Rain: Travels in New Tibet* (London: Hutchinson, 1964).

Goetz refers to John Goetz, 'On the Outs with the Dalai Lama', NOW Magazine (Toronto, Canada) Vol. 17, No. 21, 22-28 January 1998.

Goldstein (1) refers to Melvyn C. Goldstein, *The Snow Lion and the Dragon – China, Tibet and the Dalai Lama* (Berkeley: University of California Press, 1997).

Goldstein (2) refers to Melvyn C. Goldstein, *A History of Modern Tibet Volume 1: 1913-1951 The Demise of the Lamaist State* (Berkeley, Los Angeles & London: University of California, 1989).

Grunfeld refers to Tom A. Grunfeld, *The Making of Modern Tibet* (New York & London: M.E. Sharpe 1996).

Kundeling Rinpoche refers to Kundeling Rinpoche, *Interview with Gen Kelsang Tharchin, New York & Washington, May 1998*, (unpublished).

Lazar refers to *Tibet, the Issue is Independence* ed., Edward Lazar, (Parallax Press/Full Circle, 1998).

Norbu refers to Jamyang Norbu, *Shadow Tibet: Selected Writing 1989-2004* (New York: High Asia Press, 2004)

Powers refers to John Powers, *Introduction to Tibetan Buddhism*, (New York: Snow Lion Publications, 2007).

Shakabpa refers to Tsepon W. D. Shakabpa, *Tibet: A Political History* (New York: Potala Publications, 1984), pp100-103.

Swiss TV refers to Beat Regli, 'Dalai Lama: Discord in Exile', 10 vor 10, (DRS Swiss Television), January 1998.

Yamaguchi refers to Zuiho Yamaguchi, *The Sovereign Power of the Fifth Dalai Lama: sPrul sku gZims-khang-gong-ma and the Removal of Governor Norbu*, Memoirs of the Research Department of the Toyo Bunko (The Oriental Library) No.55, (Tokyo: The Tokyo Bunko, 1995).

References and notes:

1. Kyabje Trijang Rinpoche (tr. David Molk), *Music Delighting an Ocean of Protectors*, [http://dorjeshugden.com/wp/?page_id=52].
2. Fifth Dalai Lama, in Tibetan: 'Jam.mgön rgyal.wa'i bsten. srung rdo.rje shugs.lden kyi 'phrin.bchol bhjoks.bsdus, published by Sera Mey Monastery, p14; English translation (unattributed.), *Prayer by the 5th Dalai Lama to Gyelchen Dorje Shugden*, [http://dorjeshugden.com/wp/?page_id=341, 21 September 2009]. For another English translation (unattributed.), see Fifth Dalai Lama, *Propitiation of Shugden by the Great Fifth Dalai Lama*, [www.shugdensociety.info/Bernis2EN.html, 21 September 2009].
3. [http://dorjeshugden.com/wp/?p=220] See also Trinley Kalsang, [http://www.dorjeshugdenhistory.org/trode-khang-sar.html].
4. Fourteenth Dalai Lama, in Tibetan: 'Jam mgon rgyal ba'i bstan srung rgyal chen rdo rje shugs ldan rtsal la 'phrin las bcol ba 'gag med rdo rje sgra dbyangs bzhugs so; English translation, *Melody of the Unceasing Vajra: A Propitiation of Mighty Gyalchen Dorje Shugden, Protector of Conqueror Manjushri Tsongkhapa's Teachings*, (tr. Western Shugden Society). For another and complete English translation, see www.dorjeshugden.com/ Prayers/ Melody of the Unceasing Vajra by the 14th Dalai Lama.

5. Anonymous, in Tibetan: gtam drang bden rgya mtsho. The author worked for the Tibetan government and concealed his identity. The other sources of personal testimony referred to in this chapter have requested that their identities be withheld, to protect their own lives and the lives of their friends and relatives.

6. 'Boy chosen by Dalai Lama as reincarnation of spiritual leader turns back on Buddhist order', [http://www.guardian.co.uk/world/2009/may/31/dalai-lama-osel-hita-torres, 31 May 2009].

7. 'Osel´s awakening, a kid against his destiny', *Babylon Magazine*, [http://www.magazinebabylon.com/BabylonMagazine5.pdf].

8. [http://www.westernshugdensociety.org/en/reports/hypocrite-dalai-lama-report-from-india/].

9. Tony Clifton, 'Cult Mystery', *Newsweek*, 28 April 1997.

10. [http://www.westernshugdensociety.org/en/reports/open-letter-from-western-shugden-society/].

11. Phuntsog Wangyal, 'The Influence of Religion on Tibetan Politics', *The Tibet Journal*, ed., Tsering, Vol.1, July-Sept 1975, 78-86.

12. Ibid.

13. 'Nechung – The State Oracle of Tibet', The Government of Tibet in Exile Official Website, [http://www.tibet.com, 23 August 2008].

14. Fourteenth Dalai Lama, *Freedom in Exile* (Great Britain, Abacus edition, 2002), 233-4.

15. Ibid. 233-4.

16. Ibid. 235.

17. Ibid. 236.

18. Norbu, 290-1.

19. Ibid. 291.

20. Dhondup, 148.

21. Bell, 440

22. Ibid. 436

23. Ibid. 436-7.

24. Goldstein (2), 141

25. Prince Peter of Greece and Denmark, quoted in Norbu, 290-1.

26. Norbu, 292.

27. Tibet in Exile, [www.dorjeshugden.com/articles/TibetinExile.pdf, 29 September 2008].

28. Ibid.

29. Goldstein (1), 108-9.

30. Norbu, 292.

31. Helmut Gassner, 'Dalai Lama, Dorje Shugden', Speech to Friedrich-Naumann-Foundation, Hamburg, 26 March 1998, 3, 4 & 8, [http://www.dorjeshugden.com/articles/HelmutGassner01.pdf & http://www.tibet-internal.com/SpeechAtNaumannFoundation.PDF, 23 September 2009]

32. Norbu, 293-4.

33. James Belither, 'Chronicle of Events', *The Dalai Lama: A Report on the Dalai Lama's Abuses of Human Rights and Religious Freedoms*, (Ulverston, 1997), 40.

34. Victor & Victoria Trimondi, *Shadow of the Dalai Lama* – Part II – 7. 2003, [www.iivs.de].

35. See reference 33.

36. John Goetz & Jochen Graebert, Panorama ARD – German TV, 20 November 1997.

37. The Fourteenth Dalai Lama, *Freedom in Exile*, (Great Britain, Abacus edition, 2002), 133.

38. Dorje Tseten, 'Tibetan Art of Divination', The Government of Tibet in Exile website, (Tibetan Bulletin, March-April 1995), [www.tibet.com/Buddhism/Divination.html, 22 September 2009].

39. Fourteenth Dalai Lama, Talk at Sera Monastery, 1980. The Dalai Lama also mentions making decisions by using oracles, dream and divination by throwing dough-balls in *A Talk Concerning Shugden Practice 13 July 1978*, from *An Anthology of Talks Given by His Holiness The Dalai Lama Concerning Reliance Upon the Dharma Protectors*, (Dharamsala: LTWA).

40. J. C. Deus, 'Is the Dalai Lama a Wolf in Sheep's Clothing?', *Mas Alla de la Ciencia* No.103, September 1997.

41. Grunfeld, 28.

42. Quoted in Prince H. R.H. Peter of Greece and Denmark's chapter, Tibetan Oracles, in James F. Fisher, *Himalayan Anthropology. The Indo-Tibetan Interface* (The Hague: Mouton Publishers, 1978), 287.

43. Powers, 475.

44. Ram Rahul, *Dalai Lama: The Institution* (New Delhi: Vikas Publishing House, 1995), 29.

45. Powers, 163-4; & Shakabpa, 100-3.

46. Yamaguchi.

47. Ibid.

48. Shakabpa, 103.

49. Ibid. 105.

50. Ibid. 105.

51. Goldstein (1), 9.

52. Yamaguchi, 8.

53. Powers, 168.

54. Yamaguchi, 10.

55. Marylin M. Rhie & Robert A. F. Thurman, *Wisdom and Compassion: The Sacred Art of Tibet* (Tibet House/Abradale Press, 1997), 300-1

56. Quoted in Yamaguchi, 16.

57. For details of Tulku Dragpa Gyaltsen's death see: Yamaguchi; & Kundeling Rinpoche, *An Authority in Question*, (unpublished thesis), 28-30; & *A Talk Concerning Shugden Practice 13 July 1978*, from *An Anthology of Talks Given by His Holiness The Dalai Lama Concerning Reliance Upon the Dharma Protectors*, (Dharamsala, LTWA).

58. Kundeling Rinpoche, *An Authority in Question*, (unpublished thesis), 28-30.

59. Yamaguchi, 17.

60. See reference 1.

61. This was a 'blessing empowerment' and not a 'life empowerment'.

62. From an unpublished transcript of oral teachings.

63. See reference 2.

64. Yamaguchi, 19.

65. Ibid.

66. Ibid. 23.

67. Ibid. 25.

68. Elliott Sperling 'Orientalism' and Aspects of Violence in the Tibetan Tradition, *Imagining Tibet*, Thierry Dodin & Heinz Räther (eds.), (Boston: Wisdom Publications, 2001), 319.

69. Ibid. 318.

70. Shakabpa, 123.

71. Elliott Sperling 'Orientalism' and Aspects of Violence in the Tibetan Tradition, *Imagining Tibet*, Thierry Dodin & Heinz Räther (eds.), (Boston: Wisdom Publications, 2001), 318

72. Cabinet of the Tibetan Government in Exile (Dharamsala), 'Kashag's Statement concerning Dhogyal,' May 31st 1996, [http://www.dalailama.com/page.134.htm (accessed September 24, 2009)]

73. Shakabpa, 125.

74. Ibid. 126.

75. K. Dhondup, *Songs of the Sixth Dalai Lama*, (Dharamsala: LTWA, 1996).

76. Shakabpa, 128 & 132.

77. Inder L. Malik, *Dalai Lamas of Tibet: Succession of Births* (New Delhi: Uppal Publishing House, 1984), 29.

78. Grunfeld, 43.

79. Shakabpa, 129.

80. Ibid. 129.

81. Ibid., 137-8

82. Ibid. 141.

83. Ibid. 140-1.

84. Ibid. 147.

85. Ibid. 147-50.

86. Ibid. 152.

87. Powers, 173.

88. Ram Rahul, *Dalai Lama: The Institution* (New Delhi: Vikas Publishing House), 54.

89. Dhondup, 2-3.

90. Bell, 70 & 72.

91. Goldstein (2), 49-50.

92. Goldstein (1), 27-8.

93. Dhondup, 39.

94. Ibid. 43.

95. Ibid. 44.

96. Ibid. 45-6 & 66.

97. Ibid. 46 & Bell, 141-2.

98. Thirteenth Dalai Lama, 'Political Testament', quoted in Inder L. Malik, *Dalai Lamas of Tibet: Succession of Births* (New Delhi: Uppal Publishing House, 1984), 51.

99. Dhondup, 50.

100. Bell, 141.

101. Dhondup, 56, 67-9 & 75-6; & Goldstein (2), 112-20.

102. From *A Journey to Lhasa and Central Tibet* by Sarat Chandra Das, William Woodville Rockhill, (Great Britain: Royal Geographical Society 1902), quoted in *The Opening of Tibet: An Account of Lhasa and the Country and People of Central Tibet and of the Progress of the Mission Sent There by the English Government in the Year 1903-4* by Perceval Landon (London: Doubleday Page & Co., 1905), 116. The full text of which can be found: [http://www.archive.org/stream/openingtibetana01youngoog/openingtibetana01youngoog_djvu.txt].

103. Perceval Landon, *The Opening of Tibet: An Account of Lhasa and the Country and People of Central Tibet and of the Progress of the Mission Sent There by the English Government in the Year 1903-4* (London: Doubleday Page & Co., 1905), 116. (An account of this incident also appears in L. Austine Waddell, *Lhasa and its Mysteries* (London: Methuen & Co, 1929), 7-9, where it recounts that even the Lama's relatives were imprisoned for life.)

104. Ibid. 212 & 341; & Goldstein (2), 42-3.

105. Bell, 62-3.

106. Ibid. 178.

107. Perceval Landon, *The Opening of Tibet: An Account of Lhasa and the Country and People of Central Tibet and of the Progress of the Mission Sent There by the English Government in the Year 1903-4* (London: Doubleday Page & Co., 1905).

108. Ibid.

109. Bell, 180.

110. Ibid. 179.

111. Ibid. 62.

112. Alan Winnington, *Tibet: Record of a Journey* (London: Lawrence & Wisheart 1957), 98-9.

113. Grunfeld, 24.

114. Robert W. Ford, *Wind Between the Worlds: Captured in Tibet* (1957) 37.

115. Grunfeld, 24.

116. Anna Louise Strong *When Serfs stood up in Tibet* (Peking: New World Press, 1960) Chapter 8, [http://www.marxists.org/reference/archive/strong-anna-louise/1959/tibet/ch08.htm].

117. Bell, 183.

118. Bell, 197.

119. Dhondup, 64.

120. Ibid. 65 & Bell, 438.

121. Dhondup, 148-9.

122. Quoted in John Goetz & Jochen Graebert, Panorama ARD – German TV, 20 November 1997.

123. Geshe Kelsang Gyatso, *Heart Jewel* (Ulverston: Tharpa Publications, 2009), 122.

124. Fourteenth Dalai Lama, *Union of Bliss and Emptiness* (Snow Lion Publications, 1988), 26.

125. Geshe Kelsang Gyatso, *Heart Jewel* (Ulverston: Tharpa Publications, 2009), 92.

126. Fourteenth Dalai Lama, *Freedom in Exile* (Great Britain, Abacus edition, 2002), 90.

127. Fourteenth Dalai Lama, *My Land and My People* (New York: Warner Books Edition, 1997), 24.

128. Goldstein (1), 45.

129. Ibid. 45.

130. Ibid. 44.

131. Goldstein (2), 772.

132. Fourteenth Dalai Lama, *My Land & My People* (New York: Warner Books Edition, 1997), 62.

133. Goldstein (2), 743.

134. Grunfeld, 109.

135. Goldstein (1), 47.

136. Goldstein (2), 800 & 812-3.

137. Ibid. 643-4.

138. Goldstein (1), 52.

139. Alan Winnington, *Tibet: A Record of a Journey* (Lawrence and Wisheart 1957), 132 & 135.

140. Fourteenth Dalai Lama, 'His Journey', *Time*, 4 October 1999.

141. Quoted in Grunfeld, 119.

142. Ibid. 141.

143. Gelder, 210.

144. Grunfeld, 143.

145. Fourteenth Dalai Lama, *Freedom in Exile* (Great Britain, Abacus edition, 2002), 149.

146. See reference 31.

147. Swiss TV Part 3.

148. Helmut Gassner, 'Dalai Lama, Dorje Shugden', Speech to Friedrich-Naumann-Foundation, Hamburg, 26 March 1998, 3, 4 & 8, [http://www.dorjeshugden.com/articles/HelmutGassner01.pdf & http://www.tibet-internal.com/SpeechAtNaumannFoundation.PDF, accessed 23 September 23 2009].

149. John F. Avedon, *In Exile from the Land of Snows* (Wisdom Books, 1985), 269.

150. John Roberts, 'How the CIA Saved the Dalai Lama', *George Magazine*, October 1997.

151. Grunfeld, 155.

152. Quoted, ibid. 155-6.

153. Gelder, 220.

154. Grunfeld, 138-9.

155. Ibid. 144.

156. Ibid. 144.

157. Fourteenth Dalai Lama, *My Land & My People* (New York: Warner Books Edition, 1997), 168.

158. Ibid. 167-8.

159. Ibid. 168.

160. Gelder, illustration facing 160.

161. Edward Lazar, 'Independence or Accommodation?' in *The Anguish of Tibet*, eds. Kelly, Bastien, Aiello, (Berkeley: Parallax Press, 1991), 306.

162. Lhasang Tsering, 'The Issue is Independence' in Lazar, 37.

163. Jamyang Norbu, 'The Heart of the Matter' in Lazar, 32.

164. Tashi-Tobgye Jamyangling, 'The Issue is Independence', in Lazar, 72.

165. Goldstein (1), 88.

166. Lhasang Tsering, quoted in Goetz.

167. Goldstein (1), 87-8.

168. Edward Lazar, 'Independence or Accommodation?' in *The Anguish of Tibet*, eds. Kelly, Bastien, Aiello, (Berkeley: Parallax Press, 1991), 308.

169. Ibid. 307-8.

170. Ibid. .306.

171. Grunfeld, 141.

172. Fourteenth Dalai Lama, *My Land & My People* (New York: Warner Books Edition, 1977), 85 & 87.

173. Gelder, 204-5.

174. Grunfeld, 141.

175. James Belither, 'A Cry for Help', *The Dalai Lama: A Report on the Dalai Lama's Abuses of Human Rights and Religious Freedoms*, (Ulverston, 1997), 10 & Norbu, 18.

176. *The Times of India*, Delhi, 30 May 1996.

177. Pico Iyer, 'The God in Exile', *Time*, 22 December 1997.

178. Shirong Chen, 'Tibet "Chinese issue" says Dalai: The Tibetan spiritual leader, the Dalai Lama, has said the Tibetan issue is a Chinese domestic problem', 10 August 2009, [http://news.bbc.co.uk/2/hi/asia-pacific/8194138.stm].

179. Edward Lazar, 'Independence or Accommodation?' in *The Anguish of Tibet*, eds. Kelly, Bastien, Aiello, (Berkeley: Parallax Press, 1991), 306.

180. Melvyn C. Goldstein, *The Dalai Lama's Dilemma*, Foreign Affairs, Jan-Feb. 1998.

181. Ibid.

182. Ibid.

183. Ibid.

184. Goldstein (1), 90.

185. An Appeal to the Chinese People, by the Dalai Lama, 28 March 2008 [http://www.dalailama.com/page.226.htm].

186. *BBC News*, Tibet 'Chinese Issue' says Dalai, 10 August 2009, [http://news.bbc.co.uk/2/hi/asia-pacific/8194138.stm].

187. Dalai Lama meets with Media, March 16 2008, [http://www.dalailama.com/page.214.htm].

188. March 10th Statement of the Dalai Lama, [http://www.dalailama.com/news.350.htm 9 March 2009].

189. *The Daily Telegraph*, 15 August 1998

190. Address by the Dalai Lama to the Tibetan-Chinese Conference in Geneva, Thursday 6 August 2009 [http://www.dalailama.com/news.411.htm].

191. Foreign Ministry Spokesperson Jiang Yu's Press Conference on 17 April 2008 [http://au.china-embassy.org/eng/fyrth/t426648.htm].

192. Tina Lam, *Detroit Free Press*, 18 April 2008 [http://www.dalailama.com/news.239.htm, Dalai Lama speaks on Chinese Olympics].

193. Fourteenth Dalai Lama, 'An Appeal to the Chinese People', 28 March 2008 [http://www.dalailama.com/page.226.htm].

194. John Ray, *ITV News*, 'Dalai Lama calls for Olympic Protests', 18 January 2008, [http://www.itv.com/News/Articles/Dalai-Lama-calls-for-Olympic-protests.html].

195. 'Dalai Lama reaffirms his support for Beijing Olympics', 8 March 2008, [http://tibetaffairs.blogspot.com/2008/03/dalai-lama-reaffirms-his-support-for.html].

196. *Free Tibet*, 'Dalai Lama calls on supporters to stage peaceful protests during the Olympics', 22 January 2008, [http://www.freetibet.org/newsmedia/dalai-lama-calls-supporters-stage-peaceful-protests-during-olympics].

197. *BBC News*, Report on protests in London [http://news.bbc.co.uk/2/hi/uk_news/7332942.stm] & Report on protests in Paris, [http://news.bbc.co.uk/2/hi/europe/7334545.stm]; Andrew Buncombe, *The Independent*, 'Violence in Nepal as Tibetans protest Olympics', 31 March 2008, [http://www.independent.co.uk/news/world/asia/violence-in-nepal-as-tibetans-protest-olympics-802732.html].

198. Conference Press Statement: 'Tibet Conference comes up with a Roadmap for Peace in Tibet', Central Tibetan Administration Official Website [http://www.tibet.net/en/index.php?id=266&rmenuid=11].

199. Ibid.

200. *Voice* – Tibetan Woman's Association Quarterly Newsletter, April-June 2007, Volume 2 Issue 1 [http://www.tibetanwomen.org/publications/newsletters/2007/2007.5-twa_newsletter.pdf].

201. [http://www.tibetanwomen.org/press/2008/2008.01.04-press_conf.html]

202. *Xinhua*, 'China publishes evidences of Dalai clique's master-minding of riots', 1 April 2008 [http://www.chinaembassy.org.nz/eng/xw/t420234.htm].

203. *Phayul*, 'Exiled Tibetans plan protest March to Tibet ahead of Beijing Olympics', 4 January 2008 [http://www.phayul.com/news/article.aspx?id=18982].

204. *Phayul*, 'Tibetan People's Uprising Movement to reinvigorate the Tibetan freedom movement', Wednesday, 20 February 2008 [http://www.phayul.com/news/article.aspx?id=19302].

205. *Phayul*, 'Tibetan People's Uprising Movement declares more protests worldwide', 22 July 2008 [http://www.phayul.com/news/article.aspx?id=22059].

206. TYC official site [http://www.tibetanyouthcongress.org/aboutus.html]; TWA official site [http://www.tibetanwomen.org/about/]; Gu Chu Sum official site [http://www.guchusum.org/AboutUs/WhatWeDo/tabid/86/Default.aspx], 25 September 2009.

207. TYC official site [http://www.tibetanyouthcongress.org/aboutus.html#aims_and_objectives].

208. Somini Sengupta and Hari Kumar, *New York Times*, 'Dalai Lama won't stop Tibet protests', 16 March 2008 [http://www.nytimes.com/2008/03/16/world/asia/16cnd-tibet.html]. The news conference itself can be seen on: [http://www.dalailama.com/news.217.htm (22 September 2009)].

209. Ibid.

210. Bill Schiller, *The Toronto Star*, 'Canadians caught in Tibet Violence', 17 March 2008, [http://www.thestar.com/News/World/article/346763]; Chris Johnson, *The Toronto Star*, 'I can't just let this guy die on the ground' 17 March 2008 [http://www.thestar.com/News/World/article/346769]; CCTV, 'March 14: The Lhasa Riots', [http://www.cctv.com/english/special/tibetriots/01/index.shtml].

211. *Radio France International*, 2 April 2008 [http://www.rfi.fr/actucn/articles/100/article_6734.asp (in Chinese)].

212. Isabel Hilton, *The Independent* (London), 'Tibet: Desperate nation prepares to defy might of Peking', 20 October 1997 [http://www.highbeam.com/doc/1P2-4891144.html].

213. Fourteenth Dalai Lama, 'An Appeal to the Chinese People', 28 March 2008 [http://www.dalailama.com/page.226.htm].

214. Grants awarded by the NED to Tibetan groups: [http://www.ned.org/grants/08programs/grants-asia08.html #ChinaTibet in 2008]; [http://www.ned.org/grants/07programs/grants-asia07.html#ChinaTibet in 2007]; [http://www.ned.org/grants/06programs/grants-asia06.html #ChinaTibet in 2006], etc.

215. B.Raman, 'The National Endowment for Democracy of the US', South Asia Analysis Group, 13 April 2000 [http://www.southasiaanalysis.org/papers2/paper115.html].

216. Joel Brinkly, *New York Times*, 'Iran sales linked to wide program of covert policies', 15 February 1987 [http://www.nytimes.com/1987/02/15/world/iran-sales-linked-to-wide-program-of-covert-policies.html].

217. David Ignatius, *The Washington Post*, 'Innocence Abroad: The New World of Spyless Coups', 22 September 1991 [http://www.highbeam.com/doc/1P2-1086157.html].

218. Kenneth Conboy and James Morrison, *The CIA's Secret War in Tibet*, (University Press of Kansas, 2002); BBC Documentary, 'The Shadow Circus: The CIA in Tibet', 1998, [http://www.whitecranefilms.com/film/circus.html]; Jamyang Norbu, *Warriors of Tibet* (Wisdom Publications, 1986).

219. In 1974, the Dalai Lama claimed that: 'The accusation of CIA aid has no truth behind it', (Quoted in Grunfeld:) 'Diplomacy and the Dalai Lama,' FEER (Far Eastern Economic Review)18 March 1974, 32.

220. Kenneth L Woodward, *Newsweek*, 'A Scratch in the Teflon Lama', May 1998 [http://www.newsweek.com/id/92429].

221. *Wikipedia*, Panchen Lama, 15 September 2009.

222. Goldstein (1), 100-3.

223. Ibid. 106

224. Tibet Press Watch, May 1995, 13; as quoted in Goldstein (1), 106.

225. Goldstein (1), 106-9.

226. Ibid. 108-10.

227. Dawa Norbu, *Tibet: The Road Ahead* (London: Rider, 1997), quoted in *Imagining Tibet*, eds. Thierry Dodin & Heinz Räther, 301 (Boston: Wisdom Publications, 2001).

228. Ursula Bernis, *Exiled from Exile 1996-1999*, [http://www.shugdensociety.info/Bernis0EN.html, October 6th 2008].

229. Grunfeld, 200-1.

230. Tibet - Constitution, [http://www.servat.unibe.ch/icl/t100000_.html].

231. Fourteenth Dalai Lama, *Freedom in Exile* (Great Britain, Abacus edition, 2002), 233-4.

232. Swiss TV, Part 2.

233. Ibid.

234. Ibid.

235. Ibid.

236. Ibid.

237. Palden Gyal, *Tibetan News*, 'Paper Tigers', No. 22, Spring 1997.

238. Ibid.

239. Jamyang Norbu, *Tibetan News*, 'Tibet's Cultural Confusion', No. 21, Autumn 1997.

240. Heather Stoddard, 'Tibetan Publications and National Identity', Robbie Barnett and Shirin Akiner (eds.), *Resistance and Reform in Tibet*, 121-56 (London: Hurst and Co.), quoted in *Imagining Tibet*, Thierry Dodin & Heinz Räther (eds.), 368 (Boston: Wisdom Publications, 2001)

241. Lhasang Tsering in Foreword to *Illusion and Reality* by Jamyang Norbu (Dharamsala: Tibetan Youth Congress, 1989), 10.

242. *The Times of India*, Delhi, 30 May 1996.

243. The Dalai Lama, *Tibet Foundation Newsletter* No. 22, 'Meaningful Dialogue', November 1997.

244. As quoted by James Belither, *The Dalai Lama: A Report on the Dalai Lama's Abuses of Human Rights and Religious Freedoms*, (Ulverston, 1997), 19.

245. Ursula Bernis, *Exiled from Exile 1996-1999*, [http://www.shugdensociety.info/Bernis0EN.htm, 6 October 2008].

246. Cabinet of Tibet Government in Exile – Dharamsala, 'Kashag's Statement concerning Dhogyal', May 31st 1996, [http://www.dalailama.com/page.134.htm, 1 August 2008].

247. Statement by Samdhong Rinpoche, 30 August 2009, Radio Free Asia (Tibetan Service), Washingon D.C., USA. [tibetnews@rfa.org].

248. James Belither, 'Chronicle of Events', *The Dalai Lama: A Report on the Dalai Lama's Abuses of Human Rights and Religious Freedoms*, (Ulverston, 1997).

249. C. Henry & N. Haque, 'The Dalai Lama's Demons' *France 24* Special Reports, 8 August 2008, [http://www.france24.com/en/20080808-dalai-lama-demons-india-buddhism-dorje-shugden, 21 August 2008].

250. *Al Jazeera*, 7 October 2008 [http://www.wisdombuddhadorjeshugden.blogspot.com/2008/10/al-jazeera-news-documentary-video.html, 22 September 2009]

251. C. Henry & N. Haque, *France 24* Special Reports, 'The Dalai Lama's Demons', 8 August 2008, [http://www.france24.com/en/20080808-dalai-lama-demons-india-buddhism-dorje-shugden, 21 August 2008].

252. Video interview and transcript, 29 April 2008, [http://www.westernshugdensociety.org/en/news/kelsang-pema-responds-to-comments-by-the-dalai-lamas-representative-tashi-w/, 8 October 2009].

253. *BBC News*, 'Protest at Dalai Lama prayer ban', 27 May 2008, [http://news.bbc.co.uk/1/hi/england/nottinghamshire/7421888.stm, 22 September 2009].

254. Cabinet of Tibet Government in Exile – Dharamsala: 'points of the Kashag's Statement concerning Dolgyal', 31 May 1996, [http://ww.dalailama.com.page.134.htm, 1 August 2008].

255. The Government of Tibet in Exile: 'Shugden verses pluralism and national unity controversy and clarification', 2 November 1997, [http://www.tibet.com/dholgyal/CTA-book/chapter-1.html, 29 July 2008].

256. Quoted in: 'Chronicle of Events – 2008' The Tibetan Situation Today, (Western Shugden Society, London, 2008), [http://media.westernshugdensociety.net/Tibetan_Situation_Today.pdf, August 17th 2008].

257. See reference 247.

258. Fourteenth Dalai Lama, *Union of Bliss and Emptiness* (Snow Lion Publications, 1988), 148.

259. Geshe Kelsang Gyatso 'Replies to Chris Fynn – Part One', 19 December 1997, [talk.religion.Buddhism – Google group groups.google.com/group/talk.religion.buddhism/msg/c594eecc8ff4934b, 30 July 2008].

260. Khyongla Rato, *My Life and Lives*, (New York: Rato Publications, 1977 & 1991), 12.

261. Kalu Rinpoche, *Adarsha Magazine*, 'The Spirit of all Traditions', 1997.

262. Donald Lopez, *Tricycle: The Buddhist Review*, 'An Interview with Geshe Kelsang Gyatso', Vol.3 Spring 1998.

263. Kundeling Rinpoche.

264. James Belither, 'A Cry for Help', *The Dalai Lama: A Report on the Dalai Lama's Abuses of Human Rights and Religious Freedoms*, (Ulverston, 1997).

265. Fourteenth Dalai Lama, 'Concerning Dhogyal with reference to the views of past masters and other related matters', Dharamsala, October 1997 [www.dalailama.com.page.155.htm, 25 September 2009].

266. Kundeling Rinpoche.

267 Fourteenth Dalai Lama, *Union of Bliss and Emptiness* (Ithaca: Snow Lion Publications, 1988), 90

268. Official website of the Central Tibetan Administration: Projected population in 2007, [www.tibet.net/en/index.php?id=9, 25 September 2008, 4 October 2008].

269. Grunfeld, 200.

270. *Nation Master Encyclopedia*, 'Government of Tibet in Exile' [www.nationmaster.com/encyclopedia/Government-of-Tibet-in-exile, 5 October 2008].

271. Dept. of Information, Government of Tibet in Exile, 'Structure of the Tibetan Government-In-Exile', 1996, [www.tibet.com/Govt/brief.html].

272. Grunfeld, 200-2 & 228.

273. Tsering Wangyal, *Tibetan Review* Vol XIV No.9, September 1979, [http://editola.blogspot.com, 5 October 1998].

274. Tibet in Exile, [www.dorjeshugden.com, 29 September 2008].

275. Ibid.

276. Ibid.

277. 'Lessons from Tibetans in Taiwan', [http://repository.dl.itc.u-tokyo.ac.jp/dspace/bitstream/2261/8135/1/ioc152014.pdf].

278. Ursula Bernis, *Exiled from Exile 1996-1999*, [http://www.shugdensociety.info/Bernis0EN.html, 6 October 2008].

279. Michael Backman, 'Behind the Dalai Lama's holy cloak', [http://www.theage.com.au/news/business/behind-dalai-lamas-holy-cloak/2007/05/22/1179601410290.html].

280. Kundeling Rinpoche.

281. Chagdud Tulku, *Lord of the Dance* (Junction City, CA, USA: Padma Publishing, 1992), 188.

282. From http://karmapa.controverse.free.fr/VA/VAdifficultes.html, 25 September 2009.

283. Mick Brown, *Dance of 17th Lives: The Incredible True Story of Tibet's 17th Karmapa* (London: Bloomsbury, 2004).

284. G. Chhetri, *Sunday Magazine*, New Delhi, 13-19 December 1998.

285. Shamar Rinpoche, 'Letter to the Private Office of the Dalai Lama', 7 February 1997.

286. 'Interview with Jigme Rinpoche, 20 March 1994', *Kagyu Life International* No.1, 1994.

287. Kyabje Pabongka Rinpoche, *Heart-Spoon*, 'Biographies', (Wisdom Publications, 1995).

288. The Fourteenth Dalai Lama, Talk given 27 March 2006, [www.dalailama.com/page.135.htm].

289. The Fourteenth Dalai Lama, 'Concerning Dholgyal with reference to the views of past masters and other related matters', A talk on Dholgyal by the Dalai Lama during the course of religious teachings in Dharamsala, October 1997, [www.dalailama.com/page.155.htm].

290. Goldstein (2), 362

291. Unpublished interview by student of Geshe Kelsang Gyatso.

292. Geshe Lobsang Tharchin, Foreword to Tsongkapa, *The Principal Teachings of Buddhism*, (Howell, NJ, USA: Mahayana Sutra and Tantra Press, 1988).

293. Khyongla Rato, *My Life and Lives*, (New York: Rato Publications, 1977 & 1991).

294. *Mandala* magazine, 'Holy Beings: Transforming suffering into pure joy', March/April 1997.

295. 'Pabongka Rinpoche: A Memoir by Rilbur Rinpoche', in Pabongka Rinpoche, *Liberation in the Palm of Your Hand*, (Boston: Wisdom Publications, 1991).

296 *Mandala* magazine, 'Lamas', May-June 1997.

297. Department of State Publication 11342, *Foreign Relations, 1969-1976*, Volume XVII, 'Questions pertaining to Tibet', [http://www.state.gov/documents/organization/70146.pdf]; Paul Salopek, 'The CIA's Secret War in Tibet', *Chicago Tribune*, 26 January 1997, [http://pqasb.pqarchiver.com/chicagotribune/access/10937786.html?FMT=ABS]; Jim Mann, *LA Times*, 'CIA Gave Aid to Tibetan Exiles in '60s, Files Show', Sept 1998, [http://articles.latimes.com/1998/sep/15/news/mn-22993?pg=3]; Kenneth Conboy and James Morrison, *The CIA's Secret War in Tibet*, (University Press of Kansas, 2002).

298. Melinda Liu, 'When Heaven Shed Blood', *Newsweek*, 19 April 1999, [http://www.newsweek.com/id/88042/page/1].

299. Diplomacy and the Dalai Lama, *FEER* (Far Eastern Economic Review)18 March 1974, 32. Quoted in Grunfeld, 151

300. Melinda Liu, 'When Heaven Shed Blood', *Newsweek*, 19 April 1999, [http://www.newsweek.com/id/88042/page/1]

301. *BBC* Documentary, 'The Shadow Circus: The CIA in Tibet', 1998, [http://www.whitecranefilms.com/film/circus.html].

302. Department of State Publication 11342, *Foreign Relations, 1969-1976*, Volume XVII, 'Questions pertaining to Tibet', [http://www.state.gov/documents/organization/70146.pdf, p1148].

303. Melvyn C. Goldstein, *A History of Modern Tibet: The Calm Before the Storm: 1951 – 1955*, (University of California Press, 2007), 35.

304. 'Re: Dalai Lama and officials arrived safely in India' 2 April 1959, [www.foia.cia.gov].

305. Thomas Laird, *Into Tibet: The CIA's First Atomic Spy and his Secret Expedition to Lhasa*, (Grove/Atlantic Press, 2002).

306. History of Chushigangdruk: Establishment 22, [http://www.chushigangdruk.org/history/history11.htm].

307. Michael Peissel, *The Cavaliers of Kham, the Secret War in Tibet*, p216 (London: Heinemann 1972 & Boston: Little, Brown & Co. 1973). Quoted in Grunfeld, 163

308. Grunfeld, 163

309. BBC Documentary, 'The Shadow Circus: The CIA in Tibet', 1998, [http://www.whitecranefilms.com/film/circus.html].

310. Grunfeld, 163

311. Leo E. Rose, *The Politics of Bhutan* (Ithaca, NY, USA: Cornell University Press), 122.

312. Fourteenth Dalai Lama, *Freedom in Exile* (Great Britain, Abacus edition, 2002), 209.

313. Derek Davis, *Coups, Kings, and Castles in the Sky*, Far Eastern Economic Review, 10 June 1974.

314. For example, for the common Tibetan view of the Panchen Lama, Ngabo Ngawang Jigme or Bapa Phuntsok Wangyal, see 'Interview with Kasur Thubten Juchen Namgyal (Former Chief Kalon of the Tibetan Cabinet)', Claude Arpi, Dharamsala, 15 March 1997 [http://www.claudearpi.net/maintenance/uploaded_pics/ThubtenJuchen.pdf].

315. Kensaku Okawa, 'Lessons from Tibetans in Taiwan: their history, current situation and relationship with Taiwanese Nationalism', in The memoirs of the Institute of Oriental Culture, Volume 152, (University of Tokyo, 2007), 2 & 10 [http://repository.dl.itc.u-tokyo.ac.jp/dspace/bitstream/2261/8135/1/ioc152014.pdf].

316. Ibid. 16 & 21

317. Ibid. 6-8

318. Melinda Liu, 'When Heaven Shed Blood', *Newsweek*, 19 April 1999, [http://www.newsweek.com/id/88042/page/1].

319. *Wall Street Journal*, 'Gyalo Thondup: Interview with the Wall Street Journal', 20 February 2009, [http://online.wsj.com/article/SB123510349274730343.html].

320. Peter Wonacott, *Wall Street Journal*, 'In Tibet, a Clash of Approaches', 20 February 2009, [http://online.wsj.com/article/SB123508535435527541.html].

321. *People's Daily*, Wednesday, 11 April 2001, [http://english.people.com.cn/english/200104/11/eng20010411_67409.html].

322. Claudia Dreifus, *New York Times*, 'The Dalai Lama', Sunday, 28 November 1993, [http://www.nytimes.com/1993/11/28/magazine/the-dalai-lama.html].

323. Ibid.

324. Gerald Lehner and Tilman Müller, *Stern* Magazine 23 1997, 'Ein Held mit braunen Flecken'; Gerald Lehner, *Zwischen Hitler und Himalaya – Die Gedächtnislücken des Heinrich Harrer* (Vienna, Czernin Verlag, 2007); Heinrich Harrer, *Seven Years in Tibet*, 1952.

325. Gerald Lehner, *Zwischen Hitler und Himalaya – Die Gedächtnislücken des Heinrich Harrer* (Vienna, Czernin Verlag, 2007); Heinrich Harrer, *Seven Years in Tibet*, 1952.

326. Robert J. Lifton, *The Nazi Doctors : Medical Killing and the Psychology of Genocide* (New York, NY: Basic Books, 1988), 286, [http://www.holocaust-history.org/lifton/LiftonT286.shtml]; Bruno Beger, *Meine Begegnungen mit dem Ozean des Wissens*, Konigstein 1986. Beger's memoirs of Tibet which appeared on The Government of Tibet in Exile Official Website on April 15 2008 but have since been removed, can still be seen here: [http://web.archive.org/web/20021220183452/http://www.tibet.com/Status/bruno.html].

327. Nicholas Goodrick-Clarke, *Black Sun: Aryan Cults, Esoteric Nazism and the Politics of Identity*, (New York University Press, 2002), [http://books.google.co.uk/books?id=xaiaM77s6N4C&printsec=frontcover#v=onepage&q=&f=false].

328. For interview with Serrano where he discusses being the Dalai Lama's guest in Dharamsala shortly after Indira Gandhi's funeral in 1984, [http://web.archive.org/web/19990508175302re_/www.satanism.net/iss/wot/Miguel_Serrano2.html]; Mike Billington, *Why Nazis love the Dalai Lama*, includes a photo of the Dalai Lama with Serrano in Chile in 1992 (Serrano was the head of the Nazis in Chile at the time), [http://www.larouchepub.com/eiw/public/2008/2008_10-19/2008_10-19/2008-18/pdf/69-71_3518.pdf].

329. Andrew Purvis and Angela Leuker, *Time*, 'Jorg Haider's New Clothes', 10 April 2005, [http://www.time.com/time/nation/article/0,8599,1047318,00.html].

330. Originally from *Nürnberger Abendzeitung*, 19 May 2008, 'Dalai Lama in Nürnberg': Fans Jubeln, Gegner schimpfen - Steffen Windschall; quoted by German magazine *Stern* No. 32, 30 July 2009; part of the original German article can be found: [http://www.iivs.de/~iivs01311/Lamaismus/NS-Tibet-8-Harrer.htm].

331. *Stern* No. 32, 30 July 2009, [http://www.stern.de/magazin/heft/magazin-die-zwei-gesichter-des-dalai-lama-707441.html; English translation available: [http://www.dorjeshugden.com/forum/index.php?topic=504].

332. Victor and Victoria Trimondi, "The Japanese doomsday Guru Shoko Asahara and the XIV. Dalai Lama," Shadow of the Dalai Lama (2003) [http://www.trimondi.de/SDLE/Part-2-13.htm].

333. Russell Skelton, *Sydney Morning Herald*, 'Cult gave Dalai Lama $2m', 26 April 1996.

334. Ibid.

335. Werner von Bloch, *Focus* No. 38, 'Unholy Guarantee', 18 September 1995.

336. Russel Skelton, *Sydney Morning Herald*, 'Cult gave Dalai Lama $2m', 26 April 1996.

337. BBC SWB (BBC Summary of World Broadcasts) 7th April 1995 quoting Tokyo News Services, [http://www.tibet.ca/en/newsroom/wtn/archive/old?y=1995&m=4&p=7_2].

338. See reference 237.

339. 'Chronicle of Events' August 1996, [http://www.western-shugdensociety.org, 14 August 2008].

340. Robert Thurman, 'The Dalai Lama: A Conversation with Robert Thurman', Mother Jones Nov-Dec 1997.

341. Research and Analysis Wing, Department of Security, Tibetan Administration, Dharamsala [10 Most Hated Enemies of the Dalai Lama and Tibet], Report No.28/7.8/1997.

342. http://en.wikipedia.org/wiki/Nobel_peace_prize.

343. http://nobelprize.org/nobel_prizes/peace/laureates/1989/presentation-speech.html.

344. 'The Red Terror in Tibet: Interview with the Dalai Lama', US News and World Report 24 April 1961, 79. (Quoted in Grunfeld, 151).

345. Jamyang Norbu, *Warriors of Tibet*, 1986, [http://books.google.com.au/books?id=epuSaZhmklAC&printsec=frontcover].

346. http://thechinabeat.blogspot.com/2009/04/dalai-lama-and-nobel-prize-correcting.html.

347. http://www.nytimes.com/1989/10/13/world/how-and-why-the-dalai-lama-won-the-peace-prize.html.

348. Ibid.

349. http://en.wikipedia.org/wiki/Nobel_peace_prize.

350. http://nobelprize.org/nobel_prizes/peace/laureates/1989/presentation-speech.html.

351. Michael Backman, *The Asian Insider,* 'The Dalai Lama Eats Meat', 2006, 247

352. Goetz.

353. Michael Backman, 'Selling Tibet to the world', 5 June 2008, [http://business.theage.com.au/business/selling-tibet-to-the-world-20080604-2lx7.html].

354. James Belither, 'A Cry for Help', *The Dalai Lama: A Report on the Dalai Lama's Abuses of Human Rights and Religious Freedoms*, (Ulverston, 1997), 11.

355. Grunfeld, 194-6.

356. *New York Times*,'World New Briefs: Dalai Lama Group Says it Got Money from CIA', 2 October 1998.

357. Grunfeld, 201-2.

358. Ibid. 201.

359. Ibid. 201.

360. Michael Backman, *The Asian Insider,* 'The Dalai Lama Eats Meat', 2006, 240-1

361. Michael Backman, 'Western media miss the real Tibet story', *The Age*, April 9, 2008, [http://business.theage.com.au/business/western-media-miss-the-real-tibet-story-20080408-24nz.html, 9 April 2008].

362. Alexandra David-Néel, *Initiations and Initiates in Tibet* (New York: University Books, 1959), 128-9.

363. Brendan O'Neill, 'Is the Dalai Lama a "religious dictator"?, 20 May 2008, [http://www.spiked-online.com/index.php/site/article/5170/]

364. John Roberts, *George Magazine*, 'How the CIA Saved the Dalai Lama', October 1997.

365. Grunfeld, 137.

366. Ibid. & Gelder, 212-3.

367. Gelder, 213.

368. Ibid. 213. For details of the events of March 1959, see also Grunfeld, 134-9.

369. Gelder, 214.

370. Grunfeld, 144.

371. Gelder, 216

372. Ibid. 217.

373. Ibid. 213-4.

374. Ibid. 218.

375. Ibid. 219.

376. Ibid. 219.

377. Peter Mierau, *Nationalsozialistiche Expeditionspolitik: deutsche Asien-Expeditionen 1933 – 1945*, (Munich: Herbet Utz Verlag, 2006) 357.

378. Thomas Laird, 'INTO TIBET: The CIA's First Atomic Spy and His Secret Expedition to Lhasa' Grove Press, 1st edition May 2002. Original document can be found here: [http://www.thelongridersguild.com/bessac.htm]

379. Allen W. Dulles, Foreign Relations of the United States Eisenhower Administration 1958-1960, Volume XIX, *U.S. Response to the Rebellion in Tibet*, 3-4 & 24 [http://www.claudearpi.net/maintenance/uploaded_pics/Tibet1958.pdf]

380. Capucine Henry (text) and Nicolas Haque (video), France 24, The Dalai Lama's Demons, August 08, 2008 [http://www.france24.com/en/20080808-dalai-lama-demons-india-buddhism-dorje-shugden]

381. *Al Jazeera*, The Dalai Lama: The Devil Within, September 30, 2008 [http://english.aljazeera.net/programmes/peopleandpower/2008/09/200893014344405483.html]

Index